51 MESSIER.

99 MESSIER.

Gould and Lincoln, Boston.

THE

PLURALITY OF WORLDS.

On Nature's Alps I stand,
And see a thousand firmaments beneath!
A thousand systems, as a thousand grains!
So much a stranger, *and so late arrived*,
How shall man's curious spirit not inquire
What are the natives of this world sublime,
Of this so distant, unterrestrial sphere,
Where mortal, untranslated, never strayed?
NIGHT THOUGHTS.

WITH AN INTRODUCTION

BY

EDWARD HITCHCOCK, D. D.,

PRESIDENT OF AMHERST COLLEGE, AND PROFESSOR OF THEOLOGY AND GEOLOGY.

BOSTON:
GOULD AND LINCOLN,
59 WASHINGTON STREET.
1854.

PREFACE.

ALTHOUGH the opinions presented in the following Essay are put forwards without claiming for them any value beyond what they may derive from the arguments there offered, they are not published without some fear of giving offence. It will be a curious, but not a very wonderful event, if it should now be deemed as blamable to doubt the existence of inhabitants of the Planets and Stars, as, three centuries ago, it was held heretical to teach that doctrine. Yet probably there are many who will be willing to see the question examined by all the light which modern science can throw upon it; and such an examination can be undertaken to no purpose, except the view which has of late been generally rejected have the arguments in its favor fairly stated and candidly considered.

Though Revealed Religion contains no doctrine relative to the inhabitants of planets and stars; and though, till within the last three centuries, no Christian thinker deemed such a doctrine to be required, in order to complete our view of the attributes of the Creator; yet it is possible that at the present day, when the assumption of such inhabitants is very generally made and assented to, many persons have so mingled this assumption with their religious belief, that they regard it as an essential part of Natural Religion. If any such persons find their religious convictions interfered with, and their consolatory impressions disturbed, by what is said in this Essay, the Author will deeply regret to have had any share in troubling any current of pious thought belonging to the time. But, as some excuse, it may be recollected, that if such considerations had prevailed, this very doctrine, of the Plurality of Worlds, would never have been publicly maintained. And if such considerations are to have weight, it must be recollected, on the other hand, that there are many persons to whom the assumption of an endless multitude of Worlds appears difficult to reconcile with the belief of that which, as the Christian Revelation teaches us, has been done for this our World of Earth. In this conflict of religious difficulties, on a point which rather belongs to science than to religion, perhaps philosophical arguments may be patiently listened to, if urged as arguments merely; and in that hope, they are here stated, without reserve and without exaggeration.

All speculations on subjects in which Science and Religion bear upon each other, are liable to one of the two opposite charges;—that the speculator sets Philosophy and Religion at variance; or that he warps Philosophy into a conformity with Religion. It is confidently hoped that no candid reader will bring either of these charges against the present Essay. With regard to the latter, the arguments must speak for themselves. To the Author at least, they appear to be of no small philosophical force; though he is quite ready to weigh carefully and candidly any answers which may be offered to them. With regard to the amount of agreement between our Philosophy and Religion, it may perhaps be permitted to the Author to say, that while it appears to him that some of his philosophical conclusions fall in very remarkably with certain points of religious doctrine, he is well aware that Philosophy alone can do little in providing man with the consolations, hopes, supports, and convictions which Religion offers; and he acknowledges it as a ground of deep gratitude to the Author of all good, that man is not left to Philosophy for those blessings; but has a fuller assurance of them, by a more direct communication from Him.

Perhaps, too, the Author may be allowed to say, that he has tried to give to the book, not only a moral, but a scientific interest; by collecting his scientific facts from the best authorities, and the most recent discoveries. He would flatter himself, in particular, that the view of the Nebulæ and of the Solar System, which he has here given, may be not unworthy of some attention on the part of astronomers and observers, as an occasion of future researches in the skies.

CONTENTS

OF

THE PLURALITY OF WORLDS.

CHAPTER VI.

CHAPTER VII.

CHAPTER VIII.

CHAPTER IX.

CHAPTER X.

CHAPTER XI.

CHAPTER XII.

CHAPTER XIII.

INTRODUCTORY NOTICE

TO THE

AMERICAN EDITION.

It is an interesting feature in the literature of our day, that so many minds are turning their attention to the bearings of science upon religion. With a few honorable exceptions, Christian scholars have regarded this as a most unpromising field, which they have left to the tilting and gladiatorship of scepticism. But we owe it mainly to the disclosures of geology, that the tables are beginning to be turned. For a long time suspected of being in league with infidelity, it was treated as an enemy, and Christians thought only of fortifying themselves against its attacks. But they are finding out, that if this science has been seen in the enemy's camp, it was only because of their jealousy that it was compelled to remain there; like captives that are sometimes pushed forwards to cover the front rank and receive the fire of their friends. Judging from the number of works, some of them very able, that appear almost monthly from the press, in which illustrations of religion are drawn from geology, we may infer that this science is beginning to be recognized by the friends of religion as an efficient auxiliary.

"The Plurality of Worlds," now republished, is the most recent work of this description that has fallen under our notice. We can see no reason why an Essay of so much ability, in which the reasoning is so dispassionate, and opponents are treated so candidly, should appear anonymously. True, the author takes ground against some opinions widely maintained respecting the extent of the inhabited universe, and seems to suppose that he shall meet with little sympathy; and this may be his reason, though in our view quite insufficient, for remaining incognito. We think he will find that there are a secret seven thousand, who never have bowed their understandings to a belief of many of the doctrines which he combats, and he might reasonably calculate that his reasoning will add seven thousand more to the number. We confess, however, that though we have long been of this number to a certain extent, we cannot go as far as this writer has done in his conclusions.

All the world is acquainted with Dr. Chalmers' splendid Astronomical Discourses. Assuming, or rather supposing that he has proved, that the universe contains a vast number of worlds peopled like our own, he imagines the infidel to raise an objection to the mission of the Son of God, on the ground that this world is too insignificant to receive such an extraordinary interposition. His replies to this objection, drawn chiefly from our ignorance, are ingenious and convincing. But the author of the Plurality of Worlds doubts the premises on which the objection is founded. He thinks the facts of science will not sustain the conclusion that many of the heavenly bodies are inhabited; certainly not with moral and intellectual beings like man. Nay, by making his appeal to geology, he thinks the evidence strong against such an opinion.* This science shows us that this world was once certainly in a molten state, and very probably, at a still earlier date, may have been dissipated into self-luminous vapor, like the nebulæ or the comets. Immense periods, then, must have passed before any organic structures, such as have since peopled the earth, could have existed. And during the vast cycles that have elapsed since the first animals and plants appeared upon the globe, it was not in a proper condition to have sustained any other than the inferior races. Accordingly, it has been only a few thousand years since man appeared.

Now, so far as astronomy has revealed the condition of other worlds, almost all of them appear to be passing through those preparatory changes which the earth underwent previous to man's creation. What are the unresolvable nebulæ and most of the comets also, but intensely heated vapor and gas? What is the sun but a molten globe, or perhaps gaseous matter condensed so as to possess almost the density of water? The planets beyond Mars, also, (excluding the asteroids,) appear to be in a liquid condition, but not from heat, and therefore may be composed of water, or some fluid perhaps lighter than water; or at least be covered by such fluid. Moreover, so great is their distance from the sun, that his light and heat could not sustain organic beings such as exist upon the earth. Of the inferior planets, Mercury is so near the sun that it would be equally unfit for the residence of such beings. Mars, Venus, and the Moon, then, appear to be the only worlds known to us capable of sustaining a population at all analogous to that upon earth. But of these, the Moon appears to be merely a mass of extinguished volcanos, with neither water nor atmosphere. It has proceeded farther in the process of refrigeration than the earth, because it is smaller; and in its present state, is manifestly unfit for the residence either of rational or irrational creatures. So that we are left with only Mars and Venus in the solar system to which the common arguments in favor of other worlds being inhabited, will apply.

But are not the fixed stars the suns of other systems? We will thank those who think so, to read the chapter in this work that treats of the fixed stars, and we presume they will be satisfied that at least many of these bodies exhibit characters quite irreconcilable with such an hypothesis. And if some are not central suns, the presumption that the rest are, is weakened, and we must wait till a greater perfection of instruments shall afford us some positive evidence, before we know whether our solar system is a type of any others.

Thus far, it seems to us, our author has firm ground, both geological and astronomical, to stand upon. But he does not stop here. He takes the position that probably our earth may be the only body in the solar system, nay in the universe, where an intellectual, moral and immortal being, like man, has an existence. He makes the "earth the domestic hearth of the solar system; adjusted between the hot and fiery haze on one side, and the cold and watery vapor on the other: the only fit region to be a domestic hearth, a seat of habitation." He says that "it is quite agreeable to analogy that the solar system should have borne but one fertile flower. And even if any number of the fixed stars were also found to be barren flowers of the sky, we need not think the powers of creation wasted, or frustrated, thrown away, or perverted." He does not deny that some other worlds may be the abodes of plants and animals such as peopled this earth during the long ages of preadamic history. But he regards the creation of man as the great event of our world. He looks upon the space between man and the highest of the irrational creatures, as a vast one: for though in physical structure they approach one another, in intellectual and moral powers they cannot be compared. He does not think it derogatory to Divine Wisdom to have created and arranged all the other bodies of the universe to give convenience and elegance to the abode of such a being; especially since this was to be the theatre of the work of redemption.

Now we sympathize strongly in views that give dignity and exaltation to man, and not at all with that debasing philosophy, so common at this day, that looks upon him as little more than a somewhat improved orang. But we cannot admit that man is the only exalted created being to be found among the vast array of worlds around us. Geology does, indeed, teach us, that it is no disparagement of Divine Wisdom and benevolence to make a world—and if one, why not many—the residence of inferior creatures; nay to leave it without inhabitants through untold ages. But it also shows us, that when such worlds have passed through these preparatory changes, rational and immortal beings may be placed upon them. Nay, does not the history of our world show us that this seems to be the grand object of such vast periods of preparation. And is it not incredible, that amid the countless bodies of the universe, a single globe only, and that a small one, should have reached the condition adapted to the residence of beings made in the image of God? Of what possible use to man are those numberless worlds visible only through the most powerful telescopes? Surely such a view gives us a very narrow idea of the plans and purposes of Jehovah, and one not sustained in our opinion by the analogies of science.

There is another principle to which our author attaches, as we think, too little importance in this connection. When we see how vast is the variety of organic beings on this globe, and how manifold the conditions of their existence; how exactly adapted they are to the solid, the liquid, and the gaseous states of matter, can we doubt that rational and intelligent beings may be adapted to physical conditions in other worlds widely diverse from those on this globe? May not spirits be connected with bodies much heavier, or much lighter, than on earth; nay, with mere tenuous ether; and those bodies, perhaps, be better adapted to the play of intellect than ours; and be unaffected by temperatures which, on earth, would be fatal? It does seem to us that such conclusions are legitimate inferences from the facts of science; and if so, we can hardly avoid the conclusion that there may be races of intelligent beings upon other worlds where the condition of things is widely different from that on earth. Yet there is a limit to this principle; and when we can prove another world to be in a similar condition to our earth, when it was inhabited by preadamic races, or not at all inhabited, the presumption is strong, that such a world has inhabitants of a like character, or none at all.

Our author makes but a slight allusion to some most important statements of revelation, that seem to us to bear strongly upon the hypothesis which he adopts. We refer to the existence of angels, holy and unholy. In the history of the latter, we learn that *they kept not their first estate, but left their own habitation.* Have we not here an example of other rational creatures, more exalted than man, who, like him, have fallen from their first estate; and does not the presumption hence arise, that there may be similar examples in other worlds? And is there not a probability, that holy angels now in heaven, may be rational intelligencies who have passed a successful probation in other worlds? It does seem to us, that these biblical facts make the hypothesis of our author respecting man extremely improbable.

But though we must demur as to some of the views of this work, we can cordially recommend its perusal to intelligent and reasoning minds. It is an effort in the right direction, and we think will do much to correct some false notions respecting the Plurality of Worlds. And even the author's peculiar hypothetical views are sustained with much ability. He states the facts of geology and astronomy with great clearness and correctness, and seems quite familiar with mathematical reasoning. Nor does he advance opinions that come into collision with natural or revealed religion; though, as already stated, we think his favorite notions narrow our conceptions of the Divine plans and purposes. We predict for the work an extended circulation among scientific men and theologians; and commend it with confidence to all readers—and in our country they are numerous—who are fond of tracing out the connection between science and religion. E. H.

AMHERST COLLEGE, April, 1854.

THE

PLURALITY OF WORLDS.

CHAPTER I.

ASTRONOMICAL DISCOVERIES.

"When I consider the heavens, the work of thy fingers, the moon and the stars, which thou hast ordained; What is man, that thou art mindful of him? and the son of man, that thou visitest him?"

1. These striking words of the Hebrew Psalmist have been made, by an eloquent and pious writer of our own time, the starting point of a remarkable train of speculation. Dr. Chalmers, in his *Astronomical Discourses*, has treated the reflection thus suggested, in connection with such an aspect of the heavens and the stars, the earth and the universe, as modern astronomy presents to us. Even from the point of view in which the ancient Hebrew looked at the stars; seeing only their number and splendor, their lofty position, and the vast space which they visibly occupy in the sky; compared with the earth, which lies dark, and mean, and perhaps small in extent, far beneath them, and on which man has his

habitation; it appeared wonderful, and scarcely credible, that the maker of all that array of luminaries, the lord of that wide and magnificent domain, should occupy himself with the concerns of men: and yet, without a belief in His fatherly care and goodness to us, thoughtful and religious persons, accustomed to turn their minds constantly to a Supreme Governor and constant Benefactor, are left in a desolate and bewildered state of feeling. The notion that while the heavens are the work of God's fingers, the sun, moon, and stars ordained by him, He is *not* mindful of man, does not regard him, does not visit him, was not tolerable to the thought of the Psalmist. While we read, we are sure that he believed that, however insignificant and mean man might be, in comparison with the other works of God,—however difficult it might seem to conceive, that he should be found worthy the regards and the visits of the Creator of All,—yet that God *was* mindful of him, and *did* visit him. The question, "What is man, that this is so?" implies that there is an answer, whether man can discover it or not. "*What* is man, that God is mindful of him?" indicates a belief, unshaken, however much perplexed, that man is *something*, of such a kind that God *is* mindful of him.

2. But if there was room for this questioning, and cause for this perplexity, to a contemplative person, who looked at the skies, with that belief concerning the stars, which the ancient Hebrew possessed, the question recurs with far greater force, and the perplexity is immeasurably increased, by the knowledge, concerning the stars, which is given to us by the discoveries of modern astronomy. The Jew probably believed the earth to be a region, upon the whole, level, however diversified with hills and valleys, and the skies to be a vault arched over this level;—a firmament in which the

moon and the stars were placed. What magnitude to assign to this vault, he had no means of knowing; and indeed, the very aspect of the nocturnal heavens, with the multitude of stars, of various brightness, which come into view, one set after another, as the light of day dies away, suggests rather the notion of their being scattered through a vast depth of space, at various distances, than of their being so many lights fastened to a single vaulted surface. But however he might judge of this, he regarded them as placed in a space, of which the earth was the central region. The host of heaven all had reference to the earth. The sun and the moon were there, in order to give light to it, by day and by night. And if the stars had not that for their principal office, as indeed the amount of light which they gave was not such as to encourage such a belief,—and perhaps the perception, that the stars must have been created for some other object than to give light to man, was one of the principal circumstances which suggested the train of thought that we are now considering;—yet still, the region of the stars had the earth for its centre and base. Perhaps the Psalmist, at a subsequent period of his contemplations, when he was pondering the reflections which he has expressed in this passage, might have been led to think that the stars were placed there in order to draw man's thoughts to the greatness of the Creator of all things; to give some light to his mental, rather than to his bodily eye; to show how far His mode of working transcends man's faculties; to suggest that there are things in heaven, very different from the things which are on earth. If he thought thus, he was only following a train of thought on which contemplative minds, in all ages and countries, have often dwelt; and which we cannot, even now, pronounce to be either unfounded or exhausted;

as we trust hereafter to show. But whether or not this be so, we may be certain that the Psalmist regarded the stars, as things having a reference to the earth, and yet not resembling the earth; as works of God's fingers, very different from the earth with its tribes of inhabitants; as luminaries, not worlds. In the feeling of awe and perplexity, which made him ask, "What is man that thou art mindful of him?" there was no mixture of a persuasion that there were, in those luminaries, creatures, like man, the children and subjects of God; and therefore, like man, requiring his care and attention. In asking, "What is man, that thou visitest him?" there was no latent comparison, to make the question imply, "that thou visitest *him*, rather than those who dwell in those abodes?" It was the multitude and magnificence of God's works, which made it seem strange that he should care for a *thing* so small and mean as man; not the supposed multitude of God's intelligent creatures inhabiting those works, which made it seem strange that he should attend to every *person* upon this earth. It was not that the Psalmist thought that, among a multitude of earths, all peopled like this earth, man might seem to be in danger of being overlooked and neglected by his Maker; but that, there being only one earth, occupied by frail, feeble, sinful, short-lived creatures, it might be unworthy the regards of Him who dwelt in regions of eternal light and splendor, unsullied by frailty, inaccessible to corruption.

3. This, we can have no doubt, or something resembling this, was the Psalmist's view, when he made the reflection, which we have taken as the basis of our remarks. And even in this view, (which, after all that science has done, is perhaps still the most natural and familiar,) the reflection is extremely striking; and the words cannot be uttered without finding an echo in the breast of every contemplative and religious per-

son. But this view is, as most readers at this time are aware, very different from that presented to us by Modern Astronomy. The discoveries made by astronomers are supposed by most persons to have proved, or to have made it in the highest degree probable, that this view of the earth, as the sole habitation of intelligent subjects of God's government; and of the stars, as placed in a region of which the earth is the centre, and yet differing in their nature from this lower world; is altogether erroneous. According to astronomers, the earth is not a level space, but a globe. Some of the stars which we see in the vault of heaven, are globes, like it; some smaller than the earth, some larger. There are reasons, drawn from analogy, for believing that these globes, the other planets, are inhabited by living creatures, as the earth is. The earth is not at rest, with the celestial luminaries circulating above it, as the ancients believed, but itself moves in a circle about the sun, in the course of every year; and the other planets also move round the sun in like manner, in circles, some within and some without that which the earth describes. This collection of planets, thus circulating about the sun, is the SOLAR SYSTEM: of which the earth thus forms a very small part. Jupiter and Saturn are much larger than the earth. Mars and Venus are nearly as large. If these be inhabited, as the Earth is, which the analogy of their form, movements and conditions, seems to suggest, the population of the earth is a very small portion of the population of the solar system. And if the mere number of the subjects of God's government could produce any difficulty in the application of his providence to them, a person to whom this view of the world which we inhabit had been disclosed, might well, and with far more reason than the Psalmist, exclaim, "Lord, what is man, that thou art mindful of him? the inhabitants of this Earth, that thou regardest him?"

4. But this is only the first step in the asserted revelations of astronomy. Some of the stars are, as we have said, planets of the kind just described. But these stars are a few only:—five, or at most six, of those visible to the unassisted eye of man. All the rest, innumerable as they appear, and numerous as they really are, are, it is found, objects of another kind. They are not, as the planets are, opaque globes, deriving their light from a sun, about which they circulate. They shine by a light of their own. They are of the nature of the sun, not of the planets. That they appear mere specks of light, arises from their being at a vast distance from us. At a vast distance they undoubtedly are; for even with our most powerful telescopes, they still appear mere specks of light;—mere luminous points. They do not, as the planets do, when seen through telescopes, exhibit to us a circular face or disk, capable of being magnified and distinguished into parts and features. But this impossibility of magnifying them by means of telescopes, does not at all make us doubt that they may be far larger than the planets. For we know, from other sources of information, that their distance is immensely greater than that of any of the planets. We can measure the bodies of the solar system;—the earth, by absolutely going round a part of it, or in other ways; the other bodies of the system, by comparing their positions, as seen from different parts of the earth. In this manner we find that the earth is a globe 8,000 miles in diameter. In this way, again, we find that the circle which the earth describes round the sun has, in round numbers, a radius about 24,000 times the earth's radius; that is, nearly a hundred millions of miles. The earth is, at one time, a hundred millions of miles on one

side of the sun; and at another time, half a year afterwards, a hundred millions of miles on the other side. Of the bright stars which shine by their own light,—the *fixed stars*, as we call them, (to distinguish them from the planets, the *wandering stars*,)—if any one were at any moderate distance from us, we should see it change its apparent place with regard to the others, in consequence of our thus changing our point of view two hundred millions of miles: just as a distant spire changes its apparent place with regard to the more distant mountain, when we move from one window of our house to the other. But no such change of place is discernible in any of the fixed stars: or at least, if we believe the most recent asserted discoveries of astronomers, the change is so small as to imply a distance in the star, of more than two hundred thousand times the radius of the earth's orbit, which is, itself, as we have said, one hundred millions of miles.* This distance is so vastly great, that we can very well believe that the fixed stars, though to our best telescopes they appear only as points of light, are really as large as our sun, and would give as much light as he does, if we could approach as near to them. For since they are thus, the nearest of them, two hundred thousand times as far off as he is, even if we could magnify them a thousand times, which we can hardly do, they would still be only one two-hundredth of the breadth of the sun; and thus, still a mere point.

* It is quite to our purpose to recollect the impression which such discoveries naturally make upon a pious mind.

Oh! rack me not to such extent,
These distances belong to Thee;
The world's too little for Thy tent,
A grave too big for me!

George Herbert.

5. But if each fixed star be of the nature of the sun, and not smaller than the sun, does not analogy lead us to suppose that they have, some of them at least, planets circulating about them, as our sun has? If the Sun is the centre of the Solar System, why should not Sirius, (one of the brightest of the fixed stars,) be the centre of the *Sirian System?* And why should not that system have as many planets, with the same resemblances and differences of the figure, movements, and conditions of the different planets, as this? Why should not the Sirian System be as great and as varied as the solar system? And this being granted, why should not these planets be inhabited, as men have inferred the other planets of the solar system, as well as the earth, to be? And thus we have, added to the population of the universe of which we have already spoken, a number (so far as we have reason to believe) not inferior to the number of inhabitants of the solar system: this number being, according to all the analogies, very many fold that of the population of the whole earth?

And this is the conclusion, when we reason from one star only, from Sirius. But the argument is the same, from each of the stars. For we have no reason to think that Sirius, though one of the brightest, is more like our sun than any of the others is. The others appear less bright in various degrees, probably because they are further removed from us in various degrees. They may not be all of the same size and brightness; it is very unlikely that they are. But they may as easily be larger than the sun, as smaller. The natural assumption for us to make, having no ground for any other opinion, is, that they are, upon the average, of the size of our sun. On that assumption, we have as many solar systems as we have fixed stars; and, it may be, six or ten, or twenty times as many inhabited globes; inhabited by creatures of whom we must suppose, by analogy, that God is mindful, if he is mindful of us. The question recurs with overwhelming force, if we still follow the same train of reflection: "What is man, that God is mindful of him?"

6. But we have not yet exhausted the views which thus add to the force of this reflection. The fixed stars, which appear to the eye so numerous, so innumerable, in the clear sky on a moonless night, are not really so numerous as they seem. To the naked eye, there are not visible more than four or five thousand. The astronomers of Greece, and of other countries, even in ancient times, counted them, mapped them, and gave them names and designations. But Astronomy, who thus began her career by diminishing, in some degree, the supposed numbers of the host of heaven, has ended by immeasurably increasing them. The first application of the telescope to the skies discovered a vast number of fixed stars, previously unseen: and every improvement in that instrument has disclosed myriads of new stars, visibly smaller than those which had before been seen; and smaller and smaller, as the power of vision is more and more strengthened by new aids from art; as if the regions of space contained an inexhaustible supply of such objects; as if infinite space were strewn with stars in every part of it to which vision could reach. The small patch of the sky which forms, at any moment, the field of view of one of the great telescopes of Herschel, discloses to him as many stars, and those of as many different magnitudes, as the whole vault of the sky exhibits to the naked eye. But the magnifying power of such an instrument only discloses, it does not make, these stars. There appears to be quite as much reason to believe, that each of these telescopic stars is a sun, surrounded by its special family of planets, as to believe that Sirius or Arcturus

is so. Here, then, we have again an extension, indefinite to our apprehension, of the universe, as occupied by material structures; and if so, why not by a living population, such as the material structures which are nearest to us support?

7. Even yet we have not finished the series of successive views which astronomers have had opened to them, extending more and more their spectacle of the fulness and largeness of the universe. Not only does the telescope disclose myriads of stars, unseen to the naked eye, and new myriads with each increase of the powers of the instrument; but it discloses also patches of light, which, at first at least, do not appear to consist of stars: *Nebulæ*, as they are called; bright specks, it might seem, of stellar matter, thin, diffused, and irregular; not gathered into regular and definite forms, such as we may suppose the stars to be. Every one who has noticed the starry skies, may understand what is the general aspect of such nebulæ, by looking at the milky way or galaxy, an irregular band of nebulous light, which runs quite round the sky; "A circling zone, powdered with stars;" as Milton calls it. But the nebulæ of which I more especially speak, are minute patches, discovered mainly by the telescope, and in a few instances only discernible by the naked eye. And what I have to remark especially concerning them at present is, that though to visual powers which barely suffice to discern them, they appear like mere bright clouds, patches of diffused starry matter; yet that, when examined by visual powers of a higher order, by more penetrating telescopes, these patches of continuous feeble light are, in many instances at least, distinguishable into definite points: they are found, in fact, to be aggregations of stars; which before appeared as diffused light, only because our telescopes, though strong enough to reveal to our senses the aggregate mass of light of the cluster, were

not strong enough to enable us to discern any one of the stars of which the cluster consists. The galaxy, in this way, may, in almost every part, be *resolved* into separate stars; and thus, the multitude of the stars in the region of the sky occupied by that winding stream of light, is, when examined by a powerful telescope, inconceivably numerous.

8. The small telescopic nebulæ are of various forms; some of them may be in the shape of flat strata, or cakes, as it were, of stars, of small thickness, compared with the extent of the stratum. Now, if our sun were one of the individuals of such a stratum, we, looking at the stars of the stratum from his neighborhood, should see them very numerous and close in the direction of the edge of the stratum, and comparatively few and rare in other parts of the sky. We should, in short, see a galaxy running round the sky, as we see in fact. And hence Sir William Herschel has inferred, that our sun, with its attendant planets, has its place in such a stratum; and that it thus belongs to a host of stars which are, in a certain way, detached from the other nebulæ which we see. Perhaps, he adds, some of those other nebulæ are beds and masses of stars not less numerous than those which compose our galaxy, and which occupy a larger portion of the sky, only because we are immersed in the interior of the crowd. And thus, a minute speck of nebulous light, discernible only by a good telescope, may contain not only as many stars as occupy the sky to ordinary vision, but as many as is the number into which the most powerful telescope resolves the milky light of the galaxy. And of such resolvable nebulæ the number which are discovered in the sky is very great, their forms being of the most various kind; so that many of them may be, for aught we can tell, more amply stocked with stars than the galaxy is. And if all the stars, or

a large proportion of the stars, of the galaxy, be suns attended by planets, and these planets peopled with living creatures, what notion must we form of the population of the universe, when we have thus to reckon as many galaxies as there are resolvable nebulæ! the stock of discoverable nebulæ being as yet unexhausted by the powers of our telescopes; and the possibility of resolving them into stars being also an operation which has not yet been pursued to its limit.

9. For, (and this is the last step which I shall mention in this long series of ascending steps of multitude apparently infinite,) it now begins to be suspected that not some nebulæ only, but *all*, are resolvable into separate stars. When the nebulæ were first carefully studied, it was supposed that they consisted, as they appeared to consist, of some diffused and incoherent matter, not of definite and limited masses. It was conceived that they were not stars, but Stellar Matter in the course of formation into stars; and it was conceived, further, that by the gradual concentration of such matter, whirling round its centre while it concentrated, not only stars, that is, suns, might be formed, but also systems of planets, circling round these suns; and thus this *Nebular Hypothesis*, as it has been termed, gave a kind of theory of the origin and formation of systems, such as the solar system. But the great telescope which Lord Rosse has constructed, and which is much more powerful than any optical instrument yet fabricated, has been directed to many of the nebulæ, whose appearance had given rise to this theory; and the result has been, in a great number of cases, that the nebulæ are proved to consist entirely of distinct stars; and that the diffused nebulous appearance is discovered to have been an illusion, resulting from the accumulated light of a vast number of small stars near to each other. In this manner, we are led to

regard every nebula, not as an imperfectly formed star or system, but as a vast multitude of stars, and, for aught we can tell, of systems; for the apparent smallness and nearness of these stars are, it is thought, mere results of the vast distance at which they are placed from us. And thus, perhaps, all the nebulæ are, what some of them seem certainly to be, so many vast armies of stars, each of which stars, we have reason to believe, is of the nature of our sun; and may have, and according to analogy has, an accompaniment of living creatures, such as our sun has, certainly on the earth, probably, it is thought, in the other planets.

10. It is difficult to grasp, in one view, the effect of the successive steps from number to number, from distance to distance, which we have thus been measuring over. We may, however, state them again briefly, in the way of enumeration.

From our own place on the earth, we pass, in thought, as a first step, to the whole globe of the Earth; from this, as a second step, to the Planets, the other globes which compose the Solar System. A third step carries us to the Fixed Stars, as visible to the naked eye; very numerous and immensely distant. The transition to the Telescopic Stars makes a fourth step; and in this, the number and the space are increased, almost beyond the power of numbers to express how many there are, and at what distances. But a fifth step:—perhaps all this array of stars, obvious and telescopic, only make up our Nebula; while the universe is occupied by other Nebulæ innumerable, so distant that, seen from them, our nebula, though including, it may be, stars of the 20th magnitude, which may be 20 times or 2,000 times more remote than Sirius, would become a telescopic speck, as their nebulæ are to us.

11. Various images and modes of representation have been employed, in order to convey to the mind some notion of the

dimensions of the scheme of the universe to which we are thus introduced. Thus, we may reckon that a cannon-ball, moving with its usual original velocity unabated, would describe the interval between the sun and the earth in about one year. And this being so, the same missile would, from what has been said, occupy more, we know not how much more, than 200,-000 years in going to the nearest fixed star: and perhaps a thousand times as much, in going to other stars belonging to our group; and then again, 200,000 times so much, or some number of the like order, in going from one group to another. When we have advanced a step or two in this mode of statement, the velocity of the cannon-ball hardly perceptibly affects the magnitude of the numbers which we have to use.

And the same nearly is the case if we have recourse to the swiftest motion with which we are acquainted; that of Light. Light travels, it is shown by indisputable scientific reasonings, in about eight minutes from the sun to the earth. Hence we can easily calculate that it would occupy at least three years to travel as far as Sirius, and probably, three thousand years, or a much greater number, to reach to the smallest stars, or to come from them to us. And thus, as Sir W. Herschel remarked, since light is the only vehicle by which information concerning these distant bodies is conveyed to us, we do, by seeing them, receive information, not what they are at this moment, but what they were, as to visible condition, thousands of years ago. Stars may have been created when man was created, and yet their light may not have reached him.*

* This thought is, however, older. Young expresses it in his *Night Thoughts*, Night IX., (published in 1744):

How distant some of these nocturnal suns!
So distant (says the sage) 'twere not absurd
To doubt if beams, set out at nature's birth,
Are yet arrived at this so foreign world.

Stars may have been extinguished thousands of years ago, and yet may still be visible to our eyes, by means of the light which they emitted previous to their extinction, and which has not yet died away.

12. So vast then are the distances at which the different bodies of the universe are distributed; and yet so numerous are those bodies. In the vastness of their distances, there is, indeed, nothing which need disturb our minds, or which, after a little reflection, is likely to do so: for when we have said all that can be said, about the largeness of these distances, still there is no difficulty in finding room for them. We necessarily conceive *Space* as being infinite in its extent: however much space the heavenly bodies occupy, there is space beyond them: if they are not there, space is there nevertheless. That the stars and planets are so far from each other, is an arrangement which prevents their disturbing each other with their mutual attractions, to any destructive extent; and is an arrangement which the spacious, the infinite universe, admits of, without any difficulty.

13. But we are more especially concerned with the *Numbers* of the heavenly bodies. So many planets about our sun: so many suns, each perhaps with its family of planets: and then, all these suns making but one group: and other groups coming into view, one after another, in seemingly endless succession: and all these planets being of the nature of our earth, as all these stars are of the nature of our sun:—all this, presents to us a spectacle of a world—of a countless host of worlds—of which, when we regard them as thus arranged in planetary systems, and as having, according to all probability, years and seasons, days and nights, as we have, we cannot but accept it as at least a likely suggestion, that they have also inhabitants;—intelligent beings who can reckon these

days and years; who subsist on the fruits which the season brings forth, and have their daily and yearly occupations, according to their faculties. When we take, as our scheme of the universe, such a scheme as this, we may well be overwhelmed with the number of provinces, besides that in which man dwells, which the empire of the Lord of all includes; and, recurring to the words of the Psalmist, we may say with a profundity of meaning immeasurably augmented—"Lord, what is man?"

It was this view, I conceive, which Dr. Chalmers had in his thoughts, in pursuing the speculations which I have mentioned, in the outset of this Essay.

CHAPTER II.

THE ASTRONOMICAL OBJECTION TO RELIGION.

1. SUCH astronomical views, then, as those just stated, we may suppose to be those to which Chalmers had reference, in the argument of his *Astronomical Discourses.* These real or supposed discoveries of astronomers, or a considerable part of them, were the facts which were present to his mind, and of which he there discusses the bearings upon religious truths. This multiplicity of systems and worlds, which the telescopic scrutiny of the stars is assumed to have disclosed, or to have made probable, is the main feature in the constitution of the universe, as revealed by science, to which his reflections are directed. Nor can we say that, in fixing upon this view, he has gone out of his way, to struggle with obscure and latent difficulties, such as the bulk of mankind know and care little about. For in reality, such views are generally diffused in our time and country, are common to all classes of readers, and as we may venture to express it, are the *popular* views of persons of any degree of intellectual culture, who have, directly or derivatively, accepted the doctrines of modern science. Among such persons, expressions which imply that the stars are globes of luminous matter, like the sun; that there are, among them, systems of revolving bodies, seats of

life and of intelligence; are so frequent and familiar, that those who so speak, do not seem to be aware that, in using such expressions, they are making any assumption at all; any more than they suppose themselves to be making assumptions, when they speak of the globular form of the earth, or of its motion round the sun, or of its revolution on its axis. It was, therefore, a suitable and laudable purpose, for a writer like Chalmers, well instructed in science, of large and comprehensive views with regard both to religion and to philosophy, of deep and pervasive piety, and master of a dignified and persuasive eloquence, to employ himself in correcting any erroneous opinions and impressions respecting the bearing which such scientific doctrines have upon religious truth. It was his lot to labor among men of great intellectual curiosity, acuteness, and boldness: it was his tendency to deal with new views of others on the most various subjects, religious, philosophical, and social; and, on such subjects, to originate new views of his own. It fell especially within his province, therefore, to satisfy the minds of the public who listened to him, with regard to the conflict, if a conflict there was, or seemed to be, between new scientific doctrines, and permanent religious verities. He was, by his culture and his powers, peculiarly fitted, and therefore peculiarly called, to mediate between the scientific and the religious world of his time.

2. The scientific doctrine which he especially deals with, in the work to which I refer, is the multiplicity of worlds;—the existence of many seats of life, of enjoyment, of intelligence; and it may be, as he suggests also, of moral law, of transgression, of alienation from God, and of the need, and of the means, of reconciliation to Him; or of obedience to Him and sympathy with Him. That if there be many worlds resembling our world in other respects, they may resemble it in

some of these, is an obvious, and we may say, an irresistible conjecture, in any speculative mind to which the doctrine itself has been conveyed. Nor can it fail to be very interesting, to see how such a writer as I have described deals with such a suggestion; how far he accepts or inclines to accept it; and if so, what aspect such a view leads him to give to truths, either belonging to Natural or to Revealed Theology, which, before the introduction of such a view, were regarded as bearing only upon the world of which man is the inhabitant.

3. The mode in which Chalmers treats this suggestion, is to regard it as the ground of an objection to Religion, either Natural or Revealed. He supposes an objector to take his stand upon the multiplicity of worlds, assumed or granted as true; and to argue that, since there are so many worlds beside this, all alike claiming the care, the government, the goodness, the interposition, of the Creator, it is in the highest degree extravagant and absurd, to suppose that he has done, for this world, that which Religion, both Natural and Revealed, represents him as having done, and as doing. When we are told that God has provided, and is constantly providing, for the life, the welfare, the comfort of all the living things which people this earth, we can, by an effort of thought and reflection, bring ourselves to believe that it is so. When we are further told that He has given a moral law to man, the intelligent inhabitant of the earth, and governs him by a moral government, we are able, or at least the great bulk of thoughtful men, on due consideration of all the bearings of the case, are able, to accept the conviction, that this also is so. When we are still farther asked to believe that the imperfect sway of this moral law over man has required to be remedied by a special interposition of the Governor of the world, or by a series of special interpositions, to make the Law clear, and to

remedy the effects of man's transgression of it; this doctrine also,—according to the old and unscientific view, which represents the human race as, in an especial manner, the summit and crown of God's material workmanship, the end of the rest of creation, and the selected theatre of God's dealings with transgression and with obedience,—we can conceive, and, as religious persons hold, we can find ample and satisfactory evidence to believe. But if this world be merely one of innumerable worlds, all, like it, the workmanship of God; all, the seats of life, like it; others, like it, occupied by intelligent creatures, capable of will, of law, of obedience, of disobedience, as man is; to hold that this world has been the scene of God's care and kindness, and still more, of his special interpositions, communications, and personal dealings with its individual inhabitants, in the way which Religion teaches, is, the objector is conceived to maintain, extravagant and incredible. It is to select one of the millions of globes which are scattered through the vast domain of space, and to suppose that one to be treated in a special and exceptional manner, without any reason for the assumption of such a peculiarity, except that this globe happens to be the habitation of us, who make this assumption. If Religion require us to assume, that one particular corner of the Universe has been thus singled out, and made an exception to the general rules by which all other parts of the Universe are governed; she makes, it may be said, a demand upon our credulity which cannot fail to be rejected by those who are in the habit of contemplating and admiring those general laws. Can the Earth be thus the centre of the moral and religious universe, when it has been shown to have no claim to be the centre of the physical universe? Is it not as absurd to maintain this, as it would be to hold, at the present day, the old Ptolemaic hypothesis, which places the Earth in the centre of the heavenly motions, instead of the newer Copernican doctrine, which teaches that the Earth revolves round the Sun? Is not Religion disproved, by the necessity under which she lies, of making such an assumption as this?

4. Such is, in a general way, the objection to Religion with which Chalmers deals; and, as I have said, his mode of treating it is highly interesting and instructive. Perhaps, however, we shall make our reasonings and speculations apply to a wider class of readers, if we consider the view now spoken of, not as an objection, urged by an opponent of religion, but rather as a difficulty, felt by a friend of religion. It is, I conceive, certain that many of those who are not at all disposed to argue against religion, but who, on the contrary, feel that their whole internal comfort and repose are bound up indissolubly with their religious convictions, are still troubled and dismayed at the doctrines of the vastness of the universe, and the multitude of worlds, which they suppose to be taught and proved by astronomy. They have a profound reverence for the Idea of God; they are glad to acknowledge their constant and universal dependence upon His preserving power and goodness; they are ready and desirous to recognize the working of His providence; they receive the moral law, as His law, with reverence and submission; they regard their transgressions of this law as sins against Him; and are eager to find the mode of reconciliation to Him, when thus estranged from him; they willingly think of God, as near to them. But while they listen to the evidence which science, as we have said, sets before them, of the long array of groups, and hosts, and myriads, of worlds, which are brought to our knowledge, they find themselves perturbed and distressed. They would willingly think of God as near to them; but during the pro-

gress of this enumeration, He appears, at every step, to be removed further and further from them. To discover that the Earth is so large, the number of its inhabitants so great, its form so different from what man at first imagines it, may perhaps have startled them; but in this view, there is nothing which a pious mind does not easily surmount. But if Venus and Mars also have their inhabitants; if Saturn and Jupiter, globes so much larger than the earth, have a proportional amount of population; may not man be neglected or overlooked? Is he worthy to be regarded by the Creator of all? May not, must not, the most pious mind recur to the exclamation of the Psalmist: "Lord, what is man, that thou art mindful of him?" And must not this exclamation, under the new aspect of things, be accompanied by an enfeebled and less confident belief that God *is* mindful of him? And then, this array of planets, which derive their light from the Sun, extends much further than even the astronomer at first suspected. The orbit of Saturn is ten times as wide as the orbit of the earth; but beyond Saturn, and almost twice as far from the sun, Herschel discovers Uranus, another great planet; and again, beyond Uranus, and again at nearly twice *his* distance, the subtle sagacity of the astronomers of our day, surmises, and then detects, another great planet. In such a system as this, the earth shrinks into insignificance. Can its concerns engage the attention of him who made the whole? But again, this whole Solar System itself, with all its orbits and planets, shrinks into a mere point, when compared with the nearest fixed star. And again, the distance which lies between us and such stars, shrinks into incalculable smallness, when we journey in thought to other fixed stars. And again, and again, the field of our previous contemplation suffers an immeasurable contraction, as we pass on to other points of view.

5. And in all these successive moves, we are still within the dominions of the same Creator and Governor; and at every move, we are brought, we may suppose, to new bodies of his subjects, bearing, in the expansion of their number, some proportion to the expanse of space which they occupy. And if this be so, how shall the earth, and men, its inhabitants, thus repeatedly annihilated, as it were, by the growing magnitude of the known Universe, continue to be anything in the regard of Him who embraces all? Least of all, how shall men continue to receive that special, persevering, providential, judicial, personal care, which religion implies; and without the belief of which, any man who has religious thoughts, must be disturbed and unhappy, desolate and forsaken?

6. Such are, I conceive, the thoughts of many persons, under the influence of the astronomical views which Chalmers refers to as being sometimes employed against religious belief. Of course, it is natural that the views which are used by unbelievers as arguments against religious belief, should create difficulties and troubles in the minds of believers; at least, till the argument is rebutted. And of course also, the answers to the arguments, considered as infidel arguments, would operate to remove the difficulties which believers entertain on such grounds. Chalmers' reasonings against such arguments, therefore, will, so far as they are valid, avail to relieve the mental trouble of believers, who are perplexed and oppressed by the astronomical views of which I have spoken; as well as to confute and convince those who reject religion, on such astronomical grounds. It may, however, as I have said, be of use to deal with these difficulties rather as difficulties of religious men, than as objections of irreligious men; to examine rather how we can quiet the troubled and perplexed believer, than how we can triumph over the dogmatic and

self-satisfied infidel. I, at least, should wish to have the former, rather than the latter of these tasks, regarded as that which I propose to myself.

I shall hereafter attempt to explain more fully the difficulties which the doctrine of the Plurality of Worlds appears to some persons to throw in the way of Revealed Religion; but before I do so, there is one part of Chalmers' answer, bearing especially upon Natural Religion, which it may be proper to attend to.

CHAPTER III.

THE ANSWER FROM THE MICROSCOPE.

1. It is not my business, nor my intention, to criticize the remarkable work of Chalmers to which I have so often referred. But I may say, that the arguments there employed by him, so far as they go upon astronomical or philosophical grounds, are of great weight; and upon the whole, such as we may both assent to, as scientifically true, and accept as rationally persuasive. I think, however, that there are other arguments, also drawn from scientific discoveries, which bear, in a very important and striking manner, upon the opinions in question, and which Chalmers has not referred to; and I conceive that there are philosophical views of another kind, which, for those who desire and who will venture to regard the Universe and its Creator in the wider and deeper relations which appear to be open to human speculation, may be a source of satisfaction. When certain positive propositions, maintained as true while they are really highly doubtful, have given rise to difficulties in the minds of religious persons, other positive propositions, combating these, propounded and supported by argument, that they may be accepted according to their evidence, may, at any rate, have force enough to break down and dissipate such loosely founded difficulties. To present to the reader's

mind such speculations as I have thus indicated, is the object of the following pages. They can, of course, pretend to no charm, except for persons who are willing to have their minds occupied with such difficulties and such speculations as I have referred to. Those who are willing to be so employed, may, perhaps, find in what I have to say something which may interest them. For, of the arguments which I have to expound, some, though they appear to me both very obvious and very forcible, have never, so far as I am aware, been put forth in that religious bearing which seems to belong to them; and others, though aspiring to point out in some degree the relation of the Universe and its Creator, are of a very simple kind; that is, for minds which are prepared to deal with such subjects at all.

2. As I have said, the arguments with which we are here concerned refer both to Natural Religion and to Revealed Religion; and there is one of Chalmers' arguments, bearing especially upon the former branch of the subject, which I may begin by noticing. Among the thoughts which, it was stated, might naturally arise in men's minds, when the telescope revealed to them an innumerable multitude of worlds besides the one which we inhabit, was this: that the Governor of the Universe, who has so many worlds under his management, cannot be conceived as bestowing upon this Earth, and its various tribes of inhabitants, that care which, till then, Natural Religion had taught men that he does employ, to secure to man the possession and use of his faculties of mind and body; and to all animals the requisites of animal existence and animal enjoyment. And upon this Chalmers remarks, that just about the time when science gave rise to the suggestion of this difficulty, she also gave occasion to a remarkable reply to it. Just about the same time that the invention of the

Telescope showed that there were innumerable worlds, which might have inhabitants requiring the Creator's care as much as the tribes of this earth do,—the invention of the *Microscope* showed that there were, in this world, innumerable tribes of animals, which had been all along enjoying the benefits of the Creator's care, as much as those kinds with which man had been familar from the beginning. The telescope suggested that there might be dwellers in Jupiter or in Saturn, of giant size and unknown structure, who must share with us the preserving care of God. The microscope showed that there had been, close to us, inhabiting minute crevices and crannies, peopling the leaves of plants, and the bodies of other animals, animalcules of a minuteness hitherto unguessed, and of a structure hitherto unknown, who had been always sharers with us in God's preserving care. The telescope brought into view worlds as numerous as the drops of water which make up the ocean; the microscope brought into view a world in almost every drop of water. Infinity in one direction was balanced by infinity in the other. The doubts which men might feel as to what God could do, were balanced by certainties which they discovered, as to what he had always been doing. His care and goodness could not be supposed to be exhausted by the hitherto known population of the earth, for it was proved that they had not hitherto been confined to that population. The discovery of new worlds at vast distances from us, was accompanied by the discovery of new worlds close to us, even in the very substances with which we were best acquainted; and was thus rendered ineffective to disturb the belief of those who had regarded the world as having God for its governor.

3. This is a striking reflection, and is put by Chalmers in a very striking manner; and it is well fitted to remove the

scruples to which it is especially addressed. If there be any persons to whom the astronomical discoveries which the telescope has brought to light, suggests doubts or difficulties with regard to such truths of Natural Religion as God's care for and government of the inhabitants of the earth, the discoveries of the many various forms of animalcular life which the microscope has brought to light are well fitted to remove such doubts, and to solve such difficulties. We may easily believe that the power of God to sustain and provide for animal life, animal sustenance, animal enjoyment, can suffice for innumerable worlds besides this, without being withdrawn or distracted or wearied in this earth; for we find that it does suffice for innumerable more inhabitants of this earth than we were before aware of. If we had imagined before, that, in conceiving God as able and willing to provide for the life and pleasure of all the sentient beings which we knew to exist upon the earth, we had formed an adequate notion of his power and of his goodness, these microscopical discoveries are well adapted to undeceive us. They show us that all the notions which our knowledge, hitherto, had enabled us to form of the powers and attributes of the Creator and Preserver of all living things, are vastly, are immeasurably below the real truth of the case. They show us that God, as revealed to us in the animal creation, is the Author and Giver of life, of the organization which life implies, of the contrivances by which it is conducted and sustained, of the enjoyment by which it is accompanied,—to an extent infinitely beyond what the unassisted vision of man could have suggested. The facts which are obvious to man, from which religious minds in all ages have drawn their notions and their evidence of the Divine power and goodness, care and wisdom, in providing for its creatures, require, we find, to be indefinitely extended, in virtue of the new tribes of minute creatures, and still new tribes, and still more minute, which we find existing around us. The views of our Natural Theology must be indefinitely extended on one side; and therefore we need not be startled or disturbed at having to extend them indefinitely on the other side;—at having to believe that there are, in other worlds, creatures whom God has created, whom he sustains in life, for whom he provides the pleasures of life, as he does for the long unsuspected creatures of this world.

4. This is, I say, a reflection which might quiet the mind of a person, whom astronomical discoveries had led to doubt of the ordinary doctrines of Natural Religion. But, I think, it may be questioned, whether, to produce such doubts, is a common or probable effect of an acquaintance with astronomical discoveries. Undoubtedly, by such discoveries, a person who believes in God, in his wisdom, power, and goodness, on the evidence of the natural world, is required to extend and exalt his conceptions of those Divine Attributes. He had believed God to be the Author of many forms of life;—he finds him to be the Author of still more forms of life. He had traced many contrivances in the structure of animals, for their sustentation and well-being; his new discoveries disclose to him (for that is undoubtedly among the effects of microscopic researches) still more nice contrivances. He had seen reason to think that all sentient beings have their enjoyments; he finds new fields of enjoyment of the same kind. But in all this, there is little or nothing to disturb the views and convictions of the Natural Theologian. He must, even by the evidence of facts patent to ordinary observation, have been led to believe that the Divine Wisdom and Power are not only great, but great in a degree which we cannot fathom or comprehend;—that they are, to our apprehension, infinite: his

new discoveries only confirm the impression of this infinite character of the Divine Attributes. He had before believed the existence of an intelligent and wise Creator, on the evidence of the marks of design and contrivance, which the creation exhibited: of such design and contrivance he discovers new marks, new examples. He had believed that God is good, because he found those contrivances invariably had the good of the creature for their object: he finds, still, that this is the general, the universal scheme of the creation, now when his view of it is extended. He has no difficulty in expanding his religious conceptions, to correspond with his scientific discoveries, so far as the microscope is the instrument of discovery; there is no reason why he should have any more difficulty in doing the same, when the telescope is his informant. It is true, that in this case the information is more imperfect. It does not tell him, even that there are living inhabitants in the regions which it reveals; and, consequently, it does not disclose any of those examples of design which belong to the structure of living things. But if we suppose, from analogy, that there are living things in those regions, we have no difficulty in conceiving, from analogy also, that those living things are constructed with a care and wisdom such as appear in the inhabitants of earth. It will not readily or commonly occur to a speculator on such subjects, that there is any source of perplexity or unbelief, in such an assumption of inhabitants of other worlds, even if we make the assumption. It is as easy, it may well and reasonably be thought, for God to create a population for the planets as to make the planets themselves;—as easy to supply Jupiter with tenants, as with satellites;—as easy to devise the organization of an inhabitant of Saturn, as the structure and equilibrium of Saturn's ring. It is no more difficult for the Universal Creator to extend to those bodies the powers which operate in organized matter, than the powers which operate in brute matter. It is as easy for Him to establish circulation and nutrition in material structures, as cohesion and crystallization, which we must suppose the planetary masses to possess; or attraction and inertia, which we know them to possess. No doubt, to our conception, organization appears to be a step beyond cohesion; circulation of living fluids, a step beyond crystallization of dead masses:—but then, it is in tracing such steps, that we discern the peculiar character of the Creator's agency. He does not merely work with mechanical and chemical powers, as man to a certain extent can do; but with organic and vital powers, which man cannot command. The Creator, therefore, can animate the dust of each planet, as easily as make the dust itself. And when from organic life we rise to sentient life, we have still only another step in the known order of Creative Power. To create animals, in any province of the Universe, cannot be conceived as much more incomprehensible or incredible, than to create vegetables. No doubt, the addition of the living and sentient principle to the material, and even to the organic structure, is a mighty step; and one which may, perhaps, be made the occasion of some speculative suggestions, in a subsequent part of this Essay; but still, it is not likely that any one, who had formed his conceptions of the Divine Mind from its manifestations in the production and sustentation of animal, as well as vegetable life, on this earth, would have his belief in the operation of such a Mind, shaken, by any necessity which might be impressed upon him, of granting the existence of animal life on other planets, as well as on the earth, or even on innumerable such planets, and on innumerable systems of planets and worlds, system above system.

5. The remark of Chalmers, therefore, to which I have referred, striking as it is, does not appear to bear directly upon a difficulty of any great force. If astronomy gives birth to scruples which interfere with religion, they must be found in some other quarter than in the possibility of mere animal life existing in other parts of the Universe, as well as on our earth. That possibility may require us to enlarge our idea of the Deity, but it has little or no tendency to disturb our apprehension of his attributes.

CHAPTER IV.

FURTHER STATEMENT OF THE DIFFICULTY.

1. We have attempted to show that if the discoveries made by the Telescope should excite in any one's mind, difficulties respecting those doctrines of Natural Religion,—the adequacy of the Creator to the support and guardianship of all the animal life which may exist in the universe,—the discoveries of the Microscope may remove such difficulties; but we have remarked also, that the train of thought which leads men to dwell upon such difficulties does not seem to be common.

But what will be the train of thought to which we shall be led, if we suppose that there are, on other planets, and in other systems, not animals only, living things, which, however different from the animals of this earth, are yet in some way analogous to them, according to the difference of circumstances; but also creatures analogous to man;—intellectual creatures, living, we must suppose, under a moral law, responsible for transgression, the subjects of a Providential Government? If we suppose that, in the other planets of our solar systems, and of other systems, there are creatures of such a kind, and under such conditions as these, how far will the religious opinions which we had previously entertained be disturbed or modified? Will any new difficulty be introduced into our views of the government of the world by such a supposition?

2. I have spoken of man as an Intellectual Creature; meaning thereby that he has a Mind;—powers of thought, by which he can contemplate the relations and properties of things in a general and abstract form; and among other relations, moral relations, the distinction of *right* and *wrong* in his actions. Those powers of thought lead him to think of a Creator and Ordainer of all things; and his perception of right and wrong leads him to regard this Creator as also the Governor and Judge of his creatures. The operation of his mind directs him to believe in a Supreme Mind: his moral nature directs him to believe that the course of human affairs, and the condition of men, both as individuals and as bodies, is determined by the providential government of God.

3. With regard to the bearing of a merely *intellectual* nature on such questions, it does not appear that any considerable difficulty would be *at once* occasioned in our religious views, by supposing such a nature to belong to other creatures, the inhabitants of other planets, as well as to man. The existence of our own minds directs us, as I have said, to a Supreme Mind; and the nature of Mind is conceived to be, in all its manifestations, so much the same, that we can conceive minds to be multiplied indefinitely, without fear of confusion, interference, or exhaustion. There may be, in Jupiter, creatures endowed with an intellect which enables them to discover and demonstrate the relations of space; and if so, they cannot have discovered and demonstrated anything of that kind as true, which is not true for us also: their Geometry must coincide with ours, as far as each goes:—thus showing how absurdly, as Plato long ago observed, we give to the science which deals with the relations of space, a name (*geometry*),

borrowed from the art of measuring the earth. The earth with its properties is no more the special basis of geometry, than are Jupiter or Saturn, or, so far as we can judge, Sirius or Arcturus and their systems, with their properties. Wherever pure intellect is, we are compelled to conceive that, when employed upon the same objects, its results and conclusions are the same. If there be intelligent inhabitants of the Moon, they may, like us, have employed their intelligence in reasoning upon the properties of lines and angles and triangles; and must, so far as they have gone, have arrived, in their thoughts, at the same properties of lines and angles and triangles, at which we have arrived. They must, like us, have had to distinguish between right angles and oblique angles. They may have come to know, as some of the inhabitants of the earth came to know, four thousand years ago, that, in a right-angled triangle, the square on the larger side is equal to the sum of the squares on the other two sides. We can conceive occurrences which would give us evidence that the Moon, as well as the Earth, contains geometers. If we were to see, on the face of the full moon, a figure gradually becoming visible, representing a right-angled triangle with a square constructed on each of its three sides as a base; we should regard it as the work of intelligent creatures there, who might be thus making a signal to the inhabitants of the earth, that they possessed such knowledge, and were desirous of making known to their nearest neighbors in the solar system, their existence and their speculations. In such an event, curious and striking as it would be, we should see nothing but what we could understand and accept, without unsettling our belief in the Supreme and Divine Intelligence. On the contrary, we could hardly fail to receive such a manifestation as a fresh evidence that the Divine Mind had imparted to the inhabitants of the Moon, as he has to us, a power of apprehending, in a very general and abstract form, the relations of that space in which he performs his works. We should judge, that having been led so far in their speculations, they must, in all probability, have been led also to a conception of the Universe, as the field of action of a universal and Divine Mind; that having thus become geometers, they must have ascended to the Idea of a God who works by geometry.

4. But yet, by such a supposition, on further consideration, we find ourselves introduced to views entirely different from those to which we are led by the supposition of mere animal life, existing in other worlds than the earth. For, not to dwell here upon any speculations as to how far the operations of our minds may resemble the operations of the Divine Mind;—a subject which we shall hereafter endeavor to discuss;—we know that the advance to such truths as those of geometry has been, among the inhabitants of the earth, gradual and progressive. Though the human mind have had the same powers and faculties, from the beginning of the existence of the race up to the present time, (as we cannot but suppose,) the results of the exercise of these powers and faculties have been very different in different ages; and have gradually grown up, from small beginnings, to the vast and complex body of knowledge concerning the scheme and relations of the Universe, which is at present accessible to the minds of human speculators. It is, as we have said, probably about four thousand years, since the first steps in such knowledge were made. Geometry is said to have had its origin in Egypt; but it assumed its abstract and speculative character first among the Greeks. Pythagoras is related to have been the first who saw, in the clear light of demonstration, the property of the right-angled triangle, of which we have spoken. The Greeks, from

the time of Socrates, stimulated especially by Plato, pursued, with wonderful success, the investigation of this kind of truths. They saw that such truths had their application in the heavens, far more extensively than on the earth. They were enabled, by such speculations, to unravel, in a great degree, the scheme of the universe, before so seemingly entangled and perplexed. They determined, to a very considerable extent, the relative motions of the planets and of the stars. And in modern times, after a long interval, in which such knowledge was nearly stationary, the progress again began; and further advances were successively made in man's knowledge of the scheme and structure of the visible heavens; till at length the intellect of man was led to those views of the extent of the Universe and the nature of the stars, which are the basis of the discussions in which we are now engaged. And thus man, having probably been, in the earliest ages of the existence of the species, entirely ignorant of abstract truth, and of the relations which, by the knowledge of such truth, we can trace in nature, (as the barbarous tribes which occupy the greater part of the earth's surface still are;) has, by a long series of progressive steps, come into the possession of knowledge, which we cannot regard without wonder and admiration; and which seems to elevate him in no inconsiderable degree, towards a community of thought with that Divine Mind, into the nature and scheme of whose works he is thus permitted to penetrate.

5. Now the knowledge which man is capable, by the nature of his mental faculties, of acquiring, being thus blank and rudimentary at first, and only proceeding gradually, by the steps of a progress, numerous, slow, and often long interrupted, to that stage in which it is the basis of our present speculations; the view which we have just taken, of the nature of Intellect, as a faculty always of the same kind, always

uniform in its operations, always consistent in its results, appears to require reconsideration; and especially with reference to the application which we made of that view, to the intelligent inhabitants of other planets and other worlds, if such inhabitants there be. For if we suppose that there are, in the Moon, or in Jupiter, creatures possessing intellectual faculties of the same kind as those of man; capable of apprehending the same abstract and general truths; able, like man, to attain to a knowledge of the scheme of the Universe; yet this supposition merely gives the capacity and the ability; and does not include any security, or even high probability, as it would seem, of the exercise of such capacity, or of the successful application of such ability. Even if the surface of the Moon be inhabited by creatures as intelligent as men, why must we suppose that they know anything more of the geometry and astronomy, than the great bulk of the less cultured inhabitants of the earth, who occupy, really, a space far larger than the surface of the Moon; and, all intelligent though they be, and in the full possession of mental faculties, are yet, on the subjects of geometry and astronomy, entirely ignorant;—their minds, as to such a knowledge, a blank? It does not follow, then, that even if there be such inhabitants in the Moon, or in the Planets, they have any sympathy with us, or any community of knowledge on the subjects of which we are now speaking. The surface of the Moon, or of Jupiter, or of Saturn, even if well peopled, may be peopled only with tribes as barbarous and ignorant as Tartars, or Esquimaux, or Australians; and therefore, by making such a supposition, we do little, even hypothetically, to extend the dominion of that intelligence, by means of which all intelligent beings have some community of thought with each other, and some suggestion of the working of the Divine and Universal Mind.

6. But, in fact, the view which we have given of the mode of existence of the human species upon the earth, as being a progressive existence, even in the development of the intellectual powers and their results, necessarily fastens down our thoughts and our speculations to the earth, and makes us feel how visionary and gratuitous it is to assume any similar kind of existence in any region occupied by other beings than man. As we have said, we have no insuperable difficulty in conceiving other parts of the Universe to be tenanted by animals. Animal life implies no progress in the species. Such as they are in one century, such are they in another. The conditions of their sustentation and generation being given, which no difference of physical circumstances can render incredible, the race may, so far as we can see, go on forever. But a race which makes a progress in the development of its faculties cannot thus, or at least cannot with the same ease, be conceived as existing through all time, and under all circumstances. Progress implies, or at least suggests, a beginning and an end. If the mere existence of a race imply a sustaining and preserving power in the Creator, the progress of a race implies a guiding and impelling power; a Governor and Director, as well as a Creator and Preserver. And progress, not merely in material conditions, not merely in the exercise of bodily faculties, but in the exercise of mental faculties, in the intellectual condition of a portion of the species, still more implies a special position and character of the race, which cannot, without great license of hypothesis, be extended to other races; and which, if so extended, becomes unmeaning, from the impossibility of our knowing what is progress in any other species;—from what and towards what it tends. The intellectual progress of the human species has been a progress in the use of thought, and in the knowledge which such use pro-

cures; it has been a progress from mere matter to mind; from the impressions of sense to ideas; from what in knowledge is casual, partial, temporary, to what is necessary, universal, and eternal. We can conceive no progress, of the nature of this, which is not identical with this; nothing like it, which is not the same. And, therefore, if we will people other planets with creatures, intelligent as man is intelligent, we must not only give to them the intelligence, but the intellectual history of the human species. They must have had their minds unfolded by steps similar to those by which the human mind has been unfolded; or at least, differing from them only as the intellectual history of one nation of the earth differs from that of another. They must have had their Pythagoras, their Plato, their Kepler, their Galileo, their Newton, if they know what we know. And thus, in order to conceive, on the Moon or on Jupiter, a race of beings intelligent like man, we must conceive, there, colonies of men, with histories resembling more or less the histories of human colonies; and indeed resembling the history of those nations whose knowledge we inherit, far more closely than the history of any other terrestrial nation resembles that part of terrestrial history. If we do this, we exercise an act of invention and imagination which may be as coherent as a fairy tale, but which, without further proof, must be as purely imaginary and arbitrary. But if we do not do this, we cannot conceive that those regions are occupied at all by intelligent beings. Intelligence, as we see in the human race, in order to have those characters which concern our argument, implies a history of intellectual development; and to assume arbitrarily a history of intellectual development for the inhabitants of a remote planet, as a ground of reasoning either for or against Religion, is a proceeding which we can hardly be expected either to assent to or to refute. If we are to form any opinions with regard to the condition of such bodies, and to trace any bearing of such opinions upon our religious views, we must proceed upon some ground which has more of reality than such a gratuitous assumption.

7. Thus the condition of man upon the earth, as a condition of intellectual progress, implies such a special guidance and government exercised over the race by the Author of his being, as produces progress; and we have not, so far as we yet perceive, any reason for supposing that He exercises a like guidance and government over any of the other bodies with which the researches of astronomers have made us acquainted. The earth and its inhabitants are under the care of God in a special manner; and we are utterly destitute of any reason for believing that other planets and other systems are under the care of God in the same manner. If we regarded merely the existence of unprogressive races of animals upon our globe, we might easily suppose that other globes also are similarly tenanted; and we might infer, that the Creator and Upholder of animal life was active on those globes, in the same manner as upon ours. But when we come to a progressive creature, whose condition implies a beginning, and therefore suggests an end, we form a peculiar judgment with respect to God's care of that creature, which we have not as yet seen the slightest grounds to extend to other possible fields of existence, where we discern no indication of progress, of beginning, or of end. So far as we can judge, God is mindful of man, and has launched and guided his course in a certain path which makes his lot and state different from that of all other creatures.

8. Now when we have arrived at this result, we have, I conceive, reached one of the points at which the difficulties which astronomical discovery puts in the way of religious conviction

begin to appear. The Earth and its human inhabitants are, as far as we yet know, in an especial manner the subjects of God's care and government, for the race is progressive. Now can this be? Is it not difficult to believe that it is so? The earth, so small a speck, only one among so many, so many thousands, so many millions of other bodies, all, probably, of the same nature with itself, wherefore should it draw to it the special regards of the Creator of all, and occupy his care in an especial manner? The teaching of the history of the human race, as intellectually progressive, agrees with the teaching of Religion, in impressing upon us that God is mindful of man; that he does regard him; but still, there naturally arises in our minds a feeling of perplexity and bewilderment, which expresses itself in the words already so often quoted, What is man, that this should be so? Can it be true that this province is thus singled out for a special and peculiar administration by the Lord of the Universal Empire?

9. Before I make any attempt to answer these questions, I must pursue the difficulty somewhat further, and look at it in other forms. As I have said, the history of Man has been, in certain nations, a history of intellectual progress, from the earliest times up to our own day. But intellectual progress has been, as I have also said, in a great measure confined to certain nations thus especially favored. The greater part of the earth's inhabitants have shared very scantily in that wealth of knowledge to which the brightest and happiest intellects among men have thus been led. But though the bulk of mankind have thus had little share in the grand treasures of science which are open to the race, their life has still been very different from that of other animals. Many nations, though they may not have been conspicuous in the history of intellectual progress, have yet not been without their place in

progress of other kinds—in arts, in arms, and, above all, in morals—in the recognition of the distinction of right and wrong in human actions, and in the practical application of this distinction. Such a progress as this has been far more extensively aimed at, than a progress in abstract and general knowledge; and, we may venture to say, has been, in many nations and in a very great measure, really effected. No doubt the imperfection of this progress, and the constant recurrence of events which appear to counteract and reverse it, are so obvious and so common as to fill with grief and indignation the minds of those who regard such a progress as the great business of the human race; but yet still, looking at the whole history of the human race, the progress is visible; and even the grief and the indignation of which we have spoken are a part of its evidences. There has been, upon the whole, a moral government of the human race. The moral law, the distinction of right and wrong, has been established in every nation; and penalties have been established for wrong-doing. The notion of right and wrong has been extended, from mere outward acts, to the springs of action, to affection, desire, and will. The course of human affairs has generally been such, that the just, the truthful, the kind, the chaste, the orderly portion of mankind have been happier than the violent and wicked. External wrong has been commonly punished by the act of human society. Internal sins, impure and dishonest designs, falsehood, cruelty, have very often led to their own punishment, by their effect upon the guilty mind itself. We do not say that the moral government which has prevailed among men has been such, that we can consider it complete and final in its visible form. We see that the aspect of things is much the contrary; and we think we see reasons why it may be expected to be so. But still, there has existed upon earth a moral government of the human race, exercised, as we must needs hold, by the Creator of man; partly through the direct operation of man's faculties, affections, and emotions; and partly through the authorities which, in all ages and nations, the nature of man has led him to establish. Now this moral progress and moral government of the human race is one of the leading facts on which Natural Religion is founded. We are thus led to regard God as the Moral Governor of man; not only his Creator and Preserver, but his Lawgiver and his Judge. And the grounds on which we entertain this belief are peculiarly the human faculties of man, and their operation in history and in society. The belief is derived from the whole complex nature of man—the working of his Affections, Desires, Convictions, Reason, Conscience, and whatever else enters into the production of human action and its consequences. God is seen to be the Moral Governor of man by evidence which is especially derived from the character of Man, and which we could not attempt to apply to any other creature than man without making our words altogether unmeaning. But would it not be too bold an assumption to speak of the Conscience of an inhabitant of Jupiter? Would it not be a rash philosophy to assume the operation of Remorse or Self-approval on the planet, in order that we may extend to it the moral government of God? Except we can point out something more solid than this to reason from, on such subjects, there is no use in our attempting to reason at all. Our doctrines must be mere results of invention and imagination. Here then, again, we are brought to the conviction that God is, so far as we yet see, in an especial and peculiar manner, the Governor of the earth and of its human inhabitants, in such a way that the like government cannot be conceived to be extended to other planets, and other systems, without arbitrary and fanciful assumptions; assumptions either of unintelligible differences with incomprehensible results, or of beings in all respects human, inhabiting the most remote regions of the universe. And here, again, therefore, we are led to the same difficulty which we have already encountered: Can the earth, a small globe among so many millions, have been selected as the scene of this especially Divine Government?

10. That when we attempt to extend our sympathies to the inhabitants of other planets and other worlds, and to regard them as living, like us, under a moral government, we are driven to suppose them to be, in all essential respects, human beings like ourselves, we have proof, in all the attempts which have been made, with whatever license of hypothesis and fancy, to present to us descriptions and representations of the inhabitants of other parts of the universe. Such representations, though purposely made as unlike human beings as the imagination of man can frame them, still are merely combinations, slightly varied, of the elements of human being; and thus show us that not only our reason, but even our imagination, cannot conceive creatures subjected to the same government to which man is subjected, without conceiving them as being men of one kind or other. A mere animal life, with no interest but animal enjoyment, we may conceive as assuming forms different from those which appear in existing animal races; though even here, there are, as we shall hereafter attempt to show, certain general principles which run through all animal life. But when in addition to mere animal impulses, we assume or suppose moral and intellectual interests, we conceive them as the moral and intellectual interests of man. Truth and falsehood, right and wrong, law and transgression, happiness and misery, reward and punishment, are the necessary elements of all that can interest us—of all that

we can call *Government.* To transfer these to Jupiter or to Sirius, is merely to imagine those bodies to be a sort of island of Formosa, or new Atlantis, or Utopia, or Platonic Polity, or something of the like kind. The boldest and most resolute attempts to devise some life different from human life, have not produced anything more different than romance-writers and political theorists have devised *as* a form of human life. And this being so, there is no more wisdom or philosophy in believing such assemblages of beings to exist in Jupiter or Sirius, without evidence, than in believing them to exist in the island of Formosa, with the like absence of evidence.

11. Any examination of what has been written on this subject would show that, in speculating about moral and intellectual beings in other regions of the universe, we merely make them to be men in another place. With regard to the plants and animals of other planets, fancy has freer play; but man cannot conceive any moral creature who is not man. Thus Fontenelle, in his *Dialogues on the Plurality of Worlds*, makes the inhabitants of Venus possess, in an exaggerated degree, the characteristics of the men of the warm climates of the earth. They are like the Moors of Grenada; or rather, the Moors of Grenada would be to them as cold as Greenlanders and Laplanders to us. And the inhabitants of Mercury have so much vivacity, that they would pass with us for insane. "Enfin c'est dans Mercure que sont les Petites-Maisons de l'Univers." The inhabitants of Jupiter and Saturn are immensely slow and phlegmatic. And though he and other writers attempt to make these inhabitants of remote regions in some respects superior to man, telling us that instead of only five senses, they may have six, or ten, or a hundred, still these are mere words which convey no meaning; and the great astronomer Bessel had reason to say, that those who imagined inhabitants in the

Moon and Planets, supposed them, in spite of all their protestations, as like to men as one egg to another.*

12. But there is one step more, which we still have to make, in order to bring out this difficulty in its full force. As we have said, the moral law has been, to a certain extent, established, developed, and enforced among men. But, as I have also said, looking carefully at the law, and at the degree of man's obedience to it, and at the operation of the sanctions by which it is supported, we cannot help seeing, that man's knowledge of the law is imperfect, his conviction of its authority feeble, his transgressions habitual, their punishment and consequences obscure. When, therefore, we regard God, as the Lawgiver and Judge of man, it will not appear strange to us, that he should have taken some mode of promulgating his Law, and announcing his Judgments, in addition to that ordinary operation of the faculties of man, of which we have spoken. Revealed Religion teaches us that he has done so: that from the first placing of the race of man upon the earth, it was his purpose to do so: that by his dealing with the race of man in the earlier times, and at various intervals, he made preparation for the mission of a special Messenger, whom, in the fulness of time, he sent upon the earth in the form of a man; and who both taught men the Law of God in a purer and clearer form than any in which it had yet been given; and revealed His purpose, of rewards for obedience, and punishments for disobedience, to be executed in a state of being to which this human life is only an introduction; and established the means by which the spirit of man, when alienated from God by transgression, may be again reconciled to Him. The arrival of this especial Messenger of Holiness, Judgment, and Redemption, forms the great event in the his-

* Populäre Vorlesungen über Wissenschaftliche Gegenstände, p. 31.

tory of the earth, considered in a religious view, as the abode of God's servants. It was attended with the sufferings and cruel death of the Divine Messenger thus sent; was preceded by prophetic announcements of his coming; and the history of the world, for the two thousand years that have since elapsed, has been in a great measure occupied with the consequences of that advent. Such a proceeding shows, of course, that God has an especial care for the race of man. The earth, thus selected as the theatre of such a scheme of Teaching and of Redemption, cannot, in the eyes of any one who accepts this Christian faith, be regarded as being on a level with any other domiciles. It is the Stage of the great Drama of God's Mercy and Man's Salvation; the Sanctuary of the Universe; the Holy Land of Creation; the Royal Abode, for a time at least, of the Eternal King. This being the character which has thus been conferred upon it, how can we assent to the assertions of Astronomers, when they tell us that it is only one among millions of similar habitations, not distinguishable from them, except that it is smaller than most of them that we can measure; confused and rude in its materials like them? Or if we believe the Astronomers, will not such a belief lead us to doubt the truth of the great scheme of Christianity, which thus makes the earth the scene of a special dispensation.

13. This is the form in which Chalmers has taken up the argument. This is the difficulty which he proposes to solve; or rather, (such being as I have said the mode in which he presents the subject,) the objection which he proposes to refute. It is the bearing of the Astronomical discoveries of modern times, not upon the doctrines of Natural Religion, but upon the scheme of Christianity, which he discusses. And the question which he supposes his opponent to propound, as

an objection to the Christian scheme, is :—How is it consistent with the dignity, the impartiality, the comprehensiveness, the analogy of God's proceedings, that he should make so special and pre-eminent a provision for the salvation of the inhabitants of this Earth, where there are such myriads of other worlds, all of which may require the like provision, and all of which have an equal claim to their Creator's care ?

14. The answer which Chalmers gives to this objection, is one drawn, in the first instance, from our ignorance. He urges that, when the objector asserts that other worlds may have the like need with our own, of a special provision for the rescue of their inhabitants from the consequences of the transgression of God's laws, he is really making an assertion without the slightest foundation. Not only does Science not give us any information on such subjects, but the whole spirit of the scientific procedure, which has led to the knowledge which we possess, concerning other planets and other systems, is utterly opposed to our making such assumptions, respecting other worlds, as the objection involves. Modern Science, in proportion as she is confident when she has good grounds of proof, however strange may be the doctrines proved, is not only diffident, but is utterly silent, and abstains even from guessing, when she has no grounds of proof. Chalmers takes Newton's reasoning, as offering a special example of this mixed temper, of courage in following the evidence, and temperance in not advancing when there is no evidence. He puts, in opposition to this, the example of the true philosophical temper,—a supposed rash theorist, who should make unwarranted suppositions and assumptions, concerning matters to which our scientific evidence does not reach ;—the animals and plants, for instance, which are to be found in the planet Jupiter. No one, he says, would more utterly reject and con-

demn such speculations than Newton, who first rightly explained the motion of Jupiter and of his attendant satellites, about which Science *can* pronounce her truths. And thus, nothing can be more opposite to the real spirit of modern science, and astronomy in particular, than arguments, such as we have stated, professing to be drawn from science and from astronomy. Since we know nothing about the inhabitants of Jupiter, true science requires that we say and suppose nothing about them; still more requires that we should not, on the ground of assumptions made with regard to them, and other supposed groups of living creatures, reject a belief, founded on direct and positive proofs, such as is the belief in the truths of Natural and of Revealed Religion.

15. To this argument of Chalmers, we may not only give our full assent, but we may venture to suggest, in accordance with what we have already said, that the argument, when so put, is not stated in all its legitimate force. The assertion that the inhabitants of Jupiter have the same need as we have, of a special dispensation for their preservation from moral ruin, is not only as merely arbitrary an assumption, as any assertion could be, founded on a supposed knowledge of an analogy between the botany of Jupiter, and the botany of the earth; but it is a great deal more so. There may be circumstances which may afford some reason to believe that something of the nature of vegetables grows on the surface of Jupiter; for instance, if we find that he is a solid globe surrounded by an atmosphere, vapor, clouds, showers. But, as we have already said, there is an immeasurable distance between the existence of unprogressive tribes of organized creatures, plants, or even animals, and the existence of a progressive creature, which can pass through the conditions of receiving, discerning, disobeying, and obeying a moral law; which can

be estranged from God, and then reconciled to him. To assume, without further proof, that there are, in Jupiter, creatures of such a nature that these descriptions apply to them, is a far bolder and more unphilosophical assumption, than any that the objector could make concerning the botany of Jupiter; and therefore, the objection thus supposed to be drawn from our supposed knowledge, is very properly answered by an appeal to our really utter ignorance, as to the points on which the argument rests.

16. This appeal to our ignorance is the main feature in Chalmer's reasonings, so far as the argument on the one side or the other has reference to science. Chalmers, indeed, pursues the argument into other fields of speculation. He urges, that not only we have no right to assume that other worlds require a redemption of the same kind as that provided for man, but that the very reverse may be the case. Man may be the only transgressor; and this, the only world that needed so great a provision for its salvation. We read in Scripture, expressions which imply that other beings, besides man, take an interest in the salvation of man. May not this be true of the inhabitants of other worlds, if such inhabitants there be? These speculations he pursues to a considerable length, with great richness of imagination, and great eloquence. But the suppositions on which they proceed are too loosely connected with the results of science, to make it safe for us to dwell upon them here.

17. I conceive, as I have said, that the argument with which Chalmers thus deals admits of answers, also drawn from modern science, which to many persons will seem more complete than that which is thus drawn from our ignorance. But before I proceed to bring forward these answers, which will require several steps of explanation, I have one or two remarks still to make.

18. Undoubtedly they who believe firmly both that the earth has been the scene of a Divine Plan for the benefit of man, and also that other bodies in the universe are inhabited by creatures who may have an interest in such a Plan, are naturally led to conjectures and imaginations as to the nature and extent of that interest. The religious poet, in his Night Thoughts, interrogates the inhabitants of a distant star, whether their race too has, in its history, events resembling the fall of man, and the redemption of man.

> Enjoy your happy realms their golden age?
> And had your Eden an abstemious Eve?
> Or, if your mother fell are you redeemed?
> And if redeemed, is your Redeemer scorned?

And such imaginations may be readily allowed to the preacher or the poet, to be employed in order to impress upon man the conviction of his privileges, his thanklessness, his inconsistency, and the like. But every form in which such reflections can be put shows how intimately they depend upon the nature and history of man. And when such reflections are made the source of difficulty or objection in the way of religious thought, and when these difficulties and objections are represented as derived from astronomical discoveries, it cannot be superfluous to inquire whether astronomy has really discovered any ground for such objections. To some persons it may be more grateful to remedy one assumption by another: the assumption of moral agents in other worlds, by the assumption of some operation of the Divine Plan in other worlds. But since many persons find great difficulty in conceiving such an operation of the Divine Plan in a satisfactory way; and many persons also think that to make such unauthorized and fanciful assumptions with regard to the Divine

Plans for the government of God's creatures is a violation of the humility, submission of mind, and spirit of reverence which religion requires; it may be useful if we can show that such assumptions, with regard to the Divine Plans, are called forth by assumptions equally gratuitous on the other side: that Astronomy no more reveals to us extra-terrestrial moral agents, than Religion reveals to us extra-terrestrial Plans of Divine government. Chalmers has spoken of the *rashness* of making assumptions on such subjects without proof; leaving it however, to be supposed, that though astronomy does not supply proof of intelligent inhabitants of other parts of the universe, she yet does offer strong analogies in favor of such an opinion. But such a procedure is more than rash: when astronomical doctrines are presented in the form in which they have been already laid before the reader, which is the ordinary and popular mode of apprehending them, the analogies in favor of "other worlds," are (to say the least) greatly exaggerated. And by taking into account what astronomy really teaches us, and what we learn also from other sciences, I shall attempt to reduce such "analogies" to their true value.

14. The privileges of man, which make the difficulty in assigning him his place in the vast scheme of the Universe, we have described as consisting in his being an *intellectual*, *moral*, and *religious* creature. Perhaps the privileges implied in the last term, and their place in our argument, may justify a word more of explanation. Religion teaches us that there is opened to man, not only a prospect of a life in the presence of God, after this mortal life, but also the possibility and the duty of spending this life as in the presence of God. This is properly the highest result and manifestation of the effect of Religion upon man. Precisely because it is this, it is difficult to speak of this effect without seeming to use the language of enthusi-

asm; and yet again, precisely because it is so, our argument would be incomplete without a reference to it. There is for man, a possibility and a duty of bringing his thoughts, purposes, and affections more and more into continual unison with the will of God. This, even Natural Religion taught men, was the highest point at which man could aim; and Revealed Religion has still more clearly enjoined the duty of aiming at such a condition. The means of a progress towards such a state belong to the Religion of the heart and mind. They include a constant purification and elevation of the thoughts, affections, and will, wrought by habits of religious reflection and meditation, of prayer and gratitude to God. Without entering into further explanation, all religious persons will agree that such a progress is, under happy influences, possible for man, and is the highest condition to which he can attain in this life. Whatever names may have been applied at different times to the steps of such a progress;—the cultivation of the divine nature in us; resignation; devotion; holiness; union with God; living in God, and with God in us;—religious persons will not doubt that there is a reality of internal state corresponding to these expressions; and that, to be capable of elevation into the condition which these expressions indicate, is one of the especial privileges of man. Man's soul, considered especially as the subject of God's government, is often called his *Spirit;* and that man is capable of such conformity to the will of God, and approximation to Him, is sometimes expressed by speaking of him as a *spiritual creature.* And though the privilege of being, or of being capable of becoming, in this sense, a spiritual creature, is a part of man's religious privileges; we may sometimes be allowed to use this additional expression, in order to remind the reader, how great those religious privileges are, and how close is the relation between man and God, which they imply.

15. We have given a view of the peculiar character of man's condition, which seem to claim for him a nature and place unique and incapable of repetition, in the scheme of the universe; and to this view astronomy, exhibiting to us the habitation of man as only one among many similar abodes, offers an objection. We are, therefore, now called upon, I conceive, to proceed to exhibit the answer which a somewhat different view of modern science suggests to this difficulty or objection.

For this purpose, we must begin by regarding the Earth in another point of view, different from that hitherto considered by us.

CHAPTER V.

GEOLOGY.

1. MAN, as I trust has been made apparent to the consciousness and conviction of the reader, is an intelligent, moral, religious, and spiritual creature; and we have to discuss the difficulty, or perplexity, or objection, which arises in our minds, when we consider such a creature as occupying an habitation, which is but one among many globes apparently equally fitted to be the dwelling-places of living things—a mere speck in the immensity of creation—an atom among such a vast array of material structures—a world, as we needs must deem it, among millions of other objects which appear to have an equal claim to be regarded as worlds.

2. The difficulty appears to be great, either way. Can the earth alone be the theatre of such intelligent, moral, religious, and spiritual action? On the other hand, can we conceive such action to go on in the other bodies of the universe? If we take the latter alternative, we must people other planets and other systems with men such as we are, even as to their history. For the intellectual and moral condition of man implies a *history* of the species; and the view of man's condition which religion presents, not only involves a scheme of which the history of the human race is a part, but also asserts a pe-

culiar reference had, in the provisions of God, to the nature of man; and even a peculiar relation and connection between the human and the divine nature. To extend such suppositions to other worlds would be a proceeding so arbitrary and fanciful, that we are led to consider whether the alternative supposition may not be more admissible. The alternative supposition is, that man is, in an especial and eminent manner, the object of God's care; that his place in the creation is, not that he merely occupies one among millions of similar domiciles provided in boundless profusion by the Creator of the Universe, but that he is the servant, subject, and child of God, in a way unique and peculiar; that his being a spiritual creature, (including his other attributes in the highest for the sake of brevity,) makes him belong to a spiritual world, which is not to be judged of merely by analogies belonging to the material universe.

3. Between these two difficulties the choice is embarrassing, and the decision must be unsatisfactory, except we can find some further ground of judgment. But perhaps this is not hopeless. We have hitherto referred to the evidence and analogies supplied by one science, namely, astronomy. But there are other sciences which give us information concerning the nature and history of the earth. From some of these, perhaps, we may obtain some knowledge of the place of the earth in the scheme of creation—how far it is, in its present condition, a thing unique, or only one thing among many like it. Any science which supplies us with evidence or information on this head, will give us aid in forming a judgment upon the question under our consideration. To such sciences, then, we will turn our attention.

One science has employed itself in investigating the nature and history of the earth by an examination of the materials of which it is composed; namely, Geology. Let us call to mind some of the results at which this science has arrived.

4. A very little attention to what is going on among the materials of which the earth's surface is composed, suffices to show us that there are causes of change constantly and effectually at work. The earth's surface is composed of land and water, hills and valleys, rocks and rivers. But these features undergo change, and produce change in each other. The mountain-rivers cut deeper and deeper into the ravines in which they run; they break up the rocks over which they rush, use the fragments as implements of further destruction, pile them up in sloping mounds where the streams issue from the mountains, spread them over the plains, fill up lakes with sediment, push into the sea great deltas. The sea batters the cliffs and eats away the land, and again, forms banks and islands where there had been deep water. Volcanoes pour out streams of lava, which destroy the vegetation over which they flow, and which again, after a series of years, are themselves clothed with vegetation. Earthquakes throw down tracts of land beneath the sea, and elevate other tracts from the bottom of the ocean. These agencies are everywhere manifest; and though at a given moment, at a given spot, their effect may seem to us almost imperceptible, too insignificant to be taken account of, yet in a long course of years almost every place has undergone considerable changes. Rivers have altered their courses, lakes have become plains, coasts have been swept away or have become inland districts, rich valleys have been ravaged by watery or fiery deluges, the country has in some way or other assumed a new face. The present aspect of the earth is in some degree different from what it was a few thousand years ago.

5. But yet, in truth, the changes of which we thus speak

have not been very considerable. The forms of countries, the lines of coasts, the ranges of mountains, the groups of valleys, the courses of rivers, are much the same now as they were in ancient times. The face of the earth, since man has had any knowledge of it, may have undergone some change, but the changeable has borne a small proportion to the permanent. Changes have taken place, and are taking place, but they do not take place rapidly. The ancient earth and the modern earth are, in all their main physical features, identical; and we must go backwards through a considerably larger interval than that which carries us back to what we usually term *antiquity*, before we are led, by the operation of causes now at work, to an aspect of the earth's surface very different from that which it now presents.

6. For instance, rivers do, no doubt, more or less alter, in the course of years, by natural causes. The Rhine, the Rhone, the Po, the Danube, have, certainly, during the last four thousand years, silted up their beds in level places, expanded the deltas at their mouths, changed the channels by which they enter the sea; and very probably, in their upper parts, altered the forms of their waterfalls and of their shingle beds. Yet even if we were thus to go backwards ten thousand, or twenty, or thirty thousand years, (setting aside great and violent causes of change, as earthquakes, volcanic eruptions, and the like,) the general form and course of these rivers, and of the ranges of mountains in which they flow, would not be different from what it is now. And the same may be said of coasts and islands, seas and bays. The present geography of the earth may be, and from all the evidence which we have, must be, very ancient, according to any measures of antiquity which can apply to human affairs.

7. But yet the further examination of the materials of the

earth carries us to a view beyond this. Though the general forms of the land and the waters of continents and seas, were, several thousand years ago, much the same as they now are; yet it was not always so. We have clear evidence that large tracts which are now dry ground, were formerly the bed of the ocean; and these, not tracts of the shore, where the varying warfare of sea and land is still going on, but the very central parts of great continents; the Alps, the Pyrenees, the Himalayas. For not only are the rocks of which these great mountain-chains consist, of such structure that they appear to have been formed as layers of sediment at the bottom of water; but also, these layers contain vast accumulations of shells, or impressions of shells, and other remains of marine animals. And these appearances are not few, limited, or partial. The existence of such marine remains, in the solid substance of continents and mountains, is a general, predominant, and almost universal fact, in every part of the earth. Nor is any other way of accounting for this fact admissible, than that those materials really have, at some time, formed bottoms of seas. The various other conjectures and hypotheses, which were put forward on this subject, when the amount, extent, multiplicity, and coherence of the phenomena were not yet ascertained, and when their natural history was not yet studied, cannot now be considered as worthy of the smallest regard. That many of our highest hills are formed of materials raised from the depths of ocean, is a proposition which cannot be doubted, by any one, who fairly examines the evidence which nature offers.

8. If we take this proposition only, we cannot immediately connect it with our knowledge respecting the surface of the earth in its present form. We learn that what is now land, has been sea; and we may suppose (since it is natural to as-

sume that the bulk of the sea has not much changed) that what is now sea was formerly land. But, except we can learn something of the manner in which this change took place, we cannot make any use of our knowledge. Was the change sudden, or gradual; abrupt, or successive; brief, or long-continuing?

9. To these questions, the further study of the facts enables us to return answers with great confidence. The change or changes which produced the effects of which we have spoken —the conversion of the bottom of the ocean into the centre of our greatest continents and highest mountains,—were undoubtedly gradual, successive, and long continued. We must state very briefly the grounds on which we make this assertion.

10. The masses which form our mountain-chains, offer evidence, as I have said, that they were deposited as sediment at the bottom of a sea, and then hardened. They consist of successive layers of such sediment, making up the whole mass of the mountain. These layers are, of course, to a certain extent, a measure of the time during which the deposition of sediment took place. The thicker the mass of sediment, the more numerous and varied its beds, and the longer period must we suppose to have been requisite for its formation. Without making any attempt at accurate or definite estimation, which would be to no purpose, it is plain that a mass of sedimentary strata five thousand or ten thousand feet thick, must have required, for its deposit, a long course of years, or rather, a long course of ages.

11. But again: on further examination it is found, that we have not merely one series of sedimentary deposits, thus forming our mountains. There are a number of different series of such layers or strata, to be found in different ranges

of hills, and in the same range, one series resting upon another. These different series of strata are distinguishable from one another by their general structure and appearance, besides more intimate characters, of which we shall shortly have to speak. Each such series appears to have a certain consistency of structure within itself; the layers of which it is composed being more or less parallel, but the successive series are not thus always parallel, the lower ones being often highly inclined and irregular, while the upper ones are more level and continuous: as if the lower strata had been broken up and thrown into disorder, and then a new series of strata had been deposited horizontally on their fragments. But in whatever way these different sedimentary series succeeded each other, each series must have required, as we have seen, a long period for its formation; and to estimate the length of the interval between the two series, we have, at the present stage of our exposition, no evidence.

12. But the mechanical structure of the strata, the result, as it seems, of aqueous sedimentary deposit, is not the only, nor the most important evidence, with regard to the length of time occupied by the formation of the rocky layers which now compose our mountains. As we have said, they contain shells, and other remains of creatures which live in the sea These they contain, not in small numbers, scattered and detached, but in vast abundance, as they are found in those parts of the ocean which is most alive with them. There are the remains of oysters and other shell-fish in layers, as they live at present in the seas near our shores; of corals, in vast patches and beds, as they now occur in the waters of the Pacific; of shoals of fishes, of many different kinds, in immense abundance. Each of these beds of shells, of corals, and of fishes, must have required many years, perhaps many cen-

turies, for the growth of the successive individuals and successive generations of which it consists: as long a time, perhaps, as the present inhabitants of the sea have lived therein: or many times longer, if there have been many such successive changes. And thus, while the present condition of the earth extends backwards to a period of vast but unknown antiquity; we have, offered to our notice, the evidence of a series of other periods, each of which, so far as we can judge, may have been as long or longer than that during which the dry land has had its present form.

13. But the most remarkable feature in the evidence is yet to come. We have spoken in general of the oysters, and corals, and fishes, which occur in the strata of our hills; as if they were creatures of the same kinds which we now designate by those names. But a more exact examination of these remains of organized beings, shows that this is not so. The tribes of animals which are found petrified in our rocks are almost all different, so far as our best natural historians can determine, from those which now live in our existing seas. They are different species; different genera. The creatures which we find thus embedded in our mountains, are not only dead as individuals, but extinct as species. They belonged, not only to a terrestrial period, but to an animal creation, which is now past away. The earth is, it seems, a domicile which has outlasted more than one race of tenants.

14. It may seem rash and presumptuous in the natural historian to pronounce thus peremptorily that certain forms of life are nowhere to be found at present, even in the unfathomable and inaccessible depths of the ocean. But even if this were so, the proposition that the earth has changed its inhabitants, since the rocks were formed, of which our hills consist, does not depend for its proof on this assumption. For in the or-

ganic bodies which our strata contain, we find remains, not only of marine animals, but of animals which inhabit the fresh waters, and the land, and of plants. And the examination of such remains having been pursued with great zeal, and with all the aids which natural history can supply, the result has been, the proofs of a vast series of different tribes of animals and plants, which have successively occupied the earth and the seas; and of which the number, variety, multiplicity, and strangeness, exceed, by far, everything which could have been previously imagined. Thus Cuvier found, in the limestone strata on which Paris stands, animals of the most curious forms, combining in the most wonderful manner the qualities of different species of existing quadrupeds. In another series of strata, the Lias, which runs as a band across England from N. E. to S. W., we have the remains of lizards, or lacertine animals, different from those which now exist, of immense size and of extraordinary structure, some approaching to the form of fishes (*ichthyosaurus*); others, with the neck of a serpent; others with wings, like the fabled forms of dragons. Then beyond these, that is, anterior to them in the series of time, we have the immense collection of fossil plants, which occur in the Coal Strata; the shells and corals of the Mountain Limestone; the peculiar fishes, different altogether from existing fishes, of the Old Red Sandstone; and though, as we descend lower and lower, the traces of organic life appear to be more rare and more limited in kind, yet still we have, beneath these, in slates and in beds of limestone, many fossil remains, still differing from those which occur in the higher, and therefore, newer strata.

15. We have no intention of instituting any definite calculation with regard to the periods of time which this succession of forms of organic life may have occupied. This, indeed, the

boldest geological speculators have not ventured to do. But the scientific discoveries thus made, have a bearing upon the analogies of creation, quite as important as the discoveries of astronomy. And therefore we may state briefly some of the divisions of the series of terrestrial strata which have suggested themselves to geological inquirers. At the outset of such speculations, it was conceived that the lower rocks, composed of granite, slate, and the like, had existed before the earth was peopled with living things; and that these, being broken up into inclined positions, there were deposited upon them, as the sediment of superincumbent waters, strata more horizontal, containing organic remains. The former were then called *Primitive* or *Primary*, the latter, *Secondary* rocks. But it was soon found that this was too sweeping and peremptory a division. Rocks which had been classed as Primary, were found to contain traces of life; and hence, an intermediate class of *Transition* strata was spoken of. But this too was soon seen to be too narrow a scheme of arrangement, to take in the rapidly-accumulating mass of facts, organic and others, which the geological record of the earth's history disclosed. It appeared that among the fossil-bearing strata there might be discerned a long series of Formations: the term *Formation* being used to imply a collection of successive strata, which, taking into account all the evidence, of materials, position, relations, and organic remains, appears to have been deposited during some one epoch or period; so as to form a natural group, chronologically and physiologically distinct from the others. In this way it appeared that, taking as the highest part of the Secondary series, the beds of chalk, which, marked by characteristic fossils, run through great tracts of Europe, with other beds, of sand and clay, which generally accompany these; there was, below this *Cretaceous Formation*, an *Oolitic Forma-*

tion, still more largely diffused, and still more abundant in its peculiar organic remains. Below this, we have, in England, the *New Red Sandstone Formation*, which, in other countries, is accompanied by beds abundant in fossils, as the *Muschelkalk* of Germany. Below this again we have the *Coal Formation*, and the *Mountain Limestone*, with their peculiar fossils. Below these, we have the Old Red Sandstone or Devonian System, with its peculiar fishes and other fossils. Beneath these, occur still numerous series of distinguishable strata; which have been arranged by Sir Roderick Murchison as the members of the *Silurian* formation; the researches by which it was established having been carried on, in the first place, in South Wales, the ancient country of the Silures. Including the lower part of this formation, and descending still lower in order, is the *Cambrian* formation of Professor Sedgwick. And since the races of organic beings, as we thus descend through successive strata, seem to be fewer and fewer in their general types, till at last they disapear; these lower members of the geological series have been termed, according to their succession, *Palæozoic*, *Protozoic*, and *Hypozoic* or *Azoic*. The general impression on the minds of geologists has been, that, as we descend in this long staircase of natural steps, we are brought in view of a state of the earth in which life was scantily manifested, so as to appear to be near its earliest stages.

16. Each of these formations is of great thickness. Several of the members of each formation are hundreds, many of them thousands of feet thick. Taken altogether, they afford an astounding record of the time during which they must have been accumulating, and during which these successive groups of animals must have been brought into being, lived, and continued their kinds.

17. We must add, that over the Secondary strata there are

found, in patches, generally of more limited extent, another, and of course, newer mass of strata, which have been termed *Tertiary Formations.* Of these, the strata, near and under Paris, lying in a hollow of the subjacent strata, and hence termed the *Paris Basin*, attracted prominent notice in the first place. And these are found to contain an immense quantity of remains of animals, which, being well preserved, and being subjected to a careful and scientific scrutiny by the great naturalist George Cuvier, had an eminent share in establishing in the minds of Geologists the belief of the extinct character of fossil species, and of the possibility of reconstructing, from such remains, the animals, different from those which now live, which had formerly tenanted the earth.

18. We have, in this enumeration, a series of groups of strata, each of which, speaking in a general way, has its own population of animals and plants, and is separated, by the peculiarities of these, from the groups below and above it. Each group may, in a general manner, be considered as a separate creation of animal and vegetable forms—creatures which have lived and died, as the races now existing upon the earth live and die; and of which the living existence may, and according to all appearance must, have occupied ages, and series of ages, such as have been occupied by the present living generations of the earth. This series of creations, or of successive periods of life, is, no doubt, a very striking and startling fact, very different from anything which the imagination of man, in previous stages of investigation of the earth's condition, had conceived; but still, is established by evidence so complete, drawn from an examination and knowledge of the structures of living things so exact and careful, as to leave no doubt whatever of the reality of the fact, on the minds of those who have attended to the evidence; founded, as it is, upon the analogies, offices, an-

atomy, and combinations of organic structures. The progress of human knowledge on this subject has been carried on and established by the same alternations of bold conjectures and felicitous confirmations of them,—of minute researches and large generalizations,—which have given reality and solidity to the other most certain portions of human knowledge. That the strata of the earth, as we descend from the highest to the lowest, are distinguished in general by characteristic or organic fossils, and that these forms of organization are different from those which now live on the earth, are truths as clearly and indisputably established in the minds of those who have the requisite knowledge of geology and natural history, as that the planets revolve round the sun, and satellites round the planets. That these epochs of creation are something quite different from anything which we now see taking place on the earth, no more disturbs the belief of those facts, which scientific explorers entertain, than the seemingly obvious difference between the nebulæ which are regarded as yet unformed planetary systems, and the solar system to which our earth belongs, disturbs the belief of astronomers, that such nebulæ, as well as our system, really exist. Indeed we may say, as we shall hereafter see, that the fact of our earth having passed through the series of periods of organic life which geologists recognize, is, hitherto, incomparably better established, than the fact that the nebulæ, or any of them, are passing through a series of changes, such as may lead to a system like ours; as some eminent astronomers in modern times have held. In this respect, the history of the world, and its place in the universe, are far more clearly learnt from geology than from astronomy.

19. But with regard to this series of Organic *Creations*, if, for the sake of brevity, we may call them so; we may naturally ask, in what manner, by what agencies, at what inter-

vals, they succeeded each other on the earth? Now, do the researches of geologists give us any information on these points, which may be brought to bear upon our present speculations? If we ask these questions, we receive, from different classes of geologists, different answers. A little while ago, most geologists held, probably the greater number still hold, that the transitions from one of these periods of organic life to another, were accompanied generally by seasons of violent disruption and mutation of the surface of the earth, exceeding anything which has taken place since the surface assumed its present general form; in the same proportion as the changes of its organic population go beyond any such changes which we can discern to be at present in operation. And there were found to be changes of other kinds, which seemed to show that these epochs of organic transition had also been epochs of mechanical violence, upon a vast and wonderful scale. It appeared that, at some of these epochs at least, the strata previously deposited, as if in comparative tranquillity, had been broken, thrust up from below, or drawn or cast downwards; so that strata which must at first have been nearly level, were thrown into positions highly inclined, fractured, set on edge, contorted, even inverted. Over the broken edges of these strata, thus disturbed and fractured, were found vast accumulations of the fragments which such rude treatment might naturally produce; these fragmentary ruins being spread in beds comparatively level, over the bristling edges of the subjacent rocks, as if deposited in the fluid which had overwhelmed the previous structure; and with few or no traces of life appearing in this mass of ruins; while, in the strata which lay over them, and which appeared to have been the result of quieter times, new forms of organic life made their appearance in vast abundance. Such is, for example, the relation of the coal strata in a great part of England; broken into innumerable basins, ridges, valleys, strips, and shreds, lying in all positions; and then filled into a sort of level, by the conglomerate of the magnesian limestone, and the superincumbent red sandstone and oolites. In other cases it appeared as if there were the means of tracing, in these dislocations, the agency of igneous stony matter, which had been injected from below, so as to form mountain-chains, or the cores of such; and in which the period of the convulsion could be traced, by the strata to which the disturbance extended; *those* strata being supposed to have been deposited before the eruption, which were thrust upwards by it into highly-inclined positions; while those strata which, though near to these scenes of mechanical violence, were still comparatively horizontal, as they had been originally deposited, were naturally inferred to have been formed in the waters, after the catastrophe had passed away. By such reasonings as these, M. Elie de Beaumont has conceived that he can ascertain the relative ages (according to the vast and loose measurements of age which belong to this subject) of the principal ranges of mountains of the earth's surface.

20. Such estimations of age can, indeed, as we have intimated, be only of the widest and loosest kind; yet they all concur in assigning very great and gigantic periods of time, as having been occupied by the events which have formed the earth's strata, and brought them into their present position. For not only must there have been long ages employed, as we have said, while the successive generations of each group of animals lived, and died, and were entombed in the abraded fragments of the then existing earth; but the other operations which intervened between these apparently more tranquil processes, must also have occupied, it would seem, long ages at each interval. The dislocation, disruption, and contortion

of the vast masses of previously existing mountains, by which their framework was broken up, and its ruins covered with beds of its own rubbish, many thousand feet thick, and gradually becoming less coarse and smoother, as the higher beds were deposited upon the lower, could hardly take place, it would seem, except in hundreds and thousands of years. And then again, all these processes of deposition, thus arranging loose masses of material into level beds, must have taken place in the bottom of deep oceans; and the beds of these oceans must have been elevated into the position of mountain ridges which they now occupy, by some mighty operation of nature, which must have been comparatively tranquil, since it has not much disturbed those more level beds; and which, therefore, must have been comparatively long continued. If we accept, as so many eminent geologists have done, this evidence of a vast series of successive periods of alternate violence and repose, we must assign to each such period a duration which cannot but be immense, compared with the periods of time with which we are commonly conversant. In the periods of comparative quiet, such as now exist on the earth's surface, and such as seem to be alone consistent with continued life and successive generation, deposits at the bottom of lakes and seas take place, it would seem, only at the rate of a few feet in a year, or perhaps, in a century. When, therefore, we find strata, bearing evidence of such a mode of deposit, and piled up to the amount of thousands and tens of thousands of feet, we are naturally led to regard them as the production of myriads of years; and to add new myriads, as often as, in the prosecution of geological research, we are brought to new masses of strata of the like kind; and again, to interpolate new periods of the same order, to allow for the transition from one such group to another.

21. Nor is there anything which need startle us, in the necessity of assuming such vast intervals of time, when we have once brought ourselves to deal with the question of the antiquity of the earth upon scientific evidence alone. For if geology thus carries us far backwards through thousands, it may be, millions of years, astronomy does not offer the smallest argument to check this regressive supposition. On the contrary, all the most subtle and profound investigations of astronomers have led them to the conviction, that the motions of the earth may have gone on, as they now go on, for an indefinite period of past time. There is no tendency to derangement in the mechanism of the solar system, so far as science has explored it. Minute inequalities in the movements exist, too small to produce any perceptible effect on the condition of the earth's surface; and even these inequalities, after growing up through long cycles of ages, to an amount barely capable of being detected by astronomical scrutiny, reach a maximum; and, diminishing by the same slow degrees by which they increased, correct themselves, and disappear. The solar system, and the earth as part of it, constitute, so far as we can discover, a Perpetual Motion.

22. There is therefore nothing, in what we know of the Cosmical conditions of our globe, to contradict the Terrestrial evidence for its vast antiquity, as the seat of organic life. If for the sake of giving definiteness to our notions, we were to assume that the numbers which express the antiquity of these four Periods;—the Present organic condition of the earth; the Tertiary Period of geologists, which preceded that; the Secondary Period, which was anterior to that; and the Primary Period which preceded the Secondary; were on the same scale as the numbers which express these four magnitudes:—the magnitude of the Earth; that of the Solar System com-

pared with the Earth; the distance of the nearest Fixed Stars compared with the solar system; and the distance of the most remote Nebulæ compared with the nearest fixed stars; there is, in the evidence which geological science offers, nothing to contradict such an assumption.

23. And as the infinite extent which we necessarily ascribe to space, allows us to find room, without any mental difficulty, for the vast distances which astronomy reveals, and even leaves us rather embarrassed with the infinite extent which lies beyond our farthest explorations; so the infinite duration which we, in like manner, necessarily ascribe to past time, makes it easy for us, so far as our powers of intellect are concerned, to go millions of millions of years backwards, in order to trace the beginning of the earth's existence,—the first step of terrestrial creation. It is as easy for the mind of man to reason respecting a system which is billions or trillions of miles in extent, and has endured through the like number of years, or centuries, as it is to reason about a system (the earth, for instance,) which is forty million feet in extent, and has endured for a hundred thousand million of seconds, that is, a few thousand years.

24. This statement is amply sufficient for the argument which we have to found upon it; but before I proceed to do that, I will give another view which has recently been adopted by some geologists, of the mode in which the successive periods of creation, which geological research discloses to us, have passed into one another. According to this new view, we find no sufficient reason to believe that the history of the earth, as read by us in the organic and mechanical phenomena of its superficial parts, has consisted of such an alternation of periods of violence and of repose, as we have just attempted to describe. According to these theorists, strata have suc-

ceeded strata, one group of animals and plants has followed another, through a season of uniform change; with no greater paroxysm or catastrophe, it may be, than has occurred during the time that man has been an observer of the earth. It may be asked, how is this consistent with the phenomena which we have described;—with the vast masses of ruin, which mark the end of one period and the beginning of another, as is the case in passing from the coal measures of England to the superincumbent beds;—with the highly-inclined strata of the central masses, and the level beds of the upper formations which have been described as marking the mountain ranges of Europe? To these questions, a reply is furnished, we are told, by a more extensive and careful examination of the strata. It may be, that in certain localities, in certain districts, the transition, from the mountain limestone and the coal, to the superjacent sandstones and oolites, is abrupt and seemingly violent; marked by *unconformable* positions of the upper upon the lower strata, by beds of conglomerate, by the absence of organic remains in certain of these beds. But if we follow these very strata into other parts of the world, or even into other parts of this island, we find that this abruptness and incongruity between the lower and the higher strata disappears. Between the mountain-limestone and the red sandstone which lies over it, certain new beds are found, which fill up the incoherent interval; which offer the same evidence as the strata below and above them, of having been produced tranquilly; and which do not violently differ in position from either group. The appearance of incoherence in the series arose from the occurrence, in the region first examined, of a gap, which is here filled up,—a blank which is here supplied. Hence it is inferred, that whatever of violence and extreme disturbance is indicated by the dislocations and ruins there observed, was local and partial only; and that, at the very time when these fragmentary beds, void of organized beings, were forming in one place, there were, at the same time, going on, in another part of the earth's surface, not far removed, the processes of the life, death and imbedding of species, as tranquilly as at any other period. And the same assertion is made with regard to the more general fact, before described, of the stratigraphical constitution of mountain chains. It is asserted that the unconformable relation of the strata which compose the different parts of those chains, is a local occurrence only; and that the same strata, if followed into other regions, are found conformable to each other; or are reduced to a virtually continuous scheme, by the interpolation of other strata, which make a transition, in which no evidence of exceptional violence appears.

25. We shall not attempt (it is not at all necessary for us to do so) to decide between the doctrines of the two geological schools which thus stand in this opposition to each other. But it will be useful to our argument to state somewhat further the opinions of this latter school on one main point. We must explain the view which these geologists take of the mode of succession of one group of *organized* beings to another; by which, as we have said, the different successive strata are characterized. Such a phenomenon, it would at first seem, cannot be brought within the ordinary rules of the existing state of things. The species of planets and animals which inhabit the earth, do not change from age to age; they are the same in modern times, as they were in the most remote antiquity, of which we have any record. The dogs and horses, sheep and cattle, lions and wolves, eagles and swallows, corn and vines, oaks and cedars, which occupy the earth now, are not, we have the strongest reasons to believe, essentially dif-

ferent now from what they were in the earliest ages. At least, if one or two species have disappeared, no new species have come into existence. We cannot conceive a greater violation of the known laws of nature, than that such an event as the appearance of a new species should have occurred. Even those who hold the uniformity of the mechanical changes of the earth, and of the rate of change, from age to age, and from one geological period to another; must still, it would seem, allow that the zoological and phytological changes of which geology gives her testimony, are complete exceptions to what is now taking place. The formation of strata at the bottom of the ocean from the ruin of existing continents, may be going on at present. Even the elevation of the bed of the ocean in certain places, as a process imperceptibly slow, may be in action at this moment, as these theorists hold that it is. But still, even when the beds thus formed are elevated into mountain chains, if that should happen, in the course of myriads of years, (according to the supposition it cannot be effected in a less period,) the strata of such mountain chains will still contain only the species of such creatures as now inhabit the waters; and we shall have, even then, no succession of organic epochs, such as geology discovers in the existing mountains of the earth.

26. The answer which is made to this objection appears to me to involve a license of assumption on the part of the *uniformitarian* geologist, (as such theorists have been termed,) which goes quite beyond the bounds of natural philosophy: but I wish to state it; partly, in order to show that the most ingenious men, stimulated by the exigencies of a theory, which requires some hypothesis concerning the succession of species, to make it coherent and complete, have still found it impossible to bring the creation of species of plants and ani-

mals within the domain of natural science; and partly, to show how easily and readily geological theorists are led to assume periods of time, even of a higher order than those which I have ventured to suggest.

27. It must, however, be first stated, as a fact on which the assumption is founded which I have to notice, that the organic groups by which these successive strata are characterized, are not so distinct and separate, as it was convenient, for the sake of explanation, to describe them in the first instance. Although each body of strata is marked by predominant groups of genera and species, yet it is not true, that all the species of each formation disappear, when we proceed to the next. Some species and genera endure through several successive groups of strata; while others disappear, and new forms come into view, as we ascend. And thus, the change from one set of organic forms to another, as we advance in time, is made, not altogether by abrupt transitions, but in part continuously. The uniformitarian, in the case of organic, as in the case of mechanical change, obliterates or weakens the evidence of sudden and catastrophic leaps, by interposing intermediate steps, which involve, partly the phenomena of the preceding, and partly those of the subsequent condition. As he allows no universal transition from one deposit to a succeeding discrepant and unconformable deposit, so he allows no abrupt and complete transition from one collection of organic beings, —one creation, as we may call it,—to another. If creation must needs be an act out of the region of natural science, he will have it to be at least an act not exercised at distant intervals, and on peculiar occasions; but constantly going on, and producing its effects, as much at one time in the geological history of the world, as at another.

28. And this he holds, not only with regard to the geological

periods which have preceded the existing condition of the earth, but also with regard to the transition from those previous periods to that in which we live. The present population of the earth is not one in which all previous forms are extinct. The past population of the earth was not one in which there are found no creatures still living. On the contrary, he finds that there exists a vast mass of strata, superior to the secondary strata, which are characterized by extinct forms, and are yet inferior to those deposits which are now going on by the agency of obvious causes. These masses of strata contain a population of creatures, partly extinct species, and partly such species as are still living on our land and in our waters. The proportion in which the old and the new species occur in such strata, is various; and the strata are so numerous, so rich in organic remains, so different from each other, and have been so well explored, that they have been classified and named according to the proportion of new and of old species which they contain. Those which contain the largest proportion of species still living, have been termed *Pliocene*, as containing a *greater* number of *new* or recent species. Below these, are strata which are termed *Miocene*, implying a *smaller* number of *new* species. Below these again, are others which have been termed *Eocene*, as containing few new species indeed, but yet enough to mark the *dawn*, the *Eos*, of the existing state of the organic world. These strata are, in many places, of very considerable thickness; and their number, their succession, and the great amount of extinct species which they contain, shows, in a manner which cannot be questioned, (if the evidence of geology is accepted at all,) in what a gradual manner, a portion at least, of the existing forms of organic life have taken the place of a different population previously existing on the surface of the globe.

29. And thus the uniformitarian is led to consider the facts which geology brings to light, as indicating a slow and almost imperceptible, but, upon the whole, constant series of changes, not only in the position of the earth's materials, but in its animal and vegetable population. Land becomes sea and sea becomes land; the beds of oceans are elevated into mountain regions, carrying with them the remains of their inhabitants; sheets of lava pour from volcanic vents and overwhelm the seats of life; and these, again, become fields of vegetation; or, it may be, descend to the depths of the sea, and are overgrown with groves of coral; lakes are filled with sediment, imbedding the remains of land animals, and form the museums of future zoologists; the deltas of mighty rivers become the centres of continents, and are excavated as coal-fields by men in remote ages. And yet all this time, so slow is the change, that man is unaware such changes are going on. He knows that the mountains of Scandinavia are rising out of the Baltic at the rate of a few feet in a century; he knows that the fertile slope of Etna has been growing for thousands of years by the addition of lava streams and parasitic volcanos; he knows that the delta of the Mississippi accumulates hundreds of miles of vegetable matter every generation; he knows that the shores of Europe are yielding to the sea; but all these appear to him minute items, not worth summing; infinitesimal quantities, which he cannot integrate. And so, in truth, they are, for him. His ephemeral existence does not allow him to form a just conception, in any ordinary state of mind, of the effects of this constant agency of change, working through countless thousands of years. But Time, inexhausted and unremitting, sums the series, integrates the formula of change; and thus passes, with sure though noiseless progress, from one geological epoch to another.

30. And in the meanwhile, to complete the view thus taken by the uniformitarian of the geological history of the earth, by some constant but inscrutable law, creative agency is perpetually at work, to introduce, into this progressive system of things, new species of vegetable and animal life. Organic forms, ever and ever new ones, are brought into being, and left, visible footsteps, as it were, of the progress which Time has made;—marks placed between the rocky leaves of the book of creation; by which man, when his time comes, may turn back and read the past history of his habitation. But the point for us to remark is, the immeasurable, the inconceivable length of time, if any length of time could be inconceivable, which is required of our thoughts, by this new assumption of the constant production of new species, as a law of creation. We might feel ourselves well nigh overwhelmed, when, by looking at processes which we see producing only a few feet of height or breadth or depth during the life of man, we are called upon to imagine the construction of Alps and Andes,—when we have to imagine a world made a few inches in a century. But there, at least, we had *something* to start from: the element of change was small, but there *was* an element of change: we had to expand, but we had not to originate. But in conceiving that all the myriads of successive species, which we find in the earth's strata, have come into being by a law which is now operating, we have *nothing* to start from. We have seen, and know of, no such change; all sober and skilful naturalists reject it, as a fact not belonging to our time. We have here to build a theory without materials;—to sum a series of which every term, so far as we know, is nothing;—to introduce into our scientific reasonings an assumption contrary to all scientific knowledge.

31. This appears to me to be the real character of the as-

sumption of the constant creation of new species. But, as I have said, it is not my business here, to pronounce upon the value or truth of this assumption. The only use which I wish to make of it is this:—If any persons, who have adopted the geological view which I have just been explaining, should feel any interest in the speculations here offered to their notice, they must needs be (as I have no doubt they will be) even more willing than other geologists, to grant to our argument a scale of time for geological succession, corresponding in magnitude to the scale of distances which astronomy teaches us, as those which measure the relation of the universe to the earth.

This being supposed to be granted, I am prepared to proceed with my argument.

CHAPTER VI.

THE ARGUMENT FROM GEOLOGY.

1. I HAVE endeavored to explain that, according to the discoveries of geologists, the masses of which the surface of the earth is composed, exhibit indisputable evidence that, at different successive periods, the land and the waters which occupy it, have been inhabited by successive races of plants and animals; which, when taken in large groups, according to the ascending or descending order of the strata, consist of species different from those above and below them. Many of these groups of species are of forms so different from any living things which now exist, as to give to the life of those ancient periods an aspect strangely diverse from that which life now displays, and to transfer us, in thought, to a creation remote in its predominant forms from that among which we live. I have shown also, that the life and successive generations of these groups of species, and the events by which the rocks which contain these remains have been brought into their present situation and condition, must have occupied immense intervals of time;—intervals so large that they deserve to be compared, in their numerical expression, with the intervals of space which separate the planets and stars from each other. It has been seen, also, that the best geologists and natural his-

torians have not been able to devise any hypothesis to account for the successive introduction of these new species into the earth's population ; except the exercise of a series of acts of creation, by which they have been brought into being ; either in groups at once, or in a perpetual succession of one or a few species, which the course of long intervals of time might accumulate into groups of species. It is true, that some speculators have held that by the agency of natural causes, such as operate upon organic forms, one species might be transmuted into another ; external conditions of climate, food, and the like, being supposed to conspire with internal impulses and tendencies, so as to produce this effect. This supposition is, however, on a more exact examination of the laws of animal life, found to be destitute of proof ; and the doctrine of the successive creation of species remains firmly established among geologists. That the *extinction* of species, and of groups of species, may be accounted for by natural causes, is a proposition much more plausible, and to a certain extent, probable ; for we have good reason to believe that, even within the time of human history, some few species have ceased to exist upon the earth. But whether the extinction of such vast groups of species as the ancient strata present to our notice, can be accounted for in this way, at least without assuming the occurrence of great catastrophes, which must for a time, have destroyed all forms of life in the district in which they occurred, appears to be more doubtful. The decision of these questions, however, is not essential to our purpose. What is important is, that immense numbers of tribes of animals have tenanted the earth for countless ages, before the present state of things began to be.

2. The present state of things is that to which the existence and the history of MAN belong ; and the remark which I now

have to make is, that the existence and the history of Man are facts of an entirely different order from any which existed in any of the previous states of the earth; and that this history has occupied a series of years which, compared with geological periods, may be regarded as very brief and limited.

3. The remains of man are nowhere found in the strata which contain the records of former states of the earth. Skeletons of vast varieties of creatures have been disinterred from their rocky tombs; but these cemeteries of nature supply no portion of a human skeleton. In earlier periods of natural science, when comparative anatomy was as yet very imperfectly understood, no doubt, many fossil bones were supposed to be human bones. The remains of giants and of antediluvians were frequent in museums. But a further knowledge of anatomy has made it appear that such bones all belong to animals, of one kind or another; often, to animals utterly different, in their form and skeleton, from man. Also some bones, really human, have been found petrified in situations in which petrification has gone on in recent times, and is still going on. Human skeletons, imbedded in rocks by this process, have been found in the island of Guadaloupe, and elsewhere. But this phenomenon is easily distinguishable from the petrified bones of other animals, which are found in rocks belonging to really geological periods; and does not at all obliterate the distinction between the geological and the historical periods.

4. Indeed not bones only, but objects of art, produced by human workmanship, are found fossilized and petrified by the like processes; and these, of course, belong to the historical period. Human bones, and human works, are found in such deposits as morasses, sand-banks, lava-streams, mounds of volcanic ashes; and many of them may be of unknown, and,

compared with the duration of a few generations, of very great antiquity; but such deposits are distinguishable, generally without difficulty, from the strata in which the geologist reads the records of former creations. It has been truly said, that the geologist is an *Antiquary;* for, like the antiquary, he traces a past condition of things in the remains and effects of it which still subsist; but it has also been truly said, at the same time, that he is an antiquary *of a new Order;* for the remains which he studies are those which illustrate the history of the earth, not of man. The geologist's antiquity is not that of ornaments and arms, utensils and habiliments, walls and mounds; but of species and of genera, of seas and of mountains. It is true, that the geologist may have to study the works of man, in order to trace the effects of causes which produce the results which he investigates; as when he examines the pholad-pierced pillars of Pateoli, to prove the rise and the fall of the ground on which they stand; or notes the anchoring-rings in the wall of some Roman edifice, once a maritime fort, but now a ruin remote from the sea; or when he remarks the streets in the towns of Scania, which are now below the level of the Baltic,* and therefore show that the land has sunk since these pavements were laid. But in studying such objects, the geologist considers the hand of man as only one among many agencies. Man is to him only one of the natural causes of change.

5. And if, with the illustrious author to whom we have just referred,† we liken the fossil remains, by which the geologist determines the age of his strata, to the Medals and Coins in which the antiquary finds the record of reigns and dynasties; we must still recollect that a *Coin* really discloses a vast body of characteristics of man, to which there is nothing approach-

* Lyell, II. 420. [6th Ed.]

† Cuvier.

ing in the previous condition of the world. For how much does a Coin or Medal indicate? Property; exchange; government; a standard of value; the arts of mining, assaying, coining, drawing, and sculpture; language, writing, and reckoning; historical recollections, and the wish to be remembered by future ages. All this is involved in that small human work, a Coin. If the fossil remains of animals may (as has been said) be termed Medals struck by Nature to record the epochs of her history; Medals must be said to be, not merely, like fossil remains, records of material things; they are the records of thought, purpose, society, long continued, long improved, supplied with multiplied aids and helps; they are the permanent results, in a minute compass, of a vast progress, extending through all the ramifications of human life.

6. Not a coin merely, but any, the rudest work of human art, carries us far beyond the domain of mere animal life. There is no transition from man to animals. No doubt, there are races of men very degraded, barbarous, and brutish. No doubt there are kinds of animals which are very intelligent and sagacious; and some which are exceedingly disposed to and adapted to companionship with man. But by elevating the intelligence of the brute, we do not make it become the intelligence of the man. By making man barbarous, we do not make him cease to be a man. Animals have their especial capacities, which may be carried very far, and may approach near to human sagacity, or may even go beyond it; but the capacity of man is of a different kind. It is a capacity, not for becoming sagacious, but for becoming rational; or rather it is a capacity which he has in virtue of being rational. It is a capacity of progress. In animals, however sagacious, however well trained, the progress in skill and knowledge is limited, and very narrowly limited. The creature soon reaches a boundary, beyond

which it cannot pass; and even if the acquired habits be transmitted by descent to another generation, (which happens in the case of dogs and several other animals,) still the race soon comes to a stand in its accomplishments. But in man, the possible progress from generation to generation, in intelligence and knowledge, and we may also say, in power, is indefinite; or if this be doubted, it is at least so vast, that compared with animals, his capacity is infinite. And this capacity extends to all races of men its characterizing efficacy: for we have good reason to believe that there is no race of human beings who may not, by a due course of culture, continued through generations, be brought into a community of intelligence and power with the most intelligent and the most powerful races. This seems to be well established, for instance, with regard to the African negroes; so long regarded by most, by some probably regarded still, as a race inferior to Europeans. It has been found that they are abundantly capable of taking a share in the arts, literature, morality and religion of European peoples. And we cannot doubt that, in the same manner, the native Australians, or the Bushmen of the Cape of Good Hope, have human faculties and human capacities; however difficult it might be to unfold these, in one or two generations, into a form of intelligence and civilization in any considerable degree resembling our own.

7. It is not requisite for us, and it might lead to unnecessary difficulties, to fix upon any one attribute of man, as peculiarly characteristic, and distinguishing him from brutes. Yet it would not be too much to say that man is, in truth, universally and specifically characterized by the possession of *Language*. It will not be questioned that language, in its highest forms, is a wonderful vehicle and a striking evidence of the intelligence of man. His bodily organs can, by a few scarcely

perceptible motions, shape the air into sounds which express the kinds, properties, actions and relations of things, under thousands of aspects, in forms infinitely more general and recondite than those in which they present themselves to his senses;—and he can, by means of these forms, aided by the use of his senses, explore the boundless regions of space, the far recesses of past time, the order of nature, the working of the Author of nature. This man does, by the exercise of his Reason, and by the use of Language, a necessary implement of his Reason for such purposes.

8. That language, in such a stage, is a special character of man, will not be doubted. But it may be thought, there is little resemblance between Language in this exalted degree of perfection, and the seemingly senseless gibberish of the most barbarous tribes. Such an opinion, however, might easily be carried too far. All human language has in it the elements of indefinite intellectual activity, and the germs of indefinite development. Even the rudest kind of speech, used by savages, denotes objects by their kinds, their attributes, their relations, with a degree of generality derived from the intellect, not from the senses. The generality may be very limited; the relations which the human intellect is capable of apprehending may be imperfectly conveyed. But to denote kinds and attributes and actions and relations *at all*, is a beginning of generalization and abstraction;—or rather, is far more than a beginning. It is the work of a faculty which can generalize and abstract; and these mental processes once begun, the field of progress which is open to them is indefinite. Undoubtedly it may happen that weak and barbarous tribes are, for many generations, so hard pressed by circumstances, and their faculties so entirely absorbed in providing for the bare wants of the poorest life, that their thoughts may never travel to anything

beyond these, and their language may not be extended so as to be applicable to any other purposes. But this is not the standard condition of mankind. It is not, by such cases, that man, or that human nature, is to be judged. The normal condition of man is one of an advance beyond the mere means of subsistence, to the arts of life, and the exercise of thought in a general form. To some extent, such an advance has taken place in almost every region of the earth and in every age.

9. Perhaps we may often have a tendency to think more meanly than they deserve, of so-called barbarous tribes, and of those whose intellectual habits differ much from our own. We may be prone to regard ourselves as standing at the summit of civilization; and all other nations and ages, as not only occupying inferior positions, but positions on a slope which descends till it sinks into the nature of brutes. And yet how little does an examination of the history of mankind justify this view! The different stages of civilization, and of intellectual culture, which have prevailed among them, have had no appearance of belonging to one single series, in which the cases differed only as higher or lower. On the contrary, there have been many very different kinds of civilization, accompanied by different forms of art and of thought; showing how universally the human mind tends to such habits, and how rich it is in the modes of manifesting its innate powers. How different have been the forms of civilization among the Chinese, the Indians, the Egyptians, the Babylonians, the Mexicans, the Peruvians! Yet in all, how much was displayed of sagacity and skill, of perseverance and progress, of mental activity and grasp, of thoughtfulness and power. Are we, in thinking of these manifestations of human capacity, to think of them as only a stage between us and brutes? or are we to think so, even of the stoical Red Indians of North America, or the en-

5*

ergetic New Zealanders, and Caffres? And if not, why of the African Negroes, or the Australians, or the Bushmen? We may call their Language a jargon. Very probable it would, in its present form, be unable to express a great deal of what we are in the habit of putting into language. But can we refuse to believe that, with regard to matters with which they are familiar, and on occasions where they are interested, they would be to each other intelligible and clear? And if we suppose cases in which their affections and emotions are strongly excited, (and affections and emotions at least we cannot deny them,) can we not believe that they would be eloquent and impressive? Do we not know, in fact, that almost all nations which we call savage, are, on such occasions, eloquent in their own language? And since this is so, must not their language, after all, be a wonderful instrument as well as ours? Since it can convey one man's thoughts and emotions to many, clothed in the form which they assume in his mind; giving to things, it may be, an aspect quite different from that which they would have if presented to their own senses; guiding their conviction, warming their hearts, impelling their purposes;—can language, even in such cases, be otherwise than a wonderful produce of man's internal, of his mental, that is, of his peculiarly *human* faculties? And is not language, therefore, even in what we regard as its lowest forms, an endowment which completely separates man from animals which have no such faculty?—which cannot regard, or which cannot convey, the impressions of the individual in any such general and abstract form? Probably we should find, as those who have studied the language of savages always have found, that every such language contains a number of curious and subtle practices,—*contrivances*, we cannot help calling them,—for marking the relations, bearings and connections of words; contrivances quite different from those of the languages which we think of as more perfect; but yet, in the mouths of those who use such speech, answering their purpose with great precision. But without going into such details, the use of any *articulate* language is, as the oldest Greeks spoke of it, a special and complete distinction of man as man.

10. It would be an obscure and useless labor, to speculate upon the question whether animals have among themselves anything which can properly be called *Language.* That they have anything which can be termed Language, in the sense in which we here speak of it, as admitting of general expressions, abstractions, address to numbers, eloquence, is utterly at variance with any interpretation which we can put upon their proceedings. The broad distinction of Instinct and Reason, however obscure it may be, yet seems to be most simply described, by saying, that animals do not apprehend their impressions under general forms, and that man does. Resemblance, and consequent association of impressions, may often show like generalization; but yet it is different. There is, in man's mind, a germ of general thoughts, suggested by resemblances, which is evolved and fixed in language; and by the aid of such an addition to the impressions of sense, man has thousands of intellectual pathways from object to object, from effect to cause, from fact to inference. His impressions are projected on a sphere of thought of which the radii can be prolonged into the farthest regions of the universe. Animals, on the contrary, are shut up in their sphere of sensation,—passing from one impression to another by various associations, established by circumstances; but still, having access to no wider intellectual region, through which lie lines of transition purely abstract and mental. That they have their modes of communicating their impressions and associations,

their affections and emotions, we know; but these modes of communication do not make a language; nor do they disturb the assignment of Language as a special character of man; nor the belief that man differs in his Kind, and we may say, using a larger phrase, in his Order, from all other creatures.

11. We may sometimes be led to assign much of the development of man's peculiar powers, to the influence of external circumstances. And that the development of those powers is so influenced, we cannot doubt; but their development only, not their existence. We have already said that savages, living a precarious and miserable life, occupied incessantly with providing for their mere bodily wants, are not likely to possess language, or any other characteristic of humanity, in any but a stunted and imperfect form. But, that manhood is debased and degraded under such adverse conditions, does not make man cease to be man. Even from such an abject race, if a child be taken and brought up among the comforts and means of development which civilized life supplies, he does not fail to show that he possesses, perhaps in an eminent degree, the powers which specially belong to man. The evidences of human tendencies, human thoughts, human capacities, human affections and sympathies, appear conspicuously, in cases in which there has been no time for external circumstances to operate in any great degree, so as to unfold any difference between the man and the brute; or in which the influence of the most general of external agencies, the impressions of several of the senses, have been intercepted. Who that sees a lively child, looking with eager and curious eyes at every object, uttering cries that express every variety of elementary human emotion in the most vivacious manner, exchanging looks and gestures, and inarticulate sounds, with his nurse, can doubt that already he possesses the germs of

human feeling, thought and knowledge? that already, before he can form or understand a single articulate word, he has within him the materials of an infinite exuberance of utterance, and an impulse to find the language into which such utterance is to be moulded by the law of his human nature? And perhaps it may have happened to others, as it has to me, to know a child who had been both deaf, dumb, and blind, from a very early age. Yet she, as years went on, disclosed a perpetually growing sympathy with the other children of the family in all their actions, with which of course she could only acquaint herself by the sense of touch. She sat, dressed, walked, as they did; even imitated them in holding a book in her hand when they read, and in kneeling when they prayed. No one could look at the change which came over her sightless countenance, when a known hand touched hers, and doubt that there was a human soul within the frame. The human soul seemed not only to be there, but to have been fully developed; though the means by which it could receive such communications as generally constitute human education, were thus cut off. And such modes of communication with her companions as had been taught her, or as she had herself invented, well bore out the belief, that her mind was the constant dwelling-place, not only of human affections, but of human thoughts. So plainly does it appear that human thought is not produced or occasioned by external circumstances only; but has a special and indestructible germ in human nature.

12. I have been endeavoring to illustrate the doctrine that man's nature is different from the nature of other animals; as subsidiary to the doctrine that the Human Epoch of the earth's history is different from all the preceding Epochs. But in truth, this subsidiary proposition is not by any means neces-

sary to my main purpose. Even if barbarous and savage tribes, even if men under unfavorable circumstances, be little better than the brutes, still no one will doubt that the most civilized races of mankind, that man under the most favorable circumstances, is far, is, indeed, immeasurably elevated above the brutes. The history of man includes not only the history of Scythians and Barbarians, Australians and Negroes, but of ancient Greeks and of modern Europeans; and therefore there can be no doubt that the period of the Earth's history, which includes the history of man, is very different indeed from any period which preceded that. To illustrate the peculiarity, the elevation, the dignity, the wonderful endowments of man, we might refer to the achievements, the recorded thoughts and actions, of the most eminent among those nations;—to their arts, their poetry, their eloquence; their philosophers, their mathematicians, their astronomers; to the acts of virtue and devotion, of patriotism, generosity, obedience, truthfulness, love, which took place among them;—to their piety, their reverence for the deity, their resignation to his will, their hope of immortality. Such characteristic traits of man as man, (which all examples of intelligence, virtue, and religion, are,) might serve to show that man is, in a sense quite different from other creatures, "fearfully and wonderfully made;" but I need not go into such details. It is sufficient for my purpose to sum up the result in the expressions which I have already used; that man is an intellectual, moral, religious, and spiritual being.

13. But the existence of man upon the earth being thus an event of an order quite different from any previous part of the earth's history, the question occurs, how long has this state of things endured? What period has elapsed since this creature, with these high powers and faculties, was placed upon the

earth? How far must we go backward in time, to find the beginning of his wonderful history?—so utterly wonderful compared with anything which had previously occurred. For as to that point, we cannot feel any doubt. The wildest imagination cannot suggest that corals and madrepores, oysters and sepias, fishes and lizards, may have been rational and moral creatures; nor even those creatures which come nearer to human organization; megatheriums and mastodons, extinct deer and elephants. Undoubtedly the earth, till the existence of man, was a world of mere brute creatures. How long then has it been otherwise? How long has it been the habitation of a rational, reflective, progressive race? Can we by any evidence, geological or other, approximate to the beginning of the Human History?

14. This is a large and curious question, and one on which a precise answer may not be within our reach. But an answer not precise, an approximation, as we have suggested, may suffice for our purpose. If we can determine, in some measure, the order and scale of the period during which man has occupied the earth, the determination may serve to support the analogy which we wish to establish.

15. The geological evidence with regard to the existence of man is altogether negative. Previous to the deposits and changes which we can trace as belonging obviously to the present state of the earth's surface, and the operation of causes now existing, there is no vestige of the existence of man, or of his works. As was long ago observed,* we do not find, among the shells and bones which are so abundant in the older strata, any weapons, medals, implements, structures, which speak to us of the hand of man, the workman. If we look forwards ten or twenty thousand years, and suppose the existing works

* By Bishop Berkeley. See Lyell, III. 346.

of man to have been, by that time, ruined and covered up by masses of rubbish, inundations, morasses, lava-streams, earthquakes; still, when the future inhabitant of the earth digs into and explores these coverings, he will discover innumerable monuments that man existed so long ago. The materials of many of his works, and the traces of his own mind, which he stamps upon them, are as indestructible as the shells and bones which give language to the oldest work. Indeed, in many cases the oldest fossil remains are the results of objects of seemingly the most frail and perishable material;—of the most delicate and tender animal and vegetable tissues and filaments. That no such remains of textures and forms, moulded by the hand of man, are anywhere found among these, must be accepted as indisputable evidence that man did not exist, so as to be contemporary with the plants and animals thus commemorated. According to geological evidence, the race of man is a novelty upon the earth;—something which has succeeded to all the great geological changes.

16. And in this, almost all geologists are agreed. Even those who hold that, in other ways, the course of change has been uniform;—that even the introduction of man, as a new species of animal, is only an event of the same kind as myriads of like events which have occurred in the history of the earth;—still allow that the introduction of man, as a moral being, is an event entirely different from any which had taken place before; and that event is, geologically speaking, recent. The changes of which we have spoken, as studied by the geologist in connection with the works of man, the destruction of buildings on sea-coasts by the incursions of the ocean, the removal of the shore many miles away from ancient harbors, the overwhelming of cities by earthquakes or volcanic eruptions; however great when compared with the changes which

take place in one or two generations; are minute and infinitesimal, when put in comparison with the changes by which ranges of mountains and continents have been brought into being, one after another, each of them filled with the remains of different organic creations.

17. Further than this, geology does not go on this question. She has no chronometer which can tell us when the first buildings were erected, when man first dwelt in cities, first used implements or arms; still less, language and reflection. Geology is compelled to give over the question to History. The external evidences of the antiquity of the species fail us, and we must have recourse to the internal. Nature can tell us so little of the age of man, that we must inquire what he can tell us himself.

18. What man can tell us of his own age—what history can say of the beginning of history—is necessarily very obscure and imperfect. We know how difficult it is to trace to its origin the History of any single Nation: how much more, the History of all Nations! We know that all such particular histories carry us back to periods of the migrations of tribes, confused mixtures of populations, perplexed and contradictory genealogies of races; and as we follow these further and further backwards, they become more and more obscure and uncertain; at least in the histories which remain to us of most nations. Still, the obscurity is not such as to lead us to the conviction that research is useless and unprofitable. It is an obscurity such as naturally arises from the lapse of time, and the complexity of the subject. The aspect of the world, however far we go back, is still historical and human; historical and human, in as high a degree, as it is at the present day. Men, as described in the records of the oldest times, are of the same nature, act with the same views, are governed

by the same motives, as at present. At all points, we see thought, purpose, law, religion, progress. If we do not find a beginning, we find at least evidence that, in approaching the beginning, the condition of man does not, in any way, cease to be that of an intellectual, moral, and religious creature.

19. There are, indeed, some histories which speak to us of the beginning of man's existence upon earth; and one such history in particular, which comes to us recommended by indisputable evidence of its own great antiquity, by numerous and striking confirmations from other histories, and from facts still current, and by its connection with that religious view of man's condition, which appears to thoughtful men to be absolutely requisite to give a meaning and purpose to man's faculties and endowments. I speak, of course, of the Hebrew Scriptures. This history professes to inform us how man was placed upon the earth; and how, from one centre, the human family spread itself in various branches into all parts of the world. This genealogy of the human race is accompanied by a chronology, from which it results that the antiquity of the human race does not exceed a few thousand years. Even if we accept this history as true and authoritative, it would not be wise to be rigidly tenacious of the chronology, as to its minute exactness. For, in the first place, of three different forms in which this history appears, the chronology is different in all the three: I mean the Hebrew, the Samaritan, and the Septuagint versions of the Old Testament. And even if this were not so, since this chronology is put in the form ef genealogies, of which many of the steps may very probably have a meaning different from the simple succession of generations in a family, (as some of them certainly have,) it would be unwise to consider ourselves bound to the exact number of years stated, in any of the three versions, or even

in all. It makes no difference to our argument, nor to any purpose in which we can suppose this narrative to have a bearing, whether we accept six thousand or ten thousand years, or even a longer period, as the interval which has now elapsed since the creation of man took place, and the peopling of the earth began.

20. And, in our speculations at least, it will be well for us to take into account the view which is given us of the antiquity of the human race, by other histories as well as by this. A satisfactory result of such an investigation would be attained if, looking at all these histories, weighing their value, interpreting their expressions fairly, discovering their sources of error, and of misrepresentation, we should find them all converge to one point; all give a consistent and harmonious view of the earliest stages of man's history; of the times and places in which he first appeared as man. If all nations of men are branches of the same family, it cannot but interest us, to find all the family traditions tending upwards towards the same quarter; indicating a divergence from the same point; exhibiting a recollection of the original domicile, or of the same original family circle.

21. To a certain extent at least, this appears to be the result of the historical investigations which have been pursued relative to this subject. A certain group of nations is brought before us by these researches which, a few thousands of years ago, were possessed of arts, and manners, and habits, and belief, which make them conspicuous, and which we can easily believe to have been contemporaneous successors of a common, though, it may be even then, remote stock. Such are the Jews, Egyptians, Chaldeans, and Assyrians. The histories of these nations are connected with and confirm each other. Their languages, or most of them, have certain affinities, which

glossologists, on independent grounds, have regarded as affinities implying an original connection. Their chronologies, though in many respects discrepant, are not incapable of being reduced into an harmony by very probable suppositions. Here we have a very early view of the condition of a portion of the earth as the habitation of man, and perhaps a suggestion of a condition earlier still.

22. It is true, that there are other nations also, which claim an antiquity for their civilization equal to or greater than that which we can ascribe to these. Such are the Indians and the Chinese. But while we do not question that these nations were at a remote period in possession of arts, knowledge, and regular polity, in a very eminent degree, we are not at all called upon to assent to the immense numbers, tens of thousands and hundreds of thousands of years, by which such nations, in their histories, express their antiquity. For, in the first place, such numbers are easily devised and transferred to the obscure early stages of tradition, when the art of numeration is once become familiar. These vast intervals, applied to series of blank genealogies, or idle fables, gratify the popular appetite for numerical wonders, but have little claim on critical conviction.

23. And in the next place, we discover that not enumeration only, but a more recondite art, had a great share in the fabrication of these gigantic numbers of years. Some of the nations of whom we have thus spoken, the Indians, for example, had, at an early period, possessed themselves of a large share of astronomical knowledge. They had observed and examined the motions of the Sun, the Moon, the Planets, and the Stars, till they had discovered Cycles, in which, after long and seemingly irregular wanderings in the skies, the heavenly bodies came round again to known and regular positions.

They had thus detected the order that reigns in the seeming disorder; and had, by this means, enabled themselves to know beforehand when certain astronomical events would occur; certain configurations of the Planets, for instance, and eclipses; and knowing how such events would occur in future, they were also able to calculate how the like events had occurred in the past. They could thus determine what eclipses and what planetary configurations had occurred, in thousands and tens of thousands of years of past time; and could, if they were disposed to falsify their early histories, and to confirm the falsification by astronomical evidence, do so with a very near approximation to astronomical truth. Such astronomical confirmation of their assertions, so incapable in any common apprehension of being derived from any other source than actual observation of the fact, naturally produced a great effect upon common minds; and still more, on those who examined the astronomical fact, enough only to see that it was, approximately, at least, true. But in recent times the fallacy of this evidence has been shown, and the fabrication detected. For though the astronomical rules which they had devised were approximately true, they were true approximately only. The more exact researches of modern European astronomy discovered that their cycles, though nearly exact, were not quite so. There was in them an error which made the cycle, at every revolution of its period, when it was applied to past ages, more and more wrong; so that the astronomical events which they asserted to have happened, as they had calculated that they would have happened, the better informed astronomer of our day knows would not have happened exactly so, but in a manner differing more and more from their statement, as the event was more and more remote. And thus the fact which they asserted to have been observed, had not really happened; and the confirmation, which it had been supposed to lend to their history, disappeared. And thus, there is not, in the asserted antiquity of Indian civilization and Indian astronomy, anything which has a well-founded claim to disturb our belief that the nations of the more western regions of Asia had a civilization as ancient as theirs. And considerations of nearly the same kind may be applied to the very remote astronomical facts which are recorded as having been observed in the history of some others of the ancient nations above mentioned.

24. Still less need we be disturbed by the long series of dynasties, each occupying a large period of years, which the Egyptians are said to have inserted in their early history, so as to carry their origin beyond the earliest times which I have mentioned. If they spoke of the Greek nations as children compared with their own long-continued age, as Plato says they did, a few thousands of years of previous existence would well entitle them to do so. So far as such a period goes, their monuments and their hieroglyphical inscriptions give a reality to their pretensions, which we may very willingly grant. And even the history of the Jews supposes that the Egyptians had attained a high point in arts, government, knowledge, when Abraham, the father of the Jewish nation, was still leading the life of a nomad. But this supposition is not inconsistent with the account which the Jewish Scriptures give, of the origin of nations; especially if, as we have said, we abstain from any rigid and narrow interpretation of the chronology of those scriptures; as on every ground, it is prudent to do.

25. It appears then not unreasonable to believe, that a very few thousands, or even a few hundreds of years before the time of Abraham, the nations of central and western Asia offer to us the oldest aspect of the life of man upon the earth;

and that in reasoning concerning the antiquity of the human race, we may suppose that at that period, he was in the earliest stages of his existence. Although, in truth, if we were to accept the antiquity claimed by the Egyptians, the Indians, or the Chinese, the nature of our argument would not be materially altered; for ten thousand, or even twenty thousand years, bears a very small proportion to the periods of time which geology requires for the revolutions which she describes; and, as I have said, we have geological evidence also, to show how brief the human period has been, when compared with the period which preceded the existence of man. And if this be so; if such peoples as those who have left to us the monuments of Egypt and of Assyria, the pyramids and ancient Thebes, the walls of Nineveh and Babylon, were the first nations which lived as nations; or if they were separated from such only by the interval by which the Germans of to-day are separated from the Germans of Tacitus; we may well repeat our remark, that the history of man, in the earliest times, is as truly a history of a wonderful, intellectual, social, political, spiritual creature, as it is at present. We see, in the monuments of those periods, evidences so great and so full of skill, that even now, they amaze us, of arts, government, property, thought, the love of beauty, the recognition of deity; evidences of memory, foresight, power. If London or Berlin were now destroyed, overwhelmed, and, four thousand years hence, disinterred, these cities would not afford stronger testimony of those attributes, as existing in modern Europeans, than we have of such qualities in the ancient Babylonians and Egyptians. The history of man, as that of a creature pre-eminent in the creation, is equally such, however far back we carry our researches.

26. Nor is there anything to disturb this view, in the fact

of the existence of the uncultured and barbarous tribes which occupy, and always have occupied, a large portion of the earth's surface. For, in the first place, there is not, in the aspect of the fact, or in the information which history gives us, any reason to believe that such tribes exhibit a form of human existence, which, in the natural order of progress, is earlier than the forms of civilized life, of which we have spoken. The opinion that the most savage kind of human life, least acquainted with arts, and least provided with resources, is the state of nature out of which civilized life has everywhere gradually emerged, is an opinion which, though at one time popular, is unsupported by proof, and contrary to probability.* Savage tribes do not so grow into civilization; their condition is, far more probably, a condition of civilization degraded and lost, than of civilization incipient and prospective. Add to this, that if we were to assume that this were otherwise; if man thus originally and naturally savage, did also naturally tend to become civilized; this *tendency* is an endowment no less wonderful, than those endowments which civilization exhibits. The capacity is as extraordinary as the developed result; for the capacity involves the result. If savage man be the germ of the most highly civilized man, he differs from all other animal germs, as man differs from brute. And add to this again, that in the tribes which we call savage, and whose condition most differs, in external circumstances, from ours, there are, after all, a vast mass of human attributes: thought, purpose, language, family relations;

* A recent popular writer, who has asserted the self-civilizing tendency of man, has not been able, it would seem, to adduce any example of the operation of this tendency, except a single tribe of North American Indians, in whom it operated for a short time, and to a small extent.

generally property, law, government, contract, arts, and knowledge, to no small extent; and in almost every case, religion. Even uncivilized man is an intellectual, moral, social, religious creature; nor is there, in his condition, any reason why he may not be a spiritual creature, in the highest sense in which the most civilized man can be so.

27. Here then we are brought to the view which, it would seem, offers a complete reply to the difficulty, which astronomical discoveries appeared to place in the way of religion:—the difficulty of the opinion that man, occupying this speck of earth, which is but as an atom in the Universe, surrounded by millions of other globes, larger, and, to appearance, nobler than that which he inhabits, should be the object of the peculiar care and guardianship, of the favor and government, of the Creator of All, in the way in which Religion teaches us that He is. For we find that man, (the human race, from its first origin till now,) has occupied but an atom of time, as he has occupied but an atom of space:—that as he is surrounded by myriads of globes which may, like this, be the habitations of living things, so he has been preceded, on this earth, by myriads of generations of living things, not possibly or probably only, but certainly; and yet that, comparing his history with theirs, he has been, certainly has been fitted to be, the object of the care and guardianship, of the favor and government, of the Master and Governor of All, in a manner entirely different from anything which it is possible to believe with regard to the countless generations of brute creatures which had gone before him. If we will doubt or overlook the difference between man and brutes, the difficulty of ascribing to man peculiar privileges, is made as great by the revelations of geology, as of astronomy. The scale of man's insignificance is, as we have said, of the same order in reference to

time, as to space. There is nothing which at all goes beyond the magnitude which observation and reasoning suggest for geological periods, in supposing that the tertiary strata occupied, in their deposition and elevation, a period as much greater than the period of human history, as the solar system is larger than the earth:—that the secondary strata were as much longer than these in their formation, as the nearest fixed star is more distant than the sun:—that the still earlier masses, call them primary, or protozoic, or what we will, did, in their production, extend through a period of time as vast, compared with the secondary period, as the most distant nebula is remoter than the nearest star. If the earth, as the habitation of man, is a speck in the midst of an infinity of space, the earth, as the habitation of man, is also a speck at the end of an infinity of time. If we are as nothing in the surrounding universe, we are as nothing in the elapsed eternity; or rather, in the elapsed organic antiquity, during which the earth has existed and been the abode of life. If man is but one small family in the midst of innumerable possible households, he is also but one small family, the successor of innumerable tribes of animals, not possible only, but actual. If the planets *may* be the seats of life, we know that the seas which have given birth to our mountains *were* the seats of life. If the stars may have hundreds of systems of tenanted planets rolling round them, we know that the secondary group of rocks does contain hundreds of tenanted beds, witnessing of as many systems of organic creation. If the nebulæ may be planetary systems in the course of formation, we know that the primary and transition rocks either show us the earth in the course of formation, as the future seat of life, or exhibit such life as already begun.

28. How far that which astronomy thus asserts as possible, is probable:—what is the value of these possibilities of life in

distant regions of the universe, we shall hereafter consider. But in what geology asserts, the case is clear. It is no possibility, but a certainty. No one will now doubt that shells and skeletons, trunks and leaves, prove animal and vegetable life to have existed. Even, therefore, if Astronomy could demonstrate all that her most fanciful disciples assume, Geology would still have a complete right to claim an equal hearing; —to insist upon having her analogies regarded. She would have a right to answer the questions of Astronomy, when she says, How can we believe this? and to have her answers accepted.

29. Astronomy claims a sort of dignity over all other sciences, from her *antiquity*, her *certainty*, and the *vastness* of her discoveries. But the antiquity of astronomy as a science had no share in such speculations as we are discussing; and if it had had, new truths are better than old conjectures; new discoveries must rectify old errors; new answers must remove old difficulties. The vigorous youth of Geology makes her fearless of the age of Astronomy. And as to the certainty of Astronomy, it has just as little to do with these speculations. The certainty stops, just when these speculations begin. There may, indeed, be some danger of delusion on this subject. Men have been so long accustomed to look upon astronomical science as the mother of certainty, that they may confound astronomical discoveries with cosmological conjectures; though these be slightly and illogically connected with those. And then, as to the vastness of astronomical discoveries,—granting that character, inasmuch as it is to a certain degree, a matter of measurement,—we must observe, that the discoveries of geology are no less vast: they extend through time, as those of astronomy do through space. They carry us through millions of years, that is, of the earth's revolutions, as those of

astronomy do through millions of the earth's diameters, or of diameters of the earth's orbit. Geology fills the regions of duration with events, as astronomy fills the regions of the universe with objects. She carries us backwards by the relation of cause and effect, as astronomy carries us upwards by the relations of geometry. As astronomy steps on from point to point of the universe by a chain of triangles, so geology steps from epoch to epoch of the earth's history by a chain of mechanical and organical laws. If the one depends on the axioms of geometry, the other depends on the axioms of causation.

30. So far then, Geology has no need to regard Astronomy as her superior; and least of all, when they apply themselves together to speculations like these. But in truth, in such speculations, Geology has an immeasurable superiority. She has the command of an implement, in addition to all that Astronomy can use; and one, for the purpose of such speculations, adapted far beyond any astronomical element of discovery. She has, for one of her studies,—one of her means of dealing with her problems,—the knowledge of Life, animal and vegetable. Vital organization is a subject of attention which has, in modern times, been forced upon her. It is now one of the main parts of her discipline. The geologist must study the traces of life in every form; must learn to decypher its faintest indications and its fullest development. On the question, then, whether there be in this or that quarter, evidence of life, he can speak with the confidence derived from familiar knowledge; while the astronomer, to whom such studies are utterly foreign, because he has no facts which bear upon them, can offer, on such questions, only the loosest and most arbitrary conjectures; which, as we have had to remark, have been rebuked by eminent men, as being altogether inconsistent with the acknowledged maxims of his science.

31. When, therefore, Geology tells us that the earth, which has been the seat of human life for a few thousand years only, has been the seat of animal life for myriads, it may be, millions of years, she has a right to offer this, as an answer to any difficulty which Astronomy, or the readers of astronomical books, may suggest, derived from the considerations that the Earth, the seat of human life, is but one globe of a few thousand miles in diameter, among millions of other globes, at distances millions of times as great.

32. Let the difficulty be put in any way the objector pleases. Is it that it is unworthy of the greatness and majesty of God, according to our conceptions of Him, to bestow such peculiar care on so small a part of His creation? But we know, from geology, that He has bestowed upon this small part of His creation, mankind, this special care;—He has made their period, though only a moment in the ages of animal life, the only period of intelligenee, morality, religion. If then, to suppose that He has done this, is contrary to our coneeptions of His greatness and majesty, it is plain that our conceptions are erroneous; they have taken a wrong direction. God has not judged, as to what is worthy of Him, as we have judged. He has found it worthy of Him to bestow upon man His special care, though he occupies so small a portion of time; and why not, then, although he occupies so small a portion of space?

33. Or is the objection this; that if we suppose the earth only to be occupied by inhabitants, all the other globes of the universe are wasted;—turned to no purpose? Is waste of this kind considered as unsuited to the character of the Creator? But here again, we have the like waste, in the occupation of the earth. All its previous ages, its seas and its continents, have been wasted upon mere brute life; often, so far as we can see, for myriads of years, upon the lowest, the least conscious

forms of life; upon shell-fish, corals, sponges. Why then should not the seas and continents of other planets be occupied at present with a life no higher than this, or with no life at all? Will it be said that, so far as material objects are occupied by life, they are not wasted; but that they are wasted, if they are entirely barren and blank of life? This is a very arbitrary saying. Why should the life of a sponge, or a coral, or an oyster, be regarded as a good employment of a spot of land and water, so as to save it from being wasted? No doubt, if the coral or the oyster be there, there is a reason why it is so, consistently with the attributes of God. But then, on the same ground, we may say that if it be not there, there is a reason why it is not so. Such a mode of regarding the parts of the universe can never give us reasons why they should or should not be inhabited, when we have no other grounds for knowing whether they are. If it be a sufficient employment of a spot of rock or water that it is the seat of organization—of organic powers; why may it not be a sufficient employment of the same spot that it is the seat of attraction, of cohesion, of crystaline powers? All the planets, all parts of the universe, we have good reason to believe, are pervaded by attraction, by forces of aggregation and atomic relation, by light and heat. Why may not these be sufficient to prevent the space being wasted, in the eyes of the Creator? as, during a great part of the earth's past history, and over large portions of its present mass, they are actually held by Him sufficient; for they are all that occupy those portions. This notion, then, of the improbability of there being, in the universe, so vast an amount of waste spaces, or waste bodies, as is implied in the opinion that the earth alone is the seat of life, or of intelligence, is confuted by the fact, that there are vast spaces, waste districts, and especially waste times, to an extent as great as such a notion deems improbable. The avoidance of such waste, according to our notions of waste, is no part of the economy of creation, so far as we can discern that economy, in its most certain exemplifications.

34. Or will the objection be made in this way; that such a peculiar dignity and importance given to the earth is contrary to the analogy of creation;—that since there are so many globes, similar to the earth,—like her, revolving round the sun, like her, revolving on her axes, several of them, like her, accompanied by satellites; it is reasonable to suppose that their destination and office is the same as hers;—that since there are so many stars, each like the sun, a source of light, and probably of heat, it is reasonable to suppose that, like the sun, they are the centres of systems of planets, to which their light and heat are imparted, to uphold life:—is it thought that such a resemblance is a strong ground for believing that the planets of our system, and of other systems, are inhabited as the earth is? If such an astronomical analogy be insisted on, we must again have recourse to geology, to see what such analogy is worth. And then, we are led to reflect, that if we were to follow such analogies, we should be led to suppose that all the successive periods of the earth's history were occupied with life of the same order; that as the earth, in its present condition, is the seat of an intelligent population, so must it have been, in all former conditions. The earth, in its former conditions, was able and fitted to support life; even the life of creatures closely resembling man in their bodily structure. Even of monkeys, fossil remains have been found. But yet, in those former conditions, it did not support human life. Even those geologists who have dwelt most on the discovery of fossil monkeys, and other animals nearest to man, have not dreamt that there existed, before man, a race of

rational, intelligent, and progressive creatures. As we have seen, geology and history alike refute such a fancy. The notion, then, that one period of time in the history of the earth must resemble another, in the character of its population, because it resembles it in physical circumstances, is negatived by the facts which we discover in the history of the earth. And so, the notion that one part of the universe must resemble another in its population, because it resembles it in physical circumstances, is negatived as a law of creation. Analogy, further examined, affords no support to such a notion. The analogy of time, the events of which we know, corrects all such guesses founded on a supposed analogy of space, the furniture of which, so far as this point is concerned, we have no sufficient means of examining.

35. But in truth, we may go further. Not only does the analogy of creation not point to any such entire resemblance of similar parts, as is thus assumed, but it points in the opposite direction. Not entire resemblance, but universal difference is what we discover; not the repetition of exactly similar cases, but a series of cases perpetually dissimiliar, presents itself; not constancy, but change, perhaps advance; not one permanent and pervading scheme, but preparation and completion of successive schemes; not uniformity and a fixed type of existences, but progression and a climax. This may be said to be the case in the geological aspect of the world; for, without occupying ourselves with the question, how far the monuments of animal life, which we find preserved in the earth's strata, exhibited a gradual progression from ruder and more imperfect forms to the types of the present terrestrial population; from sponges and mollusks, to fish and lizards, from cold-blooded to warm blooded animals, and so on, till we come to the most perfect vertebrates;—a doctrine

which many eminent geologists have held, and still hold;—without discussing this question, or assuming that the fact is so; this at least cannot be denied or doubted, that man is incomparably the most perfect and highly-endowed creature which ever has existed on the earth. How far previous periods of animal existence were a necessary preparation of the earth, as the habitation of man, or a gradual progression towards the existence of man, we need not now inquire. But this at least we may say; that man, now that he is here, forms a climax to all that has preceded; a term incomparably exceeding in value all the previous parts of the series; a complex and ornate capital to the subjacent column; a personage of vastly greater dignity and importance than all the preceding line of the procession. The analogy of nature, in this case at least, appears to be, that there should be inferior, as well as superior provinces, in the universe; and that the inferior may occupy an immensely larger portion of time than the superior; why not then of space? The intelligent part of creation is thrust into the compass of a few years, in the course of myriads of ages; why not then into the compass of a few miles, in the expanse of systems? The earth was brute and inert, compared with its present condition, dark and chaotic, so far as the light of reason and intelligence are concerned, for countless centuries before man was created. Why then may not other parts of creation be still in this brute and inert and chaotic state, while the earth is under the influence of a higher exercise of creative power? If the earth was, for ages, a turbid abyss of lava and of mud, why may not Mars or Saturn be so still? If the germs of life were, gradually, and at long intervals, inserted in the terrestrial slime, why may they not be just inserted, or not yet inserted, in Jupiter? Or why should we assume that the condition of those planets resembles ours, even so far as such suppositions imply? Why may they not, some or all of them, be barren masses of stone and metal, slag and scoriæ, dust and cinders? That some of them are composed of such materials, we have better reason to believe, than we have to believe anything else respecting their physical constitution, as we shall hereafter endeavor to show. If then, the earth be the sole inhabited spot in the work of creation, the oasis in the desert of our system, there is nothing in this contrary to the analogy of creation. But if, in some way which perhaps we cannot discover, the earth obtained, for accompaniments, mere chaotic and barren masses, as conditions of coming into its present state; as it may have required, for accompaniments, the brute and imperfect races of former animals, as conditions of coming into its present state, as the habitation of man; the analogy is against, and not in favor of, the belief that they too (the other masses, the planets, &c.) are habitations. I may hereafter dwell more fully on such speculations; but the possibility that the planets are such rude masses, is quite as tenable, on astronomical grounds, as the possibility that the planets resemble the earth, in matters of which astronomy can tell us nothing. We say, therefore, that the example of geology refutes the argument drawn from the supposed analogy of one part of the universe with another; and suggests a strong suspicion that the force of analogy, better known, may tend in the opposite direction.

36. When such possibilities are presented to the reader, he may naturally ask, if we are thus to regard man as the climax of creation, in space, as in time, can we point out any characters belonging to him, which may tend to make it conceivable that the Creator should thus distinguish him, and care for him:—should prepare his habitation if it be so, by ages of cha-

otic and rudimentary life, and by accompanying orbs of brute and barren matter. If Man be, thus, the head, the crowned head of the creation, is he worthy to be thus elevated? Has he any qualities which make it conceivable that, with such an array of preparation and accompaniment, he should be placed upon the earth, his throne? Or rather, if he be thus the chosen subject of God's care, has he any qualities, which make it conceiveable that he should be thus selected; taken under such guardianship; admitted to such a dispensation; graced with such favor. The question with which we began again recurs: What is man that God should be thus mindful of him? After the views which have been presented to us, does any answer now occur to us?

37. The answer which we have to give, is that which we have already repeatedly stated. Man is an intellectual, moral, religious, and spiritual creature. If we consider these attributes, we shall see that they are such as to give him a special relation to God, and as we conceive, and must conceive, God to be; and may therefore be, in God, the occasion of special guardianship, special regard, a special dispensation towards man.

38. As an intellectual creature, he has not only an intelligence which he can apply to practical uses, to minister to the needs of animal and social life; but also an intellect by which he can speculate about the relations of things, in their most general form; for instance, the properties of space and time, the relations of finite and infinite. He can discover truths, to which all things, existing in space and time, must conform. These are conditions of existence to which the creation conforms, that is, to which the Creator conforms; and man, capable of seeing that such conditions are true and necessary, is capable, so far, of understanding some of the conditions of

the Creator's workmanship. In this way, the mind of man has some community with the mind of God; and however remote and imperfect this community may be, it must be real. Since, then, man has thus, in his intellect, an element of community with God, it is so far conceivable that he should be, in a special manner, the object of God's care and favor. The human mind, with its wonderful and perhaps illimitable powers, is something of which we can believe God to be "mindful."

39. Again: man is a moral creature. He recognizes, he cannot help recognizing, a distinction of right and wrong in his actions; and in his internal movements which lead to action. This distinction he recognizes as the reason, the highest and ultimate reason, for doing or for not doing. And this law of his own reason, he is, by reflection, led to recognize as a Law of the Supreme Reason; of the Supreme Mind which has made him what he is. The Moral Law, he owns and feels as God's Law. By the obligation which he feels to obey this Law, he feels himself God's subject; placed under his government; compelled to expect his judgment, his rewards, and punishments. By being a moral creature, then, he is, in a special manner, the subject of God; and not only we can believe that, in this capacity, God cares for him; but we cannot believe that he *does not* care for him. He cares for him, so as to approve of what he does right, and to condemn what he does wrong. And he has given him, in his own breast, an assurance that he will do this; and thus, God cares for man, in a peculiar and special manner. As a moral creature, we have no difficulty in conceiving that God may think him worthy of his regard and government.

40. The development of man's moral nature, as we have just described it, leads to, and involves the development of

his religious nature. By looking within himself, and seeing the Moral Law, he learns to look upwards to God, the Author of the Law, and the Awarder of the rewards and penalties which follow moral good and evil. But the belief of such a dispensation carries us, or makes us long to be carried, beyond the manifestations of this dispensation, as they appear in the ordinary course of human life. By thinking on such things, man is led to ascribe a wider range to the moral Government of God :—to believe in methods of reward and punishment, which do not appear in the natural course of events : to accept events, out of the order of nature, which announce that God has provided such methods : to accept them, when duly authenticated, as messages from God ; and thus, when God provides the means, to allow himself to be placed in intercourse with God. Since man is capable of this ; since, as a religious creature, this is his tendency, his need, the craving of his heart, without which, when his religious nature is fully unfolded, he can feel no comfort nor satisfaction ; we cannot be surprised that God should deem him a proper object of a special fatherly care ; a fit subject for a special dispensation of his purposes, as to the consequences of human actions. Man being this, we can believe that God is not only " mindful of him," but " visits him."

41. As we have said, the soul of man, regarded as the subject of God's religious government, is especially termed his *Spirit:* the course of human being which results from the intercourse with God, which God permits, is a *spiritual* existence. Man is capable, in no small degree, of such an existence, of such an intercourse with God ; and, as we are authorized to term it, of such a life with God, and in God, even while he continues in his present human existence. I say *authorized*, because such expressions are used, though reverently, by the

most religious men; who are, at any rate, authority as to their own sentiments; which are the basis of our reasoning. Whatever, then, may be the imperfection, in this life, of such a union with God, yet since man can, when sufficiently assisted and favored by God, enter upon such a union, we cannot but think it most credible and most natural, that he should be the object of God's special care and regard, even of his love and presence.

42. That men are, only in a comparatively small number of cases, intellectual, moral, religious, and spiritual, in the degree which I have described, does not, by any means, deprive our argument of its force. The capacity of man is, that he may become this; and such a capacity may well make him a special object in the eyes of Him under whose guidance and by whose aid, such a development and elevation of his nature is open to him. However imperfect and degraded, however unintellectual, immoral, irreligious, and unspiritual, a great part of mankind may be, still they all have the germs of such an elevation of their nature; and a large portion of them make, we cannot doubt, no small progress in this career of advancement to a spiritual condition. And with such capacities, and such practical exercise of those capacities, we can have no difficulty in believing, if the evidence directs us to believe, that that part of the creation in which man has his present appointed place, is the special field of God's care and love; by whatever wastes of space, and multitudes of material bodies, it may be surrounded; by whatever races it may have been previously occupied, of brutes that perish, and that, compared with man, can hardly be said to have lived.

CHAPTER VII.

THE NEBULÆ.

1. I HAVE attempted to show that, even if we suppose the other bodies of the universe to resemble the Earth, so far as to seem, by their materials, forms, and motions, no less fitted than she is to be the abodes of life; yet that, knowing what we do of man, we can believe that the Earth is tenanted by a race who are the *special* objects of God's care. Even if the tendency of the analogies of creation were, to incline us to suppose that the other planets are as well suited as our globe, to have inhabitants, still it would require a great amount of evidence, to make us believe that they have such inhabitants as we are; while yet such evidence is altogether wanting. Even if we knew that the stars were the centres of revolving systems, we should have an immense difficulty in believing that an Earth, with such a population as ours, revolves about any of them. If astronomy made a plurality of words probable, we have strong reasonings, drawn from other subjects, to think that the other worlds are not like ours.

2. The admirers of astronomical triumphs may perhaps be disposed to say, that when so much has been discovered, we may be allowed to complete the scheme by the exercise of fancy. I have attempted to show that we are not in such a

state of ignorance, when we look at other relations of the earth and of man, as to allow us to do this. But now we may go a little onwards in our argument; and may ask, whether Astronomy really does what is here claimed for her:—whether she carries us so securely to the bounds of the visible universe, that our Fancy may take up the task, and people the space thus explored:—whether the bodies which Astronomy has examined, be really as fitted as our Earth, to sustain a population of living things:—whether the most distant objects in the universe do really seem to be systems, or the beginnings of systems:—whether Astronomy herself may not incline in favor of the condition of man, as being the sole creature of his kind?

3. In making this inquiry, it will of course be understood, that I do so with the highest admiration for the vast discoveries which Astronomy has really made; and for the marvellous skill and invention of the great men who have, in all ages of the world, and not least, in our time, been the authors of such discoveries. From the time when Galileo first discovered the system of Jupiter's satellites, to the last scrutiny of the structure of a nebula by Lord Rosse's gigantic telescope, the history of the telescopic exploration of the sky, has been a history of genius felicitously employed in revealing wonders. In this history, the noble labors of the first and the second Herschel relative to the distribution of the fixed stars, the forms and classes of nebulæ, and the phenomena of double stars, especially bear upon our present speculations; to which we may add, the examination of the aspect of each planet, by various observers, as Schroeter, and of the moon by others, from Huyghens to Mädler and Beer. The achievements which are most likely to occur to the reader's mind are those of the Earl of Rosse; as being the latest addition to our knowledge,

and the result of the greatest instrumental powers. By the energy and ingenuity of that eminent person, an eye is directed to the heavens, having a pupil of six feet diameter, with the most complete optical structure, and the power of ranging about for its objects over a great extent of sky; and thus the quantity of light which the eye receives from any point of the heavens is augmented, it may be, fifty thousand times. The rising Moon is seen from the Observatory in Ireland with the same increase of size and light, as if her solid globe, two thousand miles in diameter, retaining all its illumination, really rested upon the summits of the Alps, to be gazed at by the naked eye. An object which appears to the naked eye a single star, may, by this teleseope, so far as its power of seeing is concerned, be resolved into fifty thousand stars, each of the same brightnes as the obvious star. What seems to the unassisted vision a nebula, a patch of diluted light, in which no distinct luminous point can be detected, may, by such an instrument, be discriminated or resolved into a number of bright dots; as the stippled shades of an engraving are resolved into dots by the application of a powerful magnifying glass. Similar results of the application of great telescopic power had of course been attained long previously; but, as the nature of scientific research is, each step adds something to our means of knowledge; and the last addition assumes, includes, and augments the knowledge which we possessed before. The discussions in which we are engaged, belong to the very boundary region of science;—to the frontier where knowledge, at least astronomical knowledge, ends, and ignorance begins. Such discoveries, therefore, as those made by Lord Rosse's telescope, require our special notice here.

4. We may begin, at what appears to us the outskirts of creation, the Nebulæ. At one time it was conceived by as-

tronomers in general, that these patches of diffused light, which are seen by them in such profusion in the sky, are not luminous bodies of regular terms and definite boundaries, apparently solid, as the stars are supposed to be; but really, as even to good telescopes many of them seem, masses of luminous cloud or vapor, loosely held together, as clouds and vapors are, and not capable by any powers of vision of being resolved into distinct visible elements. This opinion was for a time so confidentially entertained, that there was founded upon it an hypothesis, that these were gaseous masses, out of which suns and systems might afterwards be formed, by the concentration of these luminous vapors into a solid central sun, more intensely luminous; while detached portions of the mass, flying off, and cooling down so as to be no longer self-luminous, might revolve round the central body, as planets and satellites. This is the *Nebular Hypothesis*, suggested by the elder Herschel, and adopted by the great mathematician Laplace.

5. But the result of the optical scrutiny of the nebulæ by more modern observers, especially by Lord Rosse in Ireland, and Mr. Bond in America, has been, that many celestial objects which were regarded before as truly nebulous, have been resolved into stars; and this resolution has been extended to so many cases of nebulæ, of such various kinds, as to have produced a strong suspicion in the minds of astronomers that *all* the nebulæ, however different in their appearance, may really be resolved into stars, if they be attacked with optical powers sufficiently great.

6. If this were to be assumed as done, and if each of the separate points, into which the nebulæ are thus resolved, were conceived to be a star, which looks so small only because it is so distant, and which really is as likely to have a system of planets revolving about it, as is a star of the first magnitude:

—we should then have a view of the immensity of the visible universe, such as I presented to the reader in the beginning of this essay. All the distant nebulæ appear as nebulæ, only because they are so distant; if truly seen, they are groups of stars, of which each may be as important as our sun, being, like it, the centre of a planetary system. And thus, a patch of the heavens, one hundredth or one thousandth part of the visible breadth of our sun, may contain in it more life, not only than exists in the solar system, but in as many such systems as the unassisted eye can see stars in the heavens, on the clearest winter night.

7. This is a stupendous view of the greatness of the creation; and, to many persons, its very majesty, derived from magnitude and number, will make it so striking and acceptable, that, once apprehended, they will feel as if there were a kind of irreverence in disturbing it. But if this view be really not tenable when more closely examined, it is, after all, not wise to connect our feelings of religious reverence with it, so that they shall suffer a shock when we are obliged to reject it. I may add, that we may entertain an undoubting trust that any view of the creation which is found to be true, will also be found to supply material for reverential contemplation. I venture to hope that we may, by further examination, be led to a reverence of a deeper and more solemn character than a mere wonder at the immensity of space and number.

8. But whatever the result may be, let us consider the evidence for this view. It assumes that all the Nebulæ are resolvable into stars, and that they appear as nebulæ only because they are more distant than the region in which they can appear as stars. Are there any facts, any phenomena in the heavens, which may help us to determine whether this is a probable opinion?

9. It is most satisfactory for us, when we can, in such inquiries, know the thoughts which have suggested themselves to the minds of those who have examined the phenomena with the most complete knowledge, the greatest care, and the best advantages; and have speculated upon these phenomena in a way both profound and unprejudiced. Some remarks of Sir John Herschel, recommended by these precious characters, seem to me to bear strongly upon the question which I have just had to ask :—Do all the nebulæ owe their nebulous appearance to their being too distant to be seen as groups of distinct stars, though they really are such groups?

10. Herschel, in the visit which he made to the Cape of Good Hope, for the purpose of erecting to his father the most splendid monument that son ever erected,—the completed survey of the vault of heaven,—had full opportunity of studying a certain pair of remarkable bright spaces of the skies, filled with a cloudy light, which lie near the southern pole; and which, having been unavoidably noticed by the first Antarctic voyagers, are called the *Magellanic Clouds.* When the larger of these two clouds is examined through powerful telescopes, it presents, we are told, a constitution of uncommon complexity: "large patches and tracts of nebulosity in every stage of resolution, from light, irresolvable with eighteen inches of reflecting aperture, up to perfectly separated stars like the Milky Way, and clustering groups sufficiently insulated and condensed to come under the designation of irregular, and in some cases pretty rich clusters. But besides these, there are also nebulæ in abundance, both regular and irregular; globular clusters in every stage of condensation, and objects of a nebulous character quite peculiar, and which have no analogies in any other region of the heavens."* He goes on to say, that

* Herschel, *Outl. of Astr.* Art. 893.

these nebulæ and clusters are far more crowded in this space than they are in any other, even the most crowded parts, of the nebulous heavens. This *Nubecula Major*, as it is termed, is of a round or oval form, and its diameter is about six degrees, so that it is about twelve times the apparent diameter of the moon. The *Nubecula Minor* is a smaller patch of the same kind. If we suppose the space occupied by the various objects which the nubecula major includes, to be, in a general way, spherical, its nearest and most remote parts must (as its angular size proves) differ in their distance from us by little more than a tenth part of our distance from its centre. That the two nubeculæ are thus approximately spherical spaces, is in the highest degree probable; not only from the peculiarity of their contents, which suggests the notion of a peculiar group of objects, collected into a limited space; but from the barrenness, as to such objects, of the sky in the neighborhood of these Magellanic Clouds. To suppose (the only other possible supposition) that they are two columns of space, with their ends turned towards us, and their lengths hundreds and thousands of times their breadths, would be too fantastical a proceeding to be tolerated; and would, after all, not explain the facts without further altogether arbitrary assumptions.

11. It appears, then, that, in these groups, there are stars of various magnitudes, clusters of various forms, nebulæ regular and irregular, nebulous tracts and patches of peculiar character; and all so disposed, that the most distant of them, whichever these may be, are not more than one-tenth more distant than the nearest. If the nearest star in this space be at nine times the distance of Sirius, the farthest nebulæ, contained in the same space, will not be at more than ten times the distance of Sirius. Of course, the doctrine that nebulæ are seen as nebulæ, merely because they are so distant, re-

quires us to assume all nebulæ to be hundreds and thousands of times more distant than the smallest stars. If stars of the eighth magnitude (which are hardly visible to the naked eye) be eight times as remote as Sirius, a nebula containing a thousand stars, which is invisible to the naked eye, must be more than eight thousand times as remote as Sirius. And thus if, in the whole galaxy, we reckon only the stars as far as the eighth magnitude, and suppose all the stars of the galaxy to form a nebula, which is visible to the spectators in a distant nebula, only as their nebula is visible to us; we must place them at eight thousand times two hundred thousand times the distance of the Sun; and, even so, we are obviously vastly understating the calculation. These are the gigantic estimates with which some astronomical speculators have been in the habit of overwhelming the minds of their listeners; and these views have given a kind of majesty to the aspect of the nebulæ; and have led some persons to speak of the discovery of every new streak of nebulous light in the starry heavens, as a discovery of new worlds, and still new worlds. But the Magellanic Clouds show us very clearly that all these calculations are entirely baseless. In those regions of space, there coexists, in a limited compass, and in indiscriminate position, stars, clusters of stars, nebulæ, regular and irregular, and nebulous streaks and patches. These, then, are different kinds of things in themselves, not merely different to us. There are such things as nebulæ side by side with stars, and with clusters of stars. Nebulous matter resolvable occurs close to nebulous matter irresolvable. The last and widest step by which the dimensions of the universe have been expanded in the notions of eager speculators, is checked by a completer knowledge and a sager spirit of speculation. Whatever inference we may draw from the resolvability of some of the nebulæ, we may not draw this inference ;—that they are more distant, and contain a larger array of systems and of worlds, in proportion as they are difficult to resolve.

12. But indeed, if we consider this process, of the resolution of nebulæ into luminous points, on its own ground, without looking to such facts as I have just adduced, it will be difficult, or impossible, to assign any reason why it should lead to such inferences as have been drawn from it. Let us look at this matter more clearly. An astronomer, armed with a powerful telescope, *resolves* a nebula, discerns that a luminous cloud is composed of shining dots :—but what are these dots ? Into *what* does he resolve the nebula ? Into *Stars*, it is commonly said. Let us not wrangle about words. By all means let these dots be Stars, if we know about what we are speaking : if a *Star* merely mean a luminous dot in the sky. But that these stars shall resemble, in their nature, stars of the first magnitude, and that such stars shall resemble our Sun, are surely very bold structures of assumption to build on such a basis. Some nebulæ are resolvable ; are resolvable into distinct points ; certainly a very curious, probably an important discovery. We may hereafter learn that *all* nebulæ are resolvable into distinct points : that would be a still more curious discovery. But what would it amount to ? What would be the simple way of expressing it, without hypothesis, and without assumption ? Plainly this : that the substance of all nebulæ is not continuous, but discrete ;—separable, and separate into distinct luminous elements ;—nebulæ are, it would then seem, as it were, of a curdled or granulated texture ; they have run into *lumps* of light, or have been formed originally of such lumps. Highly curious. But what are these lumps ? How large are they ? At what distances ? Of what structure ? Of what use ? It would seem that he must be a bold man

who undertakes to answer these questions. Certainly he must appear to ordinary thinkers to be *very* bold, who, in reply, says, gravely and confidently, as if he had unquestionable authority for his teaching :—"These lumps, O man, are Suns; they are distant from each other as far as the Dog-star is from us; each has its system of Planets, which revolve around it; and each of these Planets is the seat of an animal and vegetable creation. Among these Planets, some, we do not yet know how many, are occupied by rational and responsible creatures, like Man; and the only matter which perplexes us, holding this belief on astronomical grounds, is, that we do not quite see how to put our theology into its due place and form in our system."

13. In discussing such matters as these, where our knowledge and our ignorance are so curiously blended together, and where it is so difficult to make men feel that so much ignorance can lie so close to so much knowledge;—to make them believe that they have been allowed to discover so much, and yet are not allowed to discover more :—we may be permitted to illustrate our meaning, by supposing a case of blended knowledge and ignorance, of real and imaginary discovery. Suppose that there were carried from a scientific to a more ignorant nation, excellent maps of the world, finely engraved; the mountain-ranges shaded in the most delicate manner, and the sheet crowded with information of all kinds, in writing large, small, and microscopic. Suppose also, that when these maps had been studied with the naked eye, so as to establish a profound respect for the knowledge and skill of the author of them, some of those who perused them should be furnished with good microscopes, so as to carry their examination further than before. They might then find that, in several parts, what before appeared to be merely crooked lines, was really writing, stating, it may be, the amount of

population of a province, or the date of foundation of a town. To exhaust all the information thus contained on the maps, might be a work of considerable time and labor. But suppose that, when this was done, a body of resolute microscopists should insist that the information which the map contained was not exhausted: that they should continue peering perseveringly at the lines which formed the shading of the mountains, maintaining that these lines also were writing, if only it might be deciphered; and should go on increasing, with immense labor and ingenuity, the powers of their microscopes, in order to discover the legend contained in these unmeaning lines. We should, perhaps, have here an image of the employment of these astronomers, who now go on looking in nebulæ for worlds. And we may notice in passing, that several of the arguments which are used by such astronomers, might be used, and would be used, by our microscopists:—how improbable it was that a person so full of knowledge, and so able to convey it, as the author of the maps was known to be, should not have a design and purpose in every line that he drew: what a waste of space it would be to leave any part of the sheet blank of information; and the like. To which the reply is to us obvious; that the design of shading the mountains was design enough; and that the information conveyed was all that was necessary or convenient. Nor does this illustration at all tend to show that such astronomical scrutiny, directed intelligently, with a right selection of the points examined, may not be highly interesting and important. If the microscopists had examined the map with a view to determine the best way in which mountains can be indicated by shading, they would have employed themselves upon a question which has been the subject of multiplied and instructive discussion in our own day.

14. But to return to the subject of Nebulæ, we may further say, with the most complete confidence, that whether or not nebulous matter be generally resolvable into shining dots, it cannot possibly be true that its being, or not being so resolvable by our telescopes, depends merely upon its smaller or greater distance from the observer. For, in the first place, that there is matter, to the best assisted eye not distinguishable from nebulous matter, which is not so resolvable, is proved by several facts. The tails of Comets often resemble nebulæ; so much so that there are several known nebulæ, which are, by the less experienced explorers of the sky, perpetually mistaken for comets, till they are proved not to be so, by their having no cometary motion. Such is the nebula in Andromeda, which is visible to the naked eye.* But the tails and nebulous appendages of comets, though they alter their appearance very greatly, according to the power of the telescope with which they are examined, have never been resolved into stars, or any kind of dots; and seem, by all investigations, to be sheets or cylinders or cones of luminous vapor, changing their form as they approach to or recede from the sun, and perhaps by the influence of other causes. Yet some of them approach very near the earth; all of them come within the limits of our system. Here, then, we have (probably, at least,) nebulous matter, which when brought close to the eye, compared with the stellar nebulæ, still appears as nebulous.

15. Again, as another phenomenon, bearing upon the same question, we have the Zodiacal Light. This is a faint cone of light† which, at certain seasons, may be seen extending from the horizon obliquely upwards, and following the course of

* Herschel. *Outl. of Astr.* Art. 874, and Plate 11, Fig. 3.
† Ibid. Art. 897.

the ecliptic, or rather, of the sun's equator. It appears to be a lens-shaped envelope of the sun, extending beyond the orbits of Mercury and Venus, and nearly attaining that of the earth; and in Sir John Herschel's view, may be regarded as placing the sun in the list of nebulous stars. No one has ever thought that this nebulous appearance was resolvable into luminous points; but if it were, probably not even the most sanguine of speculators on the multitude of suns would call these points *suns*.

16. But indeed the nebulæ themselves, and especially the most remote of the nebulæ, or at least those which most especially require the most powerful telescopes, offer far more decisive proofs that their resolvability or non-resolvability,—their apparent constitution as diffused and vaporous masses,—does not depend upon their distance. A remarkable fact in the irregular, and in some of the regular nebulæ* is, that they consist of long patches and streaks, which stretch out in various directions, and of which the form† and extent vary according to the visual power which is applied to them. Many of the nebulæ and especially of the fainter ones, entirely change their form with the optical power of the instrument by which they are scrutinized; so that, as seen in the mightier telescopes of modern times, the astronomer scarcely recognizes the figures in which the earlier observers have recorded what they saw in the same place. Parts which, before, were separate, are connected by thin bridges of light which are now detected; and where the nebulous space appeared to be bounded, it sends off long tails of faint light into the surrounding space. Now, no one can suppose that these newly-seen portions of the nebula are immensely further off than the other parts. However little we know of the nature of the object,

* Hersch. 874. † Ibid. 881—8.

we must suppose it to be one connected object, with all its parts, as to sense, at the same distance from us. Whether therefore it be resolvable or no, there must be some other reason, besides the difference of distance, why the brighter parts were seen, while the fainter parts were not. The obvious reason is, that the latter were not seen because they were thin films which required more light to see them. We are led, irresistibly as it seems, to regard the whole mass of such a nebula, as an aggregation of vaporous rolls and streaks, assuming such forms as thin volumes of smoke or vapor often assume in our atmosphere, and assuming, like them, different shapes according to the quantity of light which comes to us from them. If, as soon as one of these new filaments or webs of a nebula comes into view, we should say, Here we have a new array of suns and of worlds, we should judge as fantastically, as any one who should com binethe like imaginations with the varying cloud-work of a summer-sky. To suppose that all the varied streaks by which the patch of nebulous light shades off into the surrounding darkness, and which change their form and extent with every additional polish which we can give to a reflecting or refracting surface, disclose, with every new streak, new worlds, is a wanton indulgence of fancy, to which astronomy gives us no countenance.*

17. Undoubtedly all true astronomers, taught caution and temperance of thought by the discipline of their magnificent science, abstain from founding such assumptions upon their

* At the recent meeting of the British Association (Sept. 1853), drawings were exhibited of the same nebulæ, as seen through Lord Rosse's large telescope, and through a telescope of three feet aperture. With the smaller telescopic power, all the characteristic features were lost. The spiral structure (see next Article but one) has been almost entirely brought to light by the large telescope.

discoveries. They know how necessary it is to be upon their guard against the tricks which fancy plays with the senses; and if they see appearances of which they cannot interpret the meaning, they are content that they should have no meaning for them, till the due explanation comes. We have innumerable examples of this wise and cautious temper, in all periods of astronomy. One has occurred lately. Several careful astronomers, observing the stars by day, had been surprised to see globes of light glide across the field of view of their telescopes, often in rapid succession and in great numbers. They did not, as may be supposed, rush to the assumption that these globes were celestial bodies of a new kind, before unseen; and that from the peculiarity of their appearance and movement, they were probably inhabited by beings of a peculiar kind. They proceeded very differently; they altered the focus of their telescopes, looked with other glasses, made various changes and trials, and finally discovered that these globes of light were the winged seeds of certain plants which were wafted through the air; and which, illuminated by the sun, were made globular by being at distances unsuited to the focus of the telescope.*

18. But perhaps something more may be founded on the ramified and straggling form which belongs to many of the nebulæ. Under the powers of Lord Rosse's telescope, a considerable number of them assume a shape consisting of several spiral films diverging from one centre, and growing broader and fainter as they diverge, so as to resemble a curled feather, or whirlpool of light.† This form, though generally de-

* See monthly Notices of the Royal Astronomical Society, Dec. 13, 1850.

† The frontispiece to this volume represents two of these Spiral Nebulæ; those denominated 51 Messier, and 99 Messier, as given by

formed by irregularities, more or less, is traceable in so many of the nebulæ, that we cannot easily divest ourselves of the persuasion that there is some general reason for such a form; —that something, in the mechanical causes which have produced the nebulæ, has tended to give them this shape. Now, when this thought has occurred to us, since mathematicians have written a great deal concerning the mechanics of the universe, it is natural to ask, whether any of the problems which they have solved give a result like that thus presented to our eyes. Do such spirals as we here see, occur in any of the diagrams which illustrate the possible motions of celestial bodies? And to this, a person acquainted with mathematical literature might reply, that in the second Book of Newton's *Principia*, in the part which has especial reference to the Vortices of Descartes, such spirals appear upon the page. They represent the path which a body would describe if, acted upon by a central force, it had to move in a medium of which the resistance was considerable;—considerable, that is, in comparison with the other forces which act; as for example, the forces which deflect the motion from a straight line. Indeed, that in such a case a body would describe a spiral, of which the general form would be more or less oval, is evident on a little consideration. And in this way, for instance, Encke's comet, which, if the resistance to its motion were insensible, would go on describing an ellipse about the sun, always returning upon the same path after every revolution; does really describe a path which, at each revolution, falls a little within the preceding revolution, and thus gradually converges to the centre. And if we suppose the comet to consist of a luminous mass, or a string of masses, which should

Lord Rosse in the *Phil. Trans. for* 1850. The former of these two has a lateral focus, besides the principal focus or pole.

occupy a considerable arc of such an orbit, the orbit would be marked by a track of light, as an oval spiral. Or if such a comet were to separate into two portions, as we have, with our own eyes, recently seen Biela's comet do; or into a greater number; then these portions would be distributed along such a spiral. And if we suppose a large mass of cometic matter thus to move in a highly resisting medium, and to consist of patches of different densities, then some would move faster and some more slowly; but all, in spirals such as have been spoken of; and the general aspect produced would be, that of the spiral nebulæ which I have endeavored to describe. The luminous matter would be more diffused in the outer and more condensed in the central parts, because to the centre of attraction all the spirals converge.

19. This would be so, we say, if the luminous matter moved in a greatly resisting medium. But what is the measure of *great* resistance? It is, as we have already said, that the resistance which opposes the motion shall bear a considerable proportion to the force which deflects the motion. But what is that force? Upon the theory of the universal gravitation of matter, on which theory we here proceed, the force which deflects the motions of the parts of each system into curves, is the mutual attraction of the parts of the system; leaving out of the account the action of other systems, as comparatively insignificent and insensible. The condition, then, for the production of such spiral figures as I have spoken of, amounts really to this; that the mutual attraction of the parts of the luminous matter is slight; or, in other words, that the matter itself is very thin and rare. In that case, indeed, we can easily see that such a result would follow. A cloud of dust, or of smoke, which was thin and light, would make but a little way through the air, and would soon fall downwards;

while a metal bullet shot horizontally with the same velocity, might fly for miles. Just so, a loose and vaporous mass of cometic matter would be pulled rapidly inwards by the attraction to the centre; and supposing it also drawn into a long train, by the different density of its different parts, it would trace, in lines of light, a circular or elliptical spiral converging to the centre of attraction, and resembling one of the branches of the spiral nebulæ. And if several such cometic masses thus travelled towards the centre, they would exhibit the wheel-like figure with bent spokes, which is seen in the spiral nebulæ. And such a figure would all the more resemble some of those nebulæ, as seen through Lord Rosse's telescope, if the spirals were accompanied by exterior branches of thinner and fainter light, which nebulous matter of smaller density might naturally form. Perhaps too, such matter, when thin, may be supposed to cool down more rapidly from its state of incandescence; and thus to become less luminous. If this were so, a great optical power would of course be required, to make the diverging branches visible at all.

20. There is one additional remark, which we may make, as to the resemblance of cometary* and nebular matter. That cometary matter is of very small density, we have many reasons to believe:—its transparency, which allows us to see stars through it undimmed;—the absence of any mechanical effect, weight, inertia, impulse, or attraction, in the nearest

* I am aware that some astronomers do not consider it as proved that cometary matter is entirely self-luminous. Arago found that the light of a Comet contained a portion of polarized light, thus proving that it had been reflected (*Cosmos*, I. p. 111, and III. p. 566). But I think the opinion that the greater part of the light is self-luminous, like the nebulæ, generally prevails. Any other supposition is scarcely consistent with the rapid changes of brightness which occur in a comet during its motion to and from the Sun.

appulses of comets to planets and satellites:—and the fact that, in the recent remarkable event in the cometic history, the separation of Biela's comet into two, the two parts did not appear to exert any perceptible attraction on each other, any more than two volumes of dust or of smoke would do on earth. Luminous cometary matter, then, is very light, that is, has very little weight or inertia. And luminous nebulous matter is also very light in this sense: if our account of the cause of spiral nebulæ has in it any truth. But yet, if we suppose the nebulæ to be governed by the law of universal gravitation, the attractive force of the luminous matter upon itself, must be sufficient to bend the spirals into their forms. How are we to reconcile this; that the matter is so loose that it falls to the centre in rapid spirals, and yet that it attracts so strongly that there is a centre, and an energetic central force to curve the spirals thither? To this, the reply which we must make is, that the size of the nebular space is such, that though its rarity is extreme, its whole mass is considerable. One part does not perceptibly attract another, but the whole does perceptibly attract every part. This indeed need the less surprise us, since it is exactly the case with our earth. One stone does not visibly attract another. It is much indeed for man, if he can make perceptible the attraction of a mountain upon a plumb-line; or of a stratum of rock a thousand feet thick upon the going of a pendulum; or of large masses of metal upon a delicate balance. By such experiments men of science have endeavored to measure that minute thing, the attraction of one portion of terrestrial matter upon another; and thus, to weigh the whole mass of the earth. And equally great, at least, may be the disproportion between the mutual attraction of two parts of a nebulous system, and the total central attraction; and thus, though the former be insensible, the latter may be important.

21. It has been shown by Newton, that if any mass of matter be distributed in a uniform sphere, or in uniform concentric spherical shells, the total attraction on a point without the sphere, will be the same as if the whole mass were collected in that single point, the centre. Now, proceeding upon the supposition of such a distribution of the matter in a nebula, (which is a reasonable average supposition,) we may say, that if our sun were expanded into a nebula reaching to the extreme bounds of the known solar system, namely, to the newly-discovered planet Neptune, or even hundreds of times further; the attraction on an external point would remain the same as it is, while the attraction on points within the sphere of diffusion would be less than it is; according to some law, depending upon the degree of condensation of the nebular matter towards the centre; but still, in the outer regions of the nebula, not differing much from the present solar attraction. If we could discover a mass of luminous matter, descending in a spiral course towards the centre of such a nebula, that is, towards the sun, we should have a sort of element of the spiral nebulæ which have now attracted so much of the attention of astronomers. But, by an extraordinary coincidence, recent discoveries have presented to us such an element. Encke's comet, of which we have just spoken, appears to be describing such a spiral curve towards the sun. It is found that its period is, at every revolution, shorter and shorter; the amplitude of its sweep, at every return within the limits of our observation, narrower and narrower; so that in the course of revolutions and ages, however numerous, still, not such as to shake the evidence of the fact, it will fall into the sun.

22. Here then we are irresistibly driven to calculate what degree of resemblance there is, between the comet of Encke, and the luminous elements of the spiral nebulæ, which have recently been found to exist in other regions of the universe. Can we compare its density with theirs? Can we learn whether the luminous matter in such nebulæ is more diffused or less diffused, than that of the comet of Encke? Can we compare the mechanical power of getting through space, as we may call it, that is, the ratio of the inertia to the resistance, in the one case, and in the other? If we can, the comparison cannot fail, it would seem, to be very curious and instructive. In this comparison, as in most others to which cosmical relations conduct us, we must expect that the numbers to which we are led, will be of very considerable amount. It is not equality in the density of the two luminous masses which we are to expect to find; if we can mark their proportions by thousands of times, we shall have made no small progress in such speculations.

23. The comet of Encke describes a spiral, gradually converging to the sun; but at what rate converging? In how many revolutions will it reach the sun? Of how many folds will its spire consist, before it attains the end of its course? The answer is:—Of very many. The retardation of Encke's Comet is very small: so small, that it has tasked the highest powers of modern calculation to detect it. Still, however, it is there: detected, and generally acknowledged, and confirmed by every revolution of the comet, which brings it under our notice; that is, commonly, about every three years. And having this fact, we must make what we can of it, in reasoning on the condition of the universe. No accuracy of calculation is necessary for our purpose: it is enough, if we bring into

view the kind of scale of numbers to which calculation would lead us.

24. Encke's comet revolves round the sun in 1,211 days. The period diminishes at present, by about one-ninth of a day every revolution. This amount of diminution will change, as the orbit narrows; but for our purpose, it will be enough to consider it unchangeable. The orbit therefore will cease to exist in a number of periods expressed by 9 times 1,211; that is, in something more that 10,000 revolutions; and of course sooner than this, in consequence of its coming in contact with the body of the sun. In 30,000 years then, it may be, this comet will complete its spiral, and be absorbed by the central mass. This long time, this long series of ten thousand revolutions, are long, because the resistance is so small, compared with the inertia of the moving mass. However thin, and rare, and unsubstantial the comet may be, the medium which resists it is much more so.

25. But this spiral, converging to its pole so slowly that it reaches it only after 10,000 circuits, is very different indeed from the spirals which we see in the nebulæ of which we have spoken. In the most conspicuous of those, there are only at most three or four circular or oval sweeps, in each spiral, or even the spiral reaches the centre before it has completed a single revolution round it. Now, what are we to infer from this? How is it, that the comet has a spiral of so many revolutions, and the nebulæ of so few? What difference of the mechanical conditions is indicated by this striking difference of form? Why, while the Comet thus lingers longer in the outer space, and approaches the sun by almost imperceptible degrees, does the Nebular Element rush, as it were, headlong to its centre, and show itself unable to circulate even for a few revolutions?

26. Regarding the question as a mechanical problem, the

answer must be this :—It is so, because the nebula is so much more rare than the matter of the comet, or the resisting medium so much more dense; or combining the two suppositions, because in the case of the comet, the luminous matter has *much* more inertia, more mechanical reality and substance, than the medium through which it moves; but in the nebula very *little* more.

27. The numbers of revolutions of the spiral, in the two cases, may not exactly represent the difference of the proportions; but, as I have said, they may serve to show the scale of them; and thus we may say, that if Encke's comet, approaching the centre by 10,000 revolutions, is 100,000 times as dense as the surrounding medium, the elements of the nebula, which reach the centre in a single revolution, are only ten times as dense as the medium through which they have to move.*

28. Nor does this result (that the bright element of the nebulæ is so few timesdenser than the medium in which it moves) offer anything which need surprise us: for, in truth, in a diffused nebula, since we suppose that its parts have mechanical properties, the nebula itself is a resisting medium. The rarer parts, which may very naturally have cooled down in consequence of their rarity, and so, become non-luminous, will resist the motions of the more dense and still-luminous portions. If we recur to the supposition, which we lately made, that the Sun were expanded into a nebulous sphere, reaching the orbit of Neptune, the diffused matter would offer a far greater resistance to the motions of comets than they now experience. In that case, Encke's comet might be brought to the centre af-

* We assume here that the number of revolutions to the centre is greater in proportion as the relative density of the resisting medium is less; which is by no means mechanically true; but the calculation may serve, as we have said, to show the scale of the numbers involved.

ter a few revolutions; and if, while it were thus descending, it were to be drawn out into a string of luminous masses, as Biela's comet has begun to be, these comets, and any others, would form separate luminous spiral tracks in the solar system; and would convert it into a spiral nebula of many branches, like those which are now the most recent objects of astronomical wonder.

29. It seems allowable to regard it as one of those coincidences, in the epochs of related yet seeming unconnected discoveries, which have so often occurred in the history of science; that we should, nearly at the same time, have had brought to our notice, the prevalence of spiral nebulæ, and the circumstances, in Biela's and in Encke's comets, which seem to explain them: the one by showing the origin of luminous broken lines, one part drifting on faster than another, according to its different density, as is usual in incoherent masses;* and the other by showing the origin of the spiral form of those lines, arising from the motion being in a resisting medium.

30. But though I have made suppositions by which our Solar System might become a spiral nebula, undoubtedly it is at present something very different; and the leading points of difference are very important for us to consider. And the main point is, that which has already been cursorily noticed: that instead of consisting of matter all nearly of the same density, and a great deal of it luminous, our Solar System consists of kinds of matter immensely different in density, and of large and regular portions which are not luminous. Instead of a diffused nebula with vaporous comets trailing spiral tracks

* Humboldt, whom nothing relative to the history of science escapes, quotes from Seneca a passage in which mention is made of a Comet which divided into two parts; and from the Chinese Annals, a notice of three "coupled Comets," which in the year 896 appeared, and described their paths together. *Cosmos*, III. p. 570, and the notes.

through a medium little rarer than themselves; we have a central sun, and the dark globes of the solid planets rolling round him, in a medium so rare, that in thousands of revolutions not a vestige of retardation can be discovered by the most subtle and persevering researches of astronomers. In the solar system, the luminous matter is collected into the body of the sun; the non-luminous matter, into the planets. And the comets and the resisting medium, which offer a small exception to this account, bear a proportion to the rest which the power of numbers scarce suffices to express.

31. Thus with regard to the density of matter in the solar system; we have supposed, as a mode of expression, that the density of a comet, Encke's comet for instance, is 100,000 times that of the resisting medium. Probably this is greatly understated; and probably also we greatly understate the matter, when we suppose that the tail of a comet is 100,000 times rarer than the matter of the sun.* And thus the resisting medium would be, at a very low calculation, 10,000 millions of times more rare than the substance of the sun.

32. And thus we are not, I think, going too far, when we say, that our Solar System, compared with spiral nebulous systems, is a system completed and finished, while they are mere confused, indiscriminate, incoherent masses. In the Nebulæ, we have loose matter of a thin and vaporous constitution, differing as more or less rare, more or less luminous, in a small degree; diffused over enormous spaces, in straggling and irregular forms; moving in devious and brief curves, with no vestige of order or system, or even of separation of different

* Laplace has proved that the masses of comets are very small. He reckons their mean mass as very much less than 1-100000th of the Earth's mass. And hence, considering their great size, we see how rare they must be. See *Expos. du Syst. du Monde.*

kinds of bodies. In the Solar System, we have the luminous separated from the non-luminous, the hot from the cold, the dense from the rare; and all, luminous and non-luminous, formed into globes, impressed with regular and orderly motions, which continue the same for innumerable revolutions and cycles.* The spiral nebulæ, compared with the solar system, cannot be considered as other than a kind of chaos; and not even a chaos, in the sense of a state preceding an orderly and stable system; for there is no indication, in those objects, of any tendency towards such a system. If we were to say that they appear mere shapeless masses, flung off in the work of creating solar systems, we might perhaps disturb those who are resolved to find everywhere worlds like ours; but it seems difficult to suggest any other reason for not saying so.

33. The same may be said of the other very irregular nebulæ, which spread out patches and paths of various degrees of brightness; and shoot out, into surrounding space, faint branches which are of different form and extent, according to the optical power with which they are seen. These irregular forms are incapable of being permanent according to the laws of mechanics. They are not figures of equilibrium; and, therefore, must change by the attraction of the matter upon itself. But if the tenuity of the matter is extreme, and the resistance of the medium in which it floats considerable, this tendency to change and to condensation may be almost nullified; and the bright specks may long keep their straggling forms, as the most fantastically shaped clouds of a summer-sky often do. It is true, it may be said that the reason why we see no change in the form of such nebulæ, is that our obser-

* Humboldt repeatedly expresses his conviction that our Solar System contains a greater variety of forms than other systems. (*Cosmos*, III. 373 and 587.)

vations have not endured long enough; all visible changes in the stars requiring an immense time, according to the gigantic scale of celestial mechanism. But even this hypothesis (it is no more) tends to establish the extreme tenuity of the nebulæ; for more solid systems, like our solar system, require, for the preservation of their form, motions which are perceptible, and indeed conspicuous, in the course of a month; namely, the motions of the planets. All, therefore, concurs to prove the extreme tenuity of the substance of irregular nebulæ.

34. Nebulæ which assume a regular, for instance, a circular or oval shape, with whatever variation of luminous density from the inner to the outer parts, may have a form of equilibrium, if their parts have a proper gyratory motion. Still, we see no reason for supposing that these differ so much from irregular nebulæ, as to be denser bodies, kept in their forms by rapid motions. We are rather led to believe that, though perhaps denser than the spiral nebulæ, they are still of extremely thin and vaporous character. It would seem very unlikely that these vast clouds of luminous vapor should be as dense as the tail of a comet; since a portion of luminous matter so small as such a tail is, must have cooled down from its most luminous condition; and must require to be more dense than nebular matter in order to be visible at all by its own light.

35. Thus we appear to have good reason to believe that nebulæ are vast masses of incoherent or gaseous matter, of immense tenuity, diffused in forms more or less irregular, but all of them destitute of any regular system of solid moving bodies. We seem, therefore, to have made it certain that *these* celestial objects at least are not inhabited. No speculators have been bold enough to place inhabitants in a comet; except, indeed, some persons who have imagined that such a

habitation, carrying its inmates alternately into the close vicinity of the sun's surface, and far beyond the orbit of Uranus, and thus exposing them to the fierce extremes of heat and cold, might be the seat of penal inflictions on those who had deserved punishment by acts done in their life on one of the planets. But even to give coherence to this wild imagination, we must further suppose that the tenants of such prison-houses, though still sensible to human suffering from extreme heat and cold, have bodies of the same vaporous and unsubstantial character as the vehicle in which they are thus carried about the system; for no frame of solid structure could be sustained by the incoherent and varying volume of a comet. And probably, to people the nebulæ with such thin and fiery forms, is a mode of providing them with population, that the most ardent advocates of the plurality of worlds are not prepared to adopt.

36. So far then as the Nebulæ are concerned, the improbability of their being inhabited, appears to mount to the highest point that can be conceived. We may, by the indulgence of fancy, people the summer-clouds, or the beams of the aurora borealis, with living beings, of the same kind of substance as those bright appearances themselves; and in doing so, we are not making any bolder assumption than we are, when we stock the Nebulæ with inhabitants, and call them in that sense, "distant worlds."

CHAPTER VIII.

THE FIXED STARS.

1. We appear, in the last chapter, to have cleared away the supposed inhabitants of the outskirts of creation, so far as the Nebulæ are the outskirts of creation. We must now approach a little nearer, in appearance at least, to our own system. We must consider the Fixed Stars; and examine any evidence which we may be able to discover, as to the probability of their containing, in themselves or in accompanying bodies, as planets, inhabitants of any kind. Any special evidence which we can discern on this subject, either way, is indeed slight. On the one side we have the asserted analogy of the parts of the universe; of which point we have spoken, and may have more to say hereafter. Each Fixed Star is conceived to be of the nature of our Sun; and therefore, like him, the centre of a planetary system. On the other side, it is extremely difficult to find any special facts relative to the nature of the fixed stars, which may enable us in any degree to judge how far they really are of a like nature with the Sun, and how far this resemblance goes. We may, however, notice a few features in the starry heavens, with which, in the absence of any stronger grounds, we may be allowed to connect our speculations on such questions. The assiduous

scrutiny of the stars which has been pursued by the most eminent astronomers, and the reflections which their researches have suggested to them, may have a new interest, when discussed under this point of view.

2. Next after the Nebulæ, the cases which may most naturally engage our attention, are Clusters of stars. The cases, indeed, in which these clusters are the closest, and the stars the smallest, and in which, therefore, it is only by the aid of a good telescope that they are resolved into stars, do not differ from the resolvable nebulæ, except in the degree of optical power which is required to resolve them. We may, therefore, it would seem, apply to such clusters, what we have said of resolvable nebulæ: that when they are thus, by the application of telescopic power, resolved into bright points, it seems to be a very bold assumption to assume, without further proof, that these bright points are suns, distant from each other as far as we are from the nearest stars. The boldness of such an assumption appears to be felt by our wisest astronomers.* That several of the clusters which are visible, some of them appearing as if the component stars were gathered together in a nearly spherical form, are systems bound together by some special force, or some common origin, we may regard, with those astronomers, as in the highest degree probable. With respect to the stability of the form of such a system, a curious remark has been made by Sir John Herschel,† that if we suppose a globular space filled with equal stars, uniformly dispersed through it, the particular stars might go on forever, describing ellipses about the centre of the globe, in all directions, and of all sizes; and all completing their revolutions in the same time. This follows, because, as Newton has shown, in such a case, the compound force which tends to the centre

* Herschel, 866.

† Ibid. 866.

of the sphere would be everywhere proportional to the distance from the centre; and under the action of such a force, ellipses about the centre would be described, all the periods being of the same amount. This kind of symmetrical and simple systematic motion, presented by Newton as a mere exemplification of the results of his mechanical principles, is perhaps realized, approximately at least, in some of the globular clusters. The motions will be swift or slow, according to the total mass of the groups. If, for instance, our Sun were thus broken into fragments, so as to fill the sphere girdled by the earth's orbit, all the fragments would revolve round the centre in a year. Now, there is no symptom, in any cluster, of its parts moving nearly so fast as this; and therefore we have, it would seem, evidence that the groups are much less dense than would be the space so filled with fragments of the sun. The slowness of the motions, in this case, as in the nebulæ, is evidence of the weakness of the forces, and therefore, of the rarity of the mass; and till we have some gyratory motion discovered in these groups, we have nothing to limit our supposition of the extreme tenuity of their total substance.

3. Let us then go on to the cases in which we have proof of such gyratory motions in the stars; for such are not wanting. Fifty years ago, Herschel the father, had already ascertained that there are certain pairs of stars, very near each other (so near, indeed, that to the unassisted eye they are seen as single stars only,) and which revolve about each other. These Binary Sidereal Systems have since been examined with immense diligence and profound skill by Herschel the son, and others; and the number of such binary systems has been found, by such observers, to be very considerable. The periods of their revolutions are of various lengths, from 30 or 40 years to several hundreds of years. Some of those pairs

which have the shortest periods, have already, since the nature of their movements was discovered, performed more than a complete revolution;* thus leaving no room for doubting that their motions are really of this gyratory kind. Not only the fact, but the law of this orbital motion, has been investigated; and the investigations, which naturally were commenced on the hypothesis that these distant bodies were governed by that Law of universal Gravitation, which prevails throughout the solar system, and so completely explains the minutest features of its motions, have ended in establishing the reality of that Law, for several Binary Systems, with as complete evidence as that which carries its operations to the orbits of Uranus and Neptune.

4. Being able thus to discern, in distant regions of the universe, bodies revolving about each other, we have the means of determining, as we do in our own solar system, the masses of the bodies so revolving. But for this purpose, we must know their distance from each other; which is, to our vision, exceedingly small, requiring, as we have said, high magnifying powers to make it visible at all. And again, to know what linear distance this small visible distance represents, we must know the distance of the stars from us, which is, for every star, as we know, immensely great; and for most, we are destitute of all means of determining how great it is. There are, however, some of these binary systems, in which astronomers conceive that they have sufficiently ascertained the value of both these elements, (the distance of the two stars from each other, and from us,) to enable them to proceed with the calculation of which I have spoken; the determination of the masses of the revolving bodies. In the case of the star *Alpha Centauri*, the first star in the constellation of the Centaur, the

* Herschel, 846.

period is reckoned to be 77 years; and as, by the same calculator, the apparent semi-axis of the orbit described is stated at 15 seconds of space, while the annual parallax of each star is about one second, it is evident that the orbit must have a radius about 15 times the radius of the earth's orbit; that is, an orbit greater than that of Saturn, and approaching to that of Uranus. In the solar system, a revolution in such an orbit would occupy a time greater than that of Saturn, which is 30 years, and less than that of Uranus, which is about 80 years: it would, in fact, be about 58 years. And since, in the binary star, the period is greater than this, namely 77 years, the attraction which holds together its two elements must be less than that which holds together the Sun and a planet at the same distance; and therefore the masses of the two stars together are considerably less than the mass of our sun.

5. A like conclusion is derived from another of these conspicuous double stars, namely, the one termed by astronomers 61 *Cygni;* of which the annual parallax has lately been ascertained to be one-third of a second of space, while the distance of the two stars is 15 seconds. Here therefore we have an orbit 45 times the size of the Earth's orbit; larger than that of the newly-discovered planet Neptune, whose orbit is 30 times as large as the earth's, and his period nearly 165 years. The period of 61 Cygni is however, it appears, probably not short of 500 years; and hence it is calculated that the sum of the masses of the two stars which make up this pair is about one-third of the mass of our Sun.*

6. These results give some countenance to the opinion, that the quantity of luminous matter, in other systems, does not differ very considerably from the mass of our Sun. It differs in these cases as 1 to 3, or thereabouts. In what degree of

* Herschel, 848.

condensation, however, the matter of these binary systems is, compared with that of our solar system, we have no means whatever of knowing. Each of the two stars may have its luminous matter diffused through a globe as large as the earth's orbit; and in that case, would probably not be more dense than the tail of a comet.* It is observed by astronomers, that in the pairs of binary stars which we have mentioned, the two stars of each pair are of different colors; the stars being of a high yellow, approaching to orange color,† but the smaller individual being in each case of a deeper tint. This might suggest to us the conjecture that the smaller mass had cooled further below the point of high luminosity than the larger; but that both these degrees of light belong to a condition still progressive, and probably still gaseous. Without attaching any great value to such conjectures, they appear to be at least as well authorized as the supposition that each of these stars, thus different, is nevertheless precisely in the condition of our sun.

7. But, even granting that each of the individuals of this pair were a sun like ours, in the nature of its material and its state of condensation, is it probable that it resembles our Sun also in having planets revolving about it? A system of planets revolving around or among a pair of suns, which are, at the same time, revolving about one another, is so complex a scheme, so impossible to arrange in a stable manner, that the assumption of the existence of such schemes, without a vestige of evidence, can hardly require confutation. No doubt, if we were really required to provide such a binary system of suns with attend-

* That these systems have not condensed to *one* centre, appears to imply a less complete degree of condensation than exists in those systems which have done so.

† Herschel, 850.

ant planets, this would be best done by putting the planets so near to one sun, that they should not be sensibly affected by the other; and this is accordingly what has been proposed.* For, as has been well said of the supposed planets, in making this proposal, "Unless closely nestled under the protecting wing of their immediate superior, the sweep of the other sun in his perihelion passage round their own, might carry them off, or whirl them into orbits utterly inconsistent with the existence of their inhabitants." To assume the existence of the inhabitants, in spite of such dangers, and to provide against the dangers by placing them so close to one sun as to be out of the reach of the other, though the whole distance of the two may not, and as we have seen, in some cases does not, exceed the dimensions of our solar system, is showing them all the favor which is possible. But in making this provision, it is overlooked that it may not be possible to keep them in permanent orbits so near to the selected centre: their sun may be a vast sphere of luminous vapor; and the planets, plunged into this atmosphere, may, instead of describing regular orbits, plough their way in spiral paths through the nebulous abyss to its central nucleus.

8. Clustered stars, then, and double stars, appear to give us but little promise of inhabitants. We must next turn our attention to the single stars, as the most hopeful cases. Indeed, it is certain that no one would have thought of regarding the individual stars of clusters, or of pairs, as the centres of planetary systems, if the view of insulated stars, as the centres of such systems, had not already become familiar, and, we may say, established. What, then, is the probability of that view? Is there good evidence that the Fixed Stars, or some of them,

* Herschel, 847.

really have planets revolving round them? What is the kind of proof which we have of this?

9. To this we must reply, that the only proof that the fixed stars are the centres of planetary systems, resides in the assumption that those stars are *like the Sun*;—resemble him in their qualities and nature, and therefore, it is inferred, must have the same offices, and the same appendages. They are, as the Sun is, independent sources of light, and thence, probably, of heat; and therefore they must have attendant planets, to which they can impart their light and heat; and these planets must have inhabitants, who live under and enjoy those influences. This is, probably, the kind of reasoning on which those rely, who regard the fixed stars as so many worlds, or centres of families of worlds.

10. Everything in this argument, therefore, depends upon this: that the Stars are *like the Sun*; and we must consider, what evidence we have of the exactness of this likeness.

11. The Stars are like the Sun in this, that they shine with an independent light, not with a borrowed light, as the planets shine. In this, however, the stars resemble, not only the Sun, but the nebulous patches in the sky, and the tales of comets; for these also, in all probability, shine with an original light. Probably it will hardly be urged that we see, by the very appearance of the stars, that they are of the nature of the Sun: for the appearance of luminaries in the sky is so far from enabling us to discriminate the nature of their light, that to a common eye, a planet and a fixed star appear alike as stars. There is no obvious distinction between the original light of the stars and the reflected light of the planets. The stars, then, being like the sun in being luminous, does it follow that they are, like the sun, definite dense masses?* Or are they,

* The density of the sun is about as great as the density of water.

or many of them, luminous masses in a far more diffused state; visually contracted to points, by the immense distance from us at which they are?

12. We have seen that some of those stars, which we have the best means of examining, are, in mass, one third, or less, of our Sun. If such a mass, at the distance of the fixed stars, were diffused through a sphere equal in radius to the earth's orbit, it would still appear to us as a point; as is evident by this, that the fixed stars, for the most part, have no discoverable annual parallax; that is, the earth's orbit appears to them a point. If one of the fixed stars, Sirius, for instance, be in this diffused condition, such a circumstance will not, mechanically speaking, prevent his having planets revolving round him; for, as we have said, the attraction of his whole mass, in whatever state of spherical diffusion, will be the same as if it were collected at the centre. But such a state of diffusion will make him so unlike our Sun, as much to break the force of the presumption that he must have planets because our Sun has. If the luminous matter of the stars gradually cools, grows dark, and solidifies, such diffusion would imply that the time of solidification is not yet begun; and therefore that the solid planets which accompany the luminous central body are not yet brought into being. If there be any truth in this hypothetical account of the changes, through which the matter of the stars successively passes; and if, by such changes, planetary systems are formed; how many of the fixed stars may never yet have reached the planetary state! how many, for want of some necessary mechanical condition, may never give rise to permanent orbits at all!

13. And that the matter of the stars does go through changes, we have evidence, in many such changes which have

actually been observed;* and perhaps in the different colors of different stars; which may, not improbably, arise from their being at different stages of their progress. That planetary systems, once formed, go through mighty changes, we have evidence in the view which geology gives us of the history of this earth; and in that view, we see also, how unique, and how far elevated in its purpose, the last period of this history may be, compared with the preceding periods; and, up to the present time at least, how comparatively brief in its duration. If, therefore, stellar globes can become planetary systems in the progress of ages, it will not be at all inconsistent with what we know of the order of nature, that only a few, or even that only one, should have yet reached that condition. All the others, but the one, may be systems yet unformed, or fragments struck off in the forming of the one. If any one is not satisfied with this account of the degree of resemblance between the fixed stars and the sun, but would make the likeness greater than this; we have only to say, that the proof that it is so lies upon him. Such a resemblance as we have supposed, is all that the facts suggest. That the stars are independent luminaries, we see; but whether they are as dense as the sun, or globes a hundred or a thousand times as rare, we have no means whatever of knowing. And, to assume that besides these luminous bodies which we see, there are dark bodies which we do not see, revolving round the others in permanent orbits, which require special mechanical conditions; and to suppose this, in order that we may build upon this assumption a still larger one, that of living inhabitants of these dark bodies; is a hypothetical procedure, which it seems strange that we should have to combat, at the present stage of the history of science, and in dealing with those whose minds have

* Herschel, 827—832.

been disciplined by the previous events in the progress of astronomy.

14. Let us consider, however, further, how far astronomy authorizes us to regard the Fixed Stars as being, like our Sun, the centres of systems of Planets. Those who hold this, consider them as having a permanent condition of brightness, as our Sun has had for an indefinite period, so far as we have any knowledge on the subject. Yet, as we have said, no small number of the stars undergo changes of brightness; and some of them undergo such changes, in a manner which is not discernibly periodical; and which must therefore be regarded as progressive. This phenomenon countenances the opinion of such a progress from one material condition to another; which, we have seen, is suggested by the analogy of the probable formation of our own solar system. The very star which is so often taken as the probable centre of a system, Sirius, has, in the course of the last 2,000 years, changed its light from red to white. Ptolemy notes it as a red star: in Tycho's time it was already, as it is now, a white one.* The star *Eta Argus* changes both its degree of light and its color; ranging, in seemingly irregular intervals of time, from the fourth to the first magnitude,† and from yellow to red. Several other examples of the like kind have been observed. Mr. Hind‡ gives an example in which he has, quite recently, observed in two years a star change its color from very red to bluish. These variable unperiodical stars are probably very numerous. Also, some stars, observed of old, are now become invisible. "The lost Pleiad," by the loss of which the cluster, called the Seven Stars, offers now only six to the naked eye, is an ex-

* *Cosmos*, III. 169, 205, and 641.

† Ibid., III. 172 and 252.

‡ *Astron. Soc. Notices*, Dec. 13, 1850.

ample of a change of this kind already noted in ancient times. There are several others, of which the extinction is recognized by astronomers as proved.* In other cases, new stars have appeared, and have then seemed to die away and vanish. The appearance of a new star in the time of the Greek astronomer Hipparchus, induced him to construct his famous Catalogue of the Stars. Others are recorded to have appeared in the middle ages. The first which was observed by modern astronomers was the celebrated star seen by Tycho Brahe in 1572. It appeared suddenly in the constellation Cassiopeia, was fixed in its place like the neighboring stars, had no nebula or tail, exceeded in splendor all other stars, being as bright as Venus when she is nearest the earth. It soon began to diminish in brightness, and passing through various diminishing degrees of magnitude, vanished altogether after seventeen months. This star also passed through various colors; being first white, then yellow, then red. In like manner, in 1604, a new star of great magnitude blazed forth in the constellation Serpentarius; and was seen by Kepler. And this also, like that of 1572, after a few months, declined and vanished.

15. These appearances led Tycho to frame an hypothesis like that which Sir William Herschel afterwards proposed, that the stars are formed by the condensation of luminous nebulous matter. Nor is it easy to think of such phenomena (of which several others have been observed, though none so conspicuous as these), without regarding them as showing that the matter of the fixed stars, occasionally at least, passes through changes of consistence as great as would be the condensation and extinction of a luminous vapor. And if such changes have been but few within the recorded period of man's observation of the stars, we must recollect how small that pe-

* See Grant's *Hist. of Physical Astronomy*, p. 538.

riod is, compared with the period during which the stars have existed. The stars themselves give us testimony of their having been in being for millions of years. For according to the best estimates we can form of their distances, the time which light would employ in reaching us from the most remote of them, would be millions of years; and, therefore, we now see those remote stars by means of the light emitted from them millions of years ago. And if, in the 2,000 years during which such observations are recorded, only 200 stars have undergone such changes in a degree visible to the earth's inhabitants; in a million of years, change going on at the same rate, 100,000 stars would exhibit visible progressive change, showing that they had not yet reached a permanent condition. And how much of change may go on in any star without its being in any degree perceptible to the most exact astronomical scrutiny!

16. The tendency of these considerations is, to lead us to think that the fixed stars are not generally in that permanent condition in which our sun is; and which appears to be alone consistent with the existence of a system such as the solar system.* These views, therefore, fall in with that which we have been led to by this consideration of the Nebulæ: that the Solar System is in a more complete and advanced state, as a system, than many at least of the stellar systems can be; it may be, than any other.

17. It has been alleged, as a proof of the likeness of the Fixed Stars to our Sun, that like him, they revolve upon their axes.† This has been supposed to be proved with regard

* I am aware of certain speculations, and especially of some recent ones, tending to show that even our Sun is wasting away by the emission of light and heat; but these opinions, even if established, do not much affect our argument, one way or the other.

† Chambers' *Astron. Disc.* p. 39.

to many of them, by their having periodical recurrences of fainter and brighter lustre; as if they were revolving orbs, with one side darkened by spots. Such facts are not very numerous or definite in the heavens. *Omicron** in the constellation *Cetus*, is the longest known of them; and is held to revolve in 331 days. From the curious phenomena now spoken of, it has been called *Mira Ceti.*† *Algol*, the second star (*Beta*) of *Perseus*, called also *Caput Medusæ*, is another, with a period of 2 days 21 hours; and in this case, the obscuration of the light, and the restoration of it, are so sudden, that from the time when it was first remarked, (by Goodricke, in 1782,) it suggested the hypothesis of an opaque body revolving round the star. The star *Delta*, in the constellation *Cephus*, is another, with a period of 5 days 9 hours. The star *Beta* in the *Lyre*, has a period of 6 days 10 hours, or perhaps 12 days 21 hours, one revolution having been taken for two. Another such star is *Eta Aquilæ*, with a period of 7 days 4 hours. These five are all the periodical stars of which astronomers can speak with precision.‡ But about thirty more are supposed to be subject to such change, though their periods, epochs, and phases of brightness, cannot at present be given exactly.

18. That these periodical changes in certain of the fixed stars are a curious and interesting astronomical fact, is indisputable. Nothing can be more probable also, than that it indicates, in the stellar masses, a revolution on their axes; which

* Hersch. 820.

† The periodical character of this star was discovered by David Fabricius, a parish priest in East Friesland, the father of John Fabricius, who discovered the solar spots. (*Cosmos*, III. 234.)

‡ Hersch. 825. In Humboldt's *Cosmos*, III. 243, Argelander, who has most carefully observed and studied these periodical stars, has given a catalogue containing 24, with the most recent determinations of their periods.

cannot surprise us, seeing that revolution upon an axis is, so far as we know, a universal law of all the large compact masses of matter which exist in the universe; and may be conceived to be a result derived from their origin, and a condition of any permanent or nearly permanent figure. But this can prove little or nothing as to their being like the sun, in any way which implies their having inhabitants, in themselves or in accompanying planets. The rotation of our Sun is not, in any intelligible way, connected with its having near it the inhabited Earth.

19. If we were to suppose some of the stars to be centres of planetary systems, we can hardly suppose it likely that these alone rotate, and that the others stand still. Probably all the stars rotate, more or less regularly, according as they are permanent or variable in form; but the most regular may still have no planets; and if they have, those planets may be as blank of inhabitants as our moon will be proved to be.

20. The revolution of Algol seems to approach the nearest to a fact in favor of a star being the centre of a revolving system; and from the first, as we have said, the periodical change, and the sudden darkening and brightening of this luminary, suggested the supposition of an opaque body revolving about it. But this body cannot be a planet. The planets which revolve about our Sun are not, any of them, nor all of them together, large enough to produce a perceptible obscuration of his light, to a spectator outside the system. But in Algol, the phenomena are very different from this.* The star

* Hersch. 821. Humboldt (*Cosmos*, III. 238 and 246,) gives the period as 68 hours 49 minutes, and says that it is 7 or 8 hours in its less bright state. If we could suppose the times of the warning, and of the greatest eclipse, given by Herschel, to be exactly determined, as $3\frac{1}{2}$ and $\frac{1}{4}$, that is, in the proportion of 14 to 1, the darkening body must have its effective breadth $\frac{14}{15}$ of that of the star. But this is on

is usually visible as a star of the second magnitude; but during each period of 2 days 21 hours, (or 69 hours,) it suffers a kind of eclipse, which reduces it to a star of the fourth magnitude. During this eclipse, the star diminishes in splendor for 3½ hours; is at its lowest brightness for a quarter of an hour; and then, in 3½ hours more, is restored to its original splendor. According to these numbers, if the obscuration be produced by a dark body revolving round a central luminary, and describing a circular orbit, as the regular recurrence of the obscuration implies, the space of the orbit during which the eclipsing body is interposed must be about one-ninth of the circumference; for the obscuration occupies 7¼ hours out of 69. And therefore the space during which the eclipsing body obscures the central one, must be about one *sixth* of the *diameter* of its orbit. Bnt in order that the revolving body may, through this space, obscure the central one, the latter must extend over this space, namely, one sixth of the diameter of the orbit. But we may remark that there is no proof, in the phenomena, that the darkening body is detached from the bright mass. The effect would be the same if the dark mass were a part of the revolving star itself. It may be that the star has not yet assumed a spherical form, but is an oblong nebular mass with one part (perhaps from being thinner in texture) cooled down and become opaque. And the amount of obscuration, reducing the star from the second to the fourth magnitude, implies that the obscuring mass is large (perhaps one half the diameter, or much more) compared with the luminous mass. If this be a probable hypothesis to account for the phenomena, they are much more against than for the sup-

the supposition that the orbit of the darkening body has the spectator's eye in its plane; if this be not so, the darkening body may be much larger.

position of the star being the centre of seats of habitation. And even if we have a planet nearly as large as its sun, revolving at the distance of only six of the sun's radii, how unlike is this to the solar system !

21. In fact, all these periodical stars, in so far as they are periodical, are proved, not to be like, but to be *unlike* our sun. It is true that the sun has spots, by means of which his rotation has been determined by astronomers. But these spots, besides being so small that they produce no perceptible alteration in his brightness, and are never, or very rarely, visible to the naked eye, are not permanent. A star with a permanent dark side would be very unlike our sun. The largest known of these stars, *Mira*, as the old astronomers called it, becomes invisible to the naked eye for 5 months during a period of 11 months. It must, therefore, have nearly one half its surface quite dark. This is very unlike the condition of the sun ; and is a condition, it would seem, very little fitted to make this star the centre of a planetary system like ours.

22. But there are other remarkable phenomena respecting these periodical stars, which have a bearing on our subject. Their periods are not quite regular, but are subject to certain variations. Thus it has been supposed that the period of Mira is subject to a cyclical fluctuation, embracing 88 of its periods ; that is, about 80 years. But this notion of a cycle of so long a duration, requires confirmation ; the fact of fluctuation in the period is alone certain. In like manner, Algol's periods are not quite uniform. All these facts agree with our suggestion, that the periodical stars are bodies of luminous matter which have not yet assumed a permanent form ; and which, therefore, as they revolve about their axes, and turn to us their darker and their brighter parts, do so at intervals, and in an order somewhat variable. And this suggestion appears

to be remarkably confirmed, by a result which recent observations have discovered relative to this star, Algol; namely, that its periods become shorter and shorter. For if the luminous matter, which is thus revolving, be gradually gathering into a more condensed form;—becoming less rare, or more compact; as, for instance, it would do, if it were collecting itself from an irregular, or elongated, into a more spherical form; such a shortening of the period of revolution would take place; for a mass which contracts while it is revolving, accelerates its rate of revolution, by mechanical principles. And thus we do appear to have, in this observed acceleration of the periods of Algol, an evidence that that luminous mass has not yet reached its final and permanent condition.

23. It is true, it has been conjectured, by high authority,* that this accelerated rapidity of the periods of Algol will not continue; but will gradually relax, and then be changed to an increase; like many other cyclical combinations in astronomy. But this conjecture seems to have little to support it. The cases in which an acceleration of motion is retarded, checked, and restored, all belong to our Solar System; and to assume that Algol, like the solar system, has assumed a permanent and balanced condition, is to take for granted precisely the point in question. We know of no such cycles among the fixed stars, at least with any certainty; for the cycle proposed for Mira must be considered as greatly needing confirmation; considering how long is the cycle, and how recent the suggestion of its existence.

24. And even in the solar system, we have accelerated motions, in which no mathematician or astronomer looks for a

* Hersch. *Outl. Astr.* 821. Another explanation of the variable period of Algol, is that the star is moving towards us, and therefore the light occupies less and less time to reach us.

check or regress of the acceleration. No one expects that Encke's comet will cease to be accelerated, and to revolve in periods continually shorter; though all the other motions hitherto observed in the system are cyclical. In the case of a fixed star, we have much less reason to look for such a cycle, than we have in Encke's comet. But further: with regard to the existence of such a cycle of faster and slower motion in the case of Algol, the most recent observed facts are strongly against it; for it has been observed by Argelander, that not only there is a diminution of the period, but that this diminution proceeds with accelerated rapidity; a course of events which, in no instance, in the whole of the cosmical movements, ends in a regression, retardation, and restoration of the former rate. We are led to believe, therefore, that this remarkable luminary will go on revolving faster and faster, till its extreme point of condensation is attained. And in the meantime, we have very strong reasons to believe that this mutable body is not, like the sun, a permanent centre of a permanent system; and that any argument drawn from its supposed likeness to the sun, in favor of the supposition that the regions which are near it are the seats of habitation, is quite baseless.

25. There are other phenomena of the Fixed Stars, and other conjectures of astronomers respecting them, which I need not notice, as they do not appear to have any bearing upon our subject. Such are the "proper motions" of the stars, and the explanation which has been suggested of some of them; that they arise from the stars revolving round other stars which are dark, and therefore invisible. Such again is the attempt to show that the Sun, carrying with it the whole Solar System, is in motion; and the further attempt to show the direction of this motion; and again, the hypothesis that the Sun itself revolves round some distant body in space. These minute in-

quiries and bold conjectures, as to the movements of the masses of matter which occupy the universe, do not throw any light on the question whether any part besides the earth is inhabited; any more than the investigation of the movements of the ocean, and of their laws, could prove or disprove the existence of marine plants and animals. They do not on that account cease to be important and interesting subjects of speculation; but they do not belong to our subject.

26. In Fontenelle's *Dialogues on the Plurality of Worlds*, a work which may be considered as having given this subject a place in popular literature, he illustrates his argument by a comparison, which it may be worth while to look at for a moment. The speaker who asserts that the moon, the planets, and the stars, are the seats of habitation, describes the person, who denies this, as resembling a citizen of Paris, who, seeing from the towers of Notre Dame the town of Saint Denis, (it being supposed that no communication between the two places had ever occurred,) denies that it is inhabited, because he cannot see the inhabitants. Of course the conclusion is easy, if we may thus take for granted that what he sees is a town. But we may modify this image, so as to represent our argument more fairly. Let it be supposed that we inhabit an island, from which innumerable other islands are visible; but the art of navigation being quite unknown, we are ignorant whether any of them are inhabited. In some of these islands, are seen masses more or less resembling churches; and some of our neighbors assert that these are churches; that churches must be surrounded by houses; and that houses must have inhabitants. Others hold that the seeming churches are only peculiar forms of rocks. In this state of the debate, everything depends upon the degree of resemblance to churches which the forms exhibit. But suppose that telescopes are in-

vented, and employed with diligence upon the questionable shapes. In a long course of careful and skilful examination, no house is seen, and the rocks do not at all become more like churches, rather the contrary. So far, it would seem, the probability of inhabitants in the islands is lessened. But there are other reasons brought into view. Our island is a long extinct volcano, with a tranquil and fertile soil; but the other islands are apparently somewhat different. Some of them are active volcanoes, the volcanic operations covering, so far as we can discern, the whole island; others undergo changes, such as weather or earthquakes may produce; but in none of them can we discover such changes as show the hand of man. For these islands, it would seem the probability of inhabitants is further lessened. And so long as we have no better materials than these for forming a judgment, it would, surely, be accounted rash, to assert that the islands in general are inhabited; and unreasonable, to blame those who deny or doubt it. Nor would such blame be justified by adducing theological or *à priori* arguments; as, that the analogy of island with island makes the assumption allowable; or that it is inconsistent with the plan of the Creator of islands to leave them uninhabited. For we know that many islands are, or were long, uninhabited. And if ours were an island occupied by a numerous, well-governed, moral, and religious race, of which the history was known, and of which the relation to the Creator was connected with its history; the assumption of a history, more or less similar to ours, for the inhabitants of the other islands, whose existence was utterly unproved, would, probably, be generally deemed a fitter field for the romance-writer than for the philosopher. It could not, at best, rise above the region of vague conjecture.

27. Fontenelle, in the agreeable book just referred to,

says, very truly, that the formula by which his view is urged on adversaries is, *Pourquoi non?* which he holds to be a powerful figure of logic. It is, however, a figure which has this peculiarity, that it may, in most cases, be used with equal force on either side. When we are asked Why the Moon, Mercury, Saturn, the system of Sirius, should *not* be inhabited by intelligent beings; we may ask, Why the earth in the ages previous to man might not be so inhabited? The answer would be, that we have proof *how* it *was* inhabited. And as to the fact in the other case, I shall shortly attempt to give proof that the Moon is certainly not, and Mercury and Saturn probably not inhabited. With regard to the Fixed Stars, it is more difficult to reason; because we have the means of knowing so little of their structure. But in this case also, we might easily ask on our side, *Pourquoi non?* Why should not the Solar System be the chief and most complete system in the universe, and the Earth the principal planet in that System? So far as we yet know, the Sun is the largest Sun among the stars; and we shall attempt to show, that the Earth is the largest solid opaque globe in the solar system. Some System must be the largest and most finished of all; why not ours? Some planet must be the largest planet; why not the Earth?

28. It should be recollected that there must be some system which is the most complete of all systems, some planet which is the largest of all planets. And if that largest planet, in the most complete system, be, after being for ages tenanted by irrational creatures, at last, and alone of all, occupied by a rational race, that race must necessarily have the power of asking such questions as these: Why they should be alone rational? Why their planet should be alone thus favored? If the case be ours, we may hope to be then able to answer these questions, when we can explain the most certain fact which they

involve; Why the Earth was occupied so long by irrational creatures, before the rational race was placed upon it? The mere power of asking such questions can prove or disaprove nothing; for it is a power which must equally subsist, whether the human inhabitants of the earth be or be not the only rational population which the universe contains. If there be a race thus favored by the Creator, they must, at that stage of their knowledge in which man now is, be able to doubt, as man does, of the extent and greatness of the privilege which they enjoy.

29. The argument that the Fixed Stars are like the Sun, and therefore the centres of inhabited systems as the Sun is, is sometimes called an argument from Analogy; and this word *Analogy* is urged, as giving great force to the reasoning. But it must be recollected, that precisely the point in question is, whether there *is* an analogy. The stars, it is said, are like the Sun. In what respects? We know of none, except in being self-luminous; and this they have in common with the nebulæ, which, as we have seen, are not centres of inhabited systems. Nor does this quality of being self-luminous at all determine the degree of condensation of a star. Sirius may be less than a hundredth or a thousandth of the density of the Sun. But the Stars, it may be further urged, are like the Sun in turning on their axes. To this we reply, that we know this only of those stars in which, the very phenomenon which proves their revolution, proves also that they are unlike the Sun, in having one side darker than the other. Add to which, their revolution is not connected with the existence of planets, still less of inhabitants of planets, in any intelligible manner. The resemblance, therefore, so far as it bears upon the question, is confined to one single point, in the highest degree ambiguous and inconclusive; and any argument drawn from this one

point of resemblance, has little claim to be termed an argument from analogy.*

30. On a subject on which we know so little, it is difficult to present any view which deserves to be regarded as an analogy. We see, among the stars, nebulæ more or less condensed, which are possibly, in some cases, stages of a connected progress towards a definite star; and it may be, to a star with planets in permanent orbits. We see, in our planet, evidence of successive stages of a connected series of brute animals, preceded perhaps by various stages of lifeless chaos. If the histories of the Sun, and of all the stars, are governed by a common analogy, the nebulous condensation, and the stages of animal life, may be parts of the same continued series of events; and different stars may be at different points of that series. But even on this supposition, but a few of the stars may be the seats of conscious life, and none, of intelligence. For among the stars which have condensed to a permanent form, how many have failed in throwing off a permanent planet! How many may be in some stage of lifeless chaos! We must needs suppose a vast number of stages between a nebular chaos and the lowest forms of conscious life. Perhaps as many as there are fixed stars; and far more than there are of stars which become fertile of life: so that no two systems may be at the same stage of the planetary progress. And if this be so,—our system being so complicated, that we must suppose

* Humboldt, very justly, regards the force of analogy as tending in the opposite direction. "After all," he asks, (*Cosmos*, III. 373,) "is the assumption of satellites to the Fixed Stars so absolutely necessary? If we were to begin from the outer planets, Jupiter, &c., analogy might seem to require that all planets have satellites. But yet this is not true for Mars, Venus, Mercury." To which we may further add the *twenty-three* Planetoids. In this case there is a much greater number of bodies which have not satellites, than which have them.

it peculiarly developed, having the largest Sun that we know of, and our Earth being (as we shall hereafter attempt to prove) the largest solid planet that we know of,—this Earth may be the sole seat of the highest stage of planetary development.

31. The assumption that there is anything of the nature of a regular law or order of progress from nebular matter to conscious life,—a law which extends to all the stars, or to many of them,—is in the highest degree precarious and unsupported; but since it is sometimes employed in such speculations as we are pursuing, we may make a remark or two connected with it. If we suppose, on the planets of other systems, a progress in some degree analogous to that which geology shows to have occurred on the Earth, there may be, in those planets, creatures in some way analogous to our vegetables and animals; but analogy also requires that they should differ far more from the terrestrial vegetables and animals of any epoch, than those of one epoch do from those of another; since they belong to a different stellar system, and probably exist under very different conditions from any that ever prevailed on the Earth. We are forbidden, therefore, by analogy, to suppose that on any other planet there was such an anatomical progression towards the form of man, as we can discern (according to some eminent physiologists) among the tribes which have occupied the Earth. Are we to conceive that the creatures on the planets of other systems are, like the most perfect terrestrial animals, symmetrical as to right and left, vertebrate, with fore limbs and hind limbs, heads, organs of sense in their heads, and the like? Every one can see how rash and fanciful it would be to make such suppositions. Those who have, in the play of their invention, imagined inhabitants of other planets, have tried to avoid this servile imitation of terrestrial forms. Here is Sir Humphry Davy's account of the inhabitants of Saturn. "I saw

moving on the surface below me, immense masses, the forms of which I find it impossible to describe. They had systems for locomotion similar to that of the morse or sea-horse, but I saw with great surprise that they moved from place to place by six extremely thin membranes, which they used as wings. I saw numerous convolutions of tubes, more analogous to the trunk of the elephant, than to anything else I can imagine, occupying what I supposed to be the upper parts of the body."* The attendant Genius informs the narrator, that though these creatures look like zoophytes, they have a sphere of sensibility and intellectual enjoyment far superior to that of the inhabitants of the Earth. If we were to reason upon a work of fancy like this, we might say, that it was just as easy to ascribe superior sensibility and intelligence to zoophyte-formed creatures upon the Earth, as in Saturn. Even fancy cannot aid us in giving consistent form to the inhabitants of other planets.

32. But even if we could assent to the opinion, as probable, that there may occur, on some other planet, progressions of organized forms analogous in some way to that series of animal forms which has appeared upon the earth, we should still have no ground to assume that this series must terminate in a rational and intelligent creature like man. For the introduction of reason and intelligence upon the Earth is no part nor consequence of the series of animal forms. It is a fact of an entirely new kind. The transition from brute to man does not come within the analogy of the transition from brute to brute. The thread of analogy, even if it could lead us so far, would break here. We may conceive analogues to other animals, but we could have no analogue to man, except man. Man is not merely a higher kind of animal; he is a creature of a superior order, participating in the attributes of a higher nature;

* *Consolations in Travel.* Dial. 1.

as we have already said, and as we hope hereafter further to show. Even, therefore, if we were to assume the general analogy of the Stars and of the Sun, and were to join to that the information which geology gives us of the history of our own planet; though we might, on this precarious path, be led to think of other planets as peopled with unimagined monsters; we should still find a chasm in our reasoning, if we tried, in this way, to find intelligent and rational creatures in planets which may revolve round Sirius or Arcturus.

33. The reasonable view of the matter appears to be this. The assumption that the Fixed Stars are of exactly the same nature as the Sun, was, at the first, when their vast distance and probable great size were newly ascertained, a bold guess; to be confirmed or refuted by subsequent observations and discoveries. Any appearances, tending in any degree to confirm this guess, would have deserved the most considerate attention. But there has not been a vestige of any such confirmatory fact. No planet, nor anything which can fairly be regarded as indicating the existence of a planet, revolving about a star, has anywhere been discerned. The discovery of nebulæ, of binary systems, of clusters of stars, of periodical stars, of varying and accelerated periods of such stars, all seem to point the other way. And if all these facts be held to be but small in amount, as to the information which they convey, about the larger, and perhaps nearer stars; still they leave the original assumption a mere guess, unsupported by all that three centuries of most diligent, and in other respects successful research, has been able to bring to light. That Copernicus, that Galileo, that Kepler, should believe the stars to be Suns, in every sense of the term, was a natural result of the expansion of thought which their great discoveries produced, in them and in their contemporaries. Nor are we yet

called upon to withdraw from them our sympathy; or entitled to contradict their conjecture. But all the knowledge that the succeeding times have given us; the extreme tenuity of much of the luminous matter in the skies; the existence of gyratory motion among the stars, quite different from planetary systems; the absence of any observed motions at all resembling such systems; the appearance of changes in stars, quite inconsistent with such permanent systems; the disclosure of the history of our own planet, as one in which changes have constantly been going on; the certainty that by far the greater part of the duration of its existence, it has been tenanted by creatures entirely different from those which give an interest, and thence, a persuasiveness, to the belief of inhabitants in worlds appended to each star; the impossibility, which appears, on the gravest consideration, of transferring to other worlds such interests as belong to our own race in this world; all these considerations should, it would seem, have prevented that old and arbitrary conjecture from growing up, among a generation professing philosophical caution, and scientific discipline, into a settled belief.

34. Some of the moral and theological views which tend to encourage and uphold this belief, may be taken under our more special consideration hereafter: but here, where we are reasoning principally upon astronomical grounds, we may conclude what we have to remark about the Fixed Stars, as the centres of inhabited systems of worlds, by saying; that it will be time enough to speculate about the inhabitants of the planets which belong to such systems, when we have ascertained that there are such planets, or one such planet. When that is done, we can then apply to them any reasons which may exist, for believing that all, or many planets, are the seats of habitation of living things. What reasons of this kind can be adduced, and what is their force with regard to our own solar system, we must now proceed to discuss.*

* What is said in Art. 15, that in consequence of the time employed in the transmission of visual impressions, our seeing a star is evidence, not that it exists now, but that it existed, it may be, many thousands of years ago; may seem, to some readers, to throw doubts upon reasonings which we have employed. It may be said that a star which was a mere chaos, when the light, by which we see it, set out from it, may, in the thousands of years which have since elapsed, have grown into an orderly world. To which bare possibility, we may oppose another supposition at least equally possible:—that the distant stars were sparks or fragments struck off in the formation of the Solar System, which are really long since extinct; and survive in appearance, only by the light which they at first emitted.

CHAPTER IX.

THE PLANETS.

1. WHEN it was discovered, by Copernicus and Galileo, that Mercury, Venus, Mars, Jupiter, Saturn, which had hitherto been regarded only as "wandering fires, that move in mystic dance," were really, in many circumstances, bodies resembling the Earth;—that they and the Earth alike, were opaque globes, revolving about the Sun in orbits nearly circular, revolving also about their own axes, and some of them accompanied by their Satellites, as the Earth is by the Moon;—it was inevitable that the conjecture should arise, that they too had inhabitants, as the Earth has. Each of these bodies were seemingly coherent and solid; furnished with an arrangement for producing day and night, summer and winter; and might therefore, it was naturally conceived, have inhabitants moving upon its solid surface, and reckoning their lives and their employment by days, and months, and years. This was an unavoidable guess. It was far less bold and sweeping than the guess that there are inhabitants in the region of the Fixed Stars, but still, like that, it was, for the time at least, only a guess; and like that, it must depend upon future explorations of these bodies and their conditions, whether the guess was confirmed or discredited. The conjecture could not, by any

moderately cautious man, be regarded as so overwhelmingly probable, that it had no need of further proof. Its final acceptance or rejection must depend on the subsequent progress of astronomy, and of science in general.

2. We have to consider then how far subsequent discoveries have given additional value to this conjecture. And, as, in the first place, important among such discoveries, we must note the addition of several new planets to our system. It was found, by the elder Herschel, (in 1781,) that, far beyond Saturn, there was another planet, which, for a time, was called by the name of its sagacious discoverer; but more recently, in order to conform the nomenclature of the planets to the mythology with which they had been so long connected, has been termed *Uranus*. This was a vast extension of the limits of the solar system. The Earth is, as we have already said, nearly a hundred millions of miles from the Sun. Jupiter is at more than five times, and Saturn nearly at ten times this distance: but Uranus, it was found, describes an orbit of which the radius is about nineteen times as great as that of the Earth. But this did not terminate the extension of the solar system which the progress of astronomy revealed. In 1846, a new planet, still more remote, was discovered: its existence having been divined, before it was seen, by two mathematicians, Mr. Adams, of Cambridge, and M. Leverrier, of Paris, from the effects of its force upon Uranus. This new planet was termed Neptune: its distance from the Sun is about thirty times the Earth's distance. Besides these discoveries of large planets, a great number of small planets were detected in the region of the solar system which lies between the orbits of Mars and Jupiter. This series of discoveries began on the first day of 1801, when Ceres was detected by Piazzi at Palermo; and has gone on up to the present time,

when twenty-three of these small bodies have been brought to light; and probably the group is not yet exhausted.

3. Now if we have to discuss the probability that all these bodies are inhabited, we may begin with the outermost of them at present known, namely Neptune. How far is it likely that this globe is occupied by living creatures which enjoy, like the creatures on the Earth, the light and heat of the Sun, about which the planet revolves? It is plain, in the first place, that this light and heat must be very feeble. Since Neptune is thirty times as far from the sun as the earth is, the diameter of the sun as seen from Neptune will only be one-thirteenth as large as it is, seen from the earth. It will, in fact, be reduced to a mere star. It will be about the diameter under which Jupiter appears when he is nearest to us. Of course its brightness will be much greater than that of Jupiter; nearly as much indeed, as the sun is brighter than the moon, both being nearly of the same size: but still, with our full-moonlight reduced to the amount of illumination which we receive from a *full Jupiter*, and our sun-light reduced in nearly the same proportion, we should have but a dark, and also a cold world. In fact, the light and the heat which reach Neptune, so far as they depend on the distance of the sun, will each be about nine hundred times smaller than they are on the earth. Now are we to conceive animals, with their vital powers unfolded, and their vital enjoyments cherished, by this amount of light and heat? Of course, we cannot say, with certainty, that any feebleness of light and heat are inconsistent with the existence of animal life: and if we had good reason to believe that Neptune is inhabited by animals, we might try to conceive in what manner their vital scheme is accommodated to this scanty supply of heat and light. If it were certain that they were there, we might inquire how they could

live there, and what manner of creatures they could be. If there were any general grounds for assuming inhabitants, we might consider what modifications of life their particular conditions would require.

4. But is there any such general ground! Such a ground we should have, if we could venture to assume that *all* the bodies of the Solar System are inhabited;—if we could proceed upon such a principle, we might reject or postpone the difficulties of particular cases.

5. But is such an assumption true? Is such a principle well founded? The best chance which we have of learning whether it is so, is to endeavor to ascertain the fact, in the body which is nearest to us; and thus, the best placed for our closer scrutiny. This is, of course, the Moon; and with regard to the Moon, we have, again, this advantage in beginning the inquiry with her:—that she, at least, is in circumstances, as to light and heat, so far as the Sun's distance affects them, which we know to be quite consistent with animal and vegetable life. For her distance from the Sun is not appreciably different from that of the Earth; her revolutions round the earth do not make nearly so great a difference, in her distance from the sun, as does the earth's different distances from the sun in summer and in winter: the fact also being, that the earth is considerably nearer to the sun in the winter of this our northern hemisphere, than in the summer. The moon's distance from the sun then, adapts her for habitation: is she inhabited?

6. The answer to this question, so far as we can answer it, may involve something more than those mere astronomical conditions, her distance from the sun, and the nature of her motions. But still, if we are compelled to answer it in the negative;—if it appear, by strong evidence, that the Moon is

not inhabited; then is there an end of the general principle, that, *all* the bodies of the solar system are inhabited, and that we must begin our speculations about each, with this assumption. If the Moon be not inhabited, then, it would seem, the belief that each special body in the system is inhabited, must depend upon reasons specially belonging to that body; and cannot be taken for granted without such reasons. Of the two bodies of the solar system which alone we can examine closely, so as to know anything about them, the Earth and the Moon, if the one be inhabited, and the other blank of inhabitants, we have no right to assume at once, that any other body in the solar system belongs to the former of these classes rather than to the latter. If, even under terrestrial conditions of light and heat, we have a total absence of the phenomenon of life, known to us only as a terrestrial phenomenon; we are surely not entitled to assume that when these conditions fail, we have still the phenomenon, life. We are not entitled to *assume* it; however it may be capable of being afterwards proved, in any special case, by special reasons; a question afterwards to be discussed.

7. Is, then, the Moon inhabited? From the moon's proximity to us, (she is distant only thirty diameters of the earth, less than ten times the earth's circumference; a railroad carriage, at its ordinary rate of travelling, would reach her in a month,) she can be examined by the astronomer with peculiar advantages. The present powers of the telescope enable him to examine her mountains as distinctly as he could the Alps at a few hundred miles distance, with the naked eye; with the additional advantage that her mountains are much more brilliantly illuminated by the Sun, and much more favorably placed for examination, than the Alps are. He can map and model the inequalities of her surface, as faithfully and exactly

as he can those of the surface of Switzerland. He can trace the streams that seem to have flowed from eruptive orifices over her plains, as he can the streams of lava from the craters of Etna or Hecla.

8. Now, this minute examination of the Moon's surface being possible, and having been made, by many careful and skilful astronomers, what is the conviction which has been conveyed to their minds, with regard to the fact of her being the seat of vegetable or animal life? Without exception, it would seem, they have all been led to the belief, that the Moon is not inhabited; that she is, so far as life and organization are concerned, waste and barren, like the streams of lava or of volcanic ashes on the earth, before any vestige of vegetation has been impressed upon them: or like the sands of Africa, where no blade of grass finds root. It is held, by such observers, that they can discern and examine portions of the moon's surface as small as a square mile;* yet, in their examination, they have never perceived any alteration, such as the cycle of vegetable changes through the revolutions of seasons would produce. Sir William Herschel did not doubt that if a change had taken place on the visible part of the Moon, as great as the growth or the destruction of a great city, as great, for instance, as the destruction of London by the great fire of 1666, it would have been perceptible to his powers of observation. Yet nothing of the kind has ever been observed. If there were lunar astronomers, as well provided as terrestrial ones are, with artificial helps of vision, they would undoubtedly be able to perceive the differences which the progress of

* More recently, at the meeting of the British Association in September, 1853, Professor Phillips has declared, that astronomers can discern the shape of a spot on the Moon's surface, which is a few hundred feet in breadth.

generations brings about on the surface of our globe; the clearing of the forests of Germany or North America; the embankment of Holland; the change of the modes of culture which alter the color of the ground in Europe; the establishment of great nests of manufactures which shroud portions of the land in smoke, as those which have their centres at Birmingham or at Manchester. However obscurely they might discern the nature of those changes, they would still see that change was going on. And so should we, if the like changes were going on upon the face of the Moon. Yet no such changes have ever been noticed. Nor even have such changes been remarked, as might occur in a mere brute mass without life;—the formation of new streams of lava, new craters, new crevices, new elevations. The Moon exhibits strong evidences, which strike all telescopic observers, of an action resembling, in many respects, volcanic action, by which its present surface has been formed.* But, if it have been produced by such internal fires, the fires seem to be extinguished; the volcanoes to be burned out. It is a mere cinder; a collection of sheets of rigid slag, and inactive craters. And if the Moon and the Earth were both, at first in a condition in which igneous eruptions from their interior produced the ridges and cones which roughen their surfaces; the Earth has had this state succeeded by a series of states of life in innumerable forms, till at last it has become the dwelling-place of man; while the Moon, smaller in dimensions, has at an earlier period completely cooled down, as to its exterior at least, without ever being judged fit or worthy by its Creator of being the seat of life; and remains, hung in the sky, as an object on which man may

* A person visiting the Eifel, a region of extinct volcanoes, west of the Rhine, can hardly fail to be struck with the resemblance of the craters there, to those seen in the moon through a telescope.

gaze, and perhaps, from which he may learn something of the constitution of the universe; and among other lessons this; that he must not take for granted, that all the other globes of the solar system are tenanted, like that on which he has his appointed place.

9. It is true, that in coming to this conclusion, the astronomers of whom I speak, have been governed by other reasons, besides those which I have mentioned, the absence of any changes, either rapid or slow, discoverable in the Moon's face. They have seen reason to believe that water and air, elements so essential to terrestrial life, do not exist in the Moon. The dark spaces on her disk, which were called *seas* by those who first depicted them, have an appearance inconsistent with their being oceans of water. They are not level and smooth, as water would be; nor uniform in their color, but marked with permanent streaks and shades, implying a rigid form. And the absence of an atmosphere of transparent vapor and air, surrounding the moon, as our atmosphere surrounds the earth, is still more clearly proved, by the absence of all the optical effects of such an atmosphere, when stars pass behind the moon's disk, and by the phenomena which are seen in solar eclipses, when her solid mass is masked by the Sun.* This absence of moisture and air in the Moon, of course, entirely confirms our previous conclusion, of the absence of vegetable and animal life; and leaves us, as we have said, to examine the question for the other bodies, on their special grounds, without any previous presumption that such life exists. Un-

* Bessel has discussed and refuted (it was hardly necessary) the conjecture of some persons (he describes them as "the feeling hearts who would find sympathy even in the Moon") that there may be in the Moon's valleys air enough to support life, though it does not rise above the hills.—*Populäre Vorlesungen*, p. 78.

doubtedly the aspect of the case will be different in one feature, when we see reason to believe that other bodies have an atmosphere; and if there be in any planet sufficient light and heat, and clouds and winds, and a due adjustment of the power of gravity, and the strength of the materials of which organized frames consist, there may be, so far as we can judge, life of some kind or other. But yet, even in those cases, we should be led to judge also, by analogy, that the life which they sustain is more different from the terrestrial life of the present period of the earth, than that is from the terrestrial life of any former geological period, in proportion as the conditions of light and heat, and attraction and density, are more different on any other planet, than they can have been on the earth, at any period of its history.

10. Let us then consider the state of these elements of being in the other planets. I have mentioned, among them, the force of gravity, and the density of materials; because these are important elements in the question. It may seem strange, that we are able, not only to measure the planets, but to weigh them; yet so it is. The wonderful discovery of universal gravitation, so firmly established, as the law which embraces every particle of matter in the solar system, enables us to do this, with the most perfect confidence. The revolutions of the satellites round their primary planets, give us a measure of the force by which the planets retain them in their orbits; and in this way, a measure of the quantity of matter of which each planet consists. And other effects of the same universal law, enable us to measure, though less easily and less exactly, the masses, even of those planets which have no satellites. And thus we can, as it were, put the Earth, and Jupiter or Saturn, in the balance against each other; and tell the proportionate number of pounds which they would weigh, if so poised. And

again, by another kind of experiment, we can, as we have said, weigh the earth against a known mountain; or even against a small sphere of lead duly adjusted for the purpose. And this has been done; and the results are extremely curious; and very important in our speculations relative to the constitution of the universe.

11. And in the first place, we may remark that the Earth is really much less heavy than we should expect, from what we know of the materials of which it consists. For, measuring the density, or specific gravity, of materials, (that is their comparative weight in the same bulk,) by their proportion to water, which is the usual way, the density of iron is 8, that of lead 11, that of gold 19: the ordinary rocks at the Earth's surface have a density of 3 or 4. Moreover, all the substances with which we are acquainted, contract into a smaller space, and have their density increased, by being subjected to pressure. Air does this, in an obvious manner; and hence it is, that the lower parts of our atmosphere are denser than the upper parts; being pressed by a greater superincumbent weight, the weight of the superior parts of the atmosphere itself. Air is thus obviously and eminently elastic. But all substances, though less obviously and eminently, are still, really, and in some degree, elastic. They all contract by compression. Water for instance, if pressed by a column of water 100000 feet high, would be reduced to a bulk one-tenth less than before. In the same manner iron, compressed by a column of iron 90000 feet high, loses one-tenth of its bulk, and of course gains so much in density. And the like takes place, in different amounts, with all material whatever. This is the rate at which compression produces its effect of increasing the density, in bodies which are in the condition of those which lie around us. But if this law were to go on at the same rate, when the compress-

ion is greatly increased, the density of bodies deep down towards the centre of the Earth must be immense. The Earth's radius is above 20 million feet. At a million feet depth we should have matter subjected to the pressure of a column of a million feet of superincumbent matter, heavier than water; and hence we should have a compression of water 10 times as great as we have mentioned; and, therefore, the bulk of the water would be reduced almost to nothing, its density increased almost indefinitely: and the same would be the case with other materials, as metals and stones. If, therefore, this law of compression were to hold for these great pressures, all materials whatever, contained in the depths of the Earth's mass, must be immensely denser, and immensely specifically heavier, than they are at the surface. And thus, the Earth consisting of these far denser materials towards the centre, but, nearer the surface, of lighter materials, such as rock, and metals, in their ordinary state, must, we should expect, be, on the whole, much heavier than if it consisted of the heaviest ordinary materials; heavier than iron, or than lead; hundreds of times perhaps heavier than stone.

12. This, however, is not found to be so. The expectation of the great density of the Earth, which we might have derived from the known laws of condensation of terrestrial substances, is not confirmed. The mass of the Earth being weighed, by means of such processes as we have already referred to, is found to be only five times heavier than so much water: less heavy than if it were made of iron: less than twice as heavy as if it were made of ordinary rock. This, of course, shows us that the condensation of the interior parts of the Earth's mass, is by no means so great as we should have expected it to be, from what we know of the laws of condensation here; and from considering the enormous pressure of superincum-

bent materials to which those interior parts are subjected. The laws of condensation, it would seem, do not go on operating for these enormous pressures, by the same progression as for smaller pressure. If a mass of a material is compressed into nine-tenths its bulk by the weight of a column of 100000 feet high, it does not follow that it will be again compressed into nine-tenths of its condensed bulk, by another column of 100000 feet high. The compression and condensation reach, or tend to, a limit; and probably, before they have gone very far. It may be possible to compress a piece of iron by one-thousandth part, even by such forces as we can use; and yet it may not be possible to compress the same piece of iron into one half its bulk, even by the weight of the whole Earth, if made to bear upon it. This appears to be probable: and this will explain, how it is, that the materials of the Earth are not so violently condensed as we should have supposed; and thus, why the Earth is so light.

13. We must avoid drawing inferences too boldly, on a subject where our means of knowledge are so obscure as they are with regard to the interior of the Earth; but yet, perhaps, we may be allowed to say, that the result which we have just stated, that the Earth is so light, suggests to us the belief that the interior consists of the same materials as the exterior, slightly condensed by pressure.* We find no encouragement to believe that there is a nucleus within, of some material, different from what we have on the outside; some metal, for instance, heavier than lead. If the earth were of granite, or of

* The doctrine that the interior nucleus of the Earth is fluid, whether accepted or rejected, does not materially affect this argument. It appears, that in some cases, at least, the melting of substances is prevented, by their being subjected to extreme pressure; but the density, the element from which we reason, is measured by methods quite independent of such questions.

lava, to the centre, it would, so far as we can judge, have much the same weight which it now has. Such a central mass, covered with the various layers of stone, which form the upper crust of the Earth, would naturally make this globe of at least the weight which it really has. And therefore, if we were to learn that a planet was much lighter than this, as to its materials,—much less dense, taking the whole mass together,—we should be compelled to infer that it was, throughout, or nearly so, formed of less compact matter than metal and stone; or else, that it had internal cavities, or some other complex structure, which it would be absurd to assume, without positive reasons.

14. Now having decided these views from an examination of the Earth, let us apply them to other planets, as bearing upon the question of their being inhabited; and in the first place, to Jupiter. We can, as we have said, easily compare the mass of Jupiter and of the Earth; for both of them have Satellites. It is ascertained, by this means, that the mass of weight of Jupiter is about 333 times the weight of the earth; but as his diameter is also 11 times that of the earth, his bulk is 1331 times that of the earth: (the *cube* of 11 is 1331); and, therefore, the density of Jupiter is to that of the earth, only as 333 to 1331, or about 1 to 4. Thus the density of Jupiter, taken as a whole, is about a quarter of the earth's density; less than that of any of the stones which form the crust of the earth; and not much greater than the density of water. Indeed, it is tolerably certain, that the density of Jupiter is not greater than it would be, if his entire globe were composed of water; making allowance for the compression which the interior parts would suffer by the pressure of those parts superincumbent. We might, therefore, offer it as a conjecture not quite arbitrary, that Jupiter is a mere sphere of water.

15. But is there anything further in the appearance of Jupiter, which may serve to contradict, or to confirm, this conjecture? There is one circumstance in Jupiter's form, which is, to say the least, perfectly consistent with the supposition, that he is a fluid mass; namely, that he is not an exact sphere, but oblate, like an orange. Such a form is produced, in a fluid sphere, by a rotation upon its axis. It is produced, even in a sphere which is (at present at least,) partly solid and partly fluid; and the oblateness of the earth is accounted for in this way. But Jupiter, who, while he is much larger than the earth, revolves much more rapidly, is much more oblate than the earth. His polar and equatorial diameters are in the proportion of 13 to 14. Now it is a remarkable circumstance, that this is the amount of oblateness, which, on mechanical principles, would result from his time of revolution, if he were entirely fluid, and of the same density throughout.* So far, then, we have some confirmation at least, of his being composed entirely of some fluid which in its density agrees with water.

16. But there are other circumstances in the appearances of Jupiter, which still further confirm this conjecture of his watery constitution. His belts,—certain bands of darker and lighter color, which run parallel to his equator, and which, in some degree, change their form, and breadth, and place, from time to time,—have been conjectured, by almost all astronomers, to arise from lines of cloud, alternating with tracts comparatively clear, and having their direction determined by currents analogous to our trade-winds, but of a much more steady and decided character, in consequence of the great

* Herschel, 512. Bessel, however, holds that the oblateness of Jupiter proves that his interior is somewhat denser than his exterior. *Pop. Vorles.* p. 91.

rotatory velocity.* Now vapors, supplying the materials of such masses of cloud, would naturally be raised from such a watery sphere as we have supposed, by the action of the Sun; would form such lines; and would change their form from slight causes of irregularity, as the belts are seen to do. The existence of these lines of cloud does of itself show that there is much water on Jupiter's surface, and is quite consistent with our conjecture, that his whole mass is water.†

17. Perhaps some persons may be disposed to doubt whether, if Jupiter be, as we suppose, merely or principally a mass of water and of vapor, we are entitled to extend to him the law of universal gravitation, which is the basis of our speculations. But this doubt may be easily dismissed. We

* Herschel, 513.

† A difficulty may be raised, founded on what we may suppose to be the fact, as to the extreme cold of those regions of the Solar System. It may be supposed that water under such a temperature could exist in no other form than ice. And that the cold must there be intense, according to our notion, there is strong reason to believe. Even in the outer regions of our atmosphere, the cold is probably very many degrees below freezing, and in the blank and airless void beyond, it may be colder still. It has been calculated by physical philosophers, on grounds which seem to be solid, that the cold of the space beyond our atmosphere is 100° below zero. The space near to Jupiter, if an absolute vacuum, in which there is no matter to receive and retain heat emitted from the Sun, may, perhaps, be no colder than it is nearer the Sun. And as to the effect the great cold would produce on Jupiter's watery material, we may remark, that if there be a free surface, there will be vapor produced by the Sun's heat; and if there be air, there will be clouds. We may add, that so far as we have reason to believe, below the freezing point, no accession of cold produces any material change in ice. Even in the expeditions of our Arctic navigators, a cold of 40° below zero was experienced, and ice was still but ice, and there were vapors and clouds as in our climate. It is quite an arbitrary assumption, to suppose that any cold which may exist in Jupiter would prevent the state of things which we suppose.

know that the waters of the earth are affected by gravitation; not only towards the earth, as shown by their weight, but towards those distant bodies, the Sun and the Moon; for this gravitation produces the tides of the ocean. And our atmosphere also has weight, as we know; and probably has also solar and lunar tides, though these are marked by many other causes of diurnal change. We have, then, the same reason for supposing that air and water, in other parts of the system, are governed by universal gravitation, and exercise themselves the attractive force of gravitation, which we have for making the like suppositions with regard to the most solid bodies. Whatever argument proves universal gravitation, proves it for all matter alike; and Newton, in the course of his magnificent generalization of the law, took care to demonstrate, by experiment, as well as by reasoning, that it might be so generalized.

18. As bearing upon the question of life in Jupiter, there is another point which requires to be considered; the force of gravity at his surface. Though, equal bulk for equal bulk, he is lighter than the earth, yet his bulk is so great that, as we have seen, he is altogether much heavier than the earth. This, his greater mass, makes bodies, at equal distances from the centres, ponderate proportionally more to him than they would do to the earth. And though his surface is 11 times further from his centre than the earth's is, and therefore the gravity at the surface is thereby diminished, yet, even after this deduction, gravity at the surface of Jupiter is nearly two and a half times that on the earth.* And thus a man transferred to the surface of Jupiter would feel a stone, carried in his hands, and would feel his own limbs also, (for his muscular power would not be altered by the transfer,) become 2½ times

* Herschel, 508.

as heavy, as difficult to raise, as they were before. Under such circumstances animals of large dimensions would be oppressed with their own weight. In the smaller creatures on the earth, as in insects, the muscular power bears a great proportion to the weight, and they might continue to run and to leap, even if gravity were tripled or quadrupled. But an elephant could not trot with two or three elephants placed upon his back. A lion or tiger could not spring, with twice or thrice his own weight hung about his neck. Such an increase of gravity would be inconsistent then, with the present constitution and life of the largest terrestrial animals; and if we are to suppose planets inhabited, in which gravity is much more energetic than it is upon the earth, we must suppose classes of animals which are adapted to such a different mechanical condition.

19. Taking into account then, these circumstances in Jupiter's state; his (probably) bottomless waters; his light, if any, solid materials; the strong hand with which gravity presses down such materials as there are; the small amount of light and heat which reaches him, at 5 times the earth's distance from the sun; what kind of inhabitants shall we be led to assign to him? Can they have skeletous, where no substance so dense as bone is found, at least in large masses? It would seem not probable.* And it would seem they must be dwellers in the waters, for against the existence there of solid land, we have much evidence. They must, with so little of light and heat, have a low degree of vitality. They must

* It may be thought fanciful to suppose that because there is little or no solid matter (of any kind known to us) in Jupiter, his animals are not likely to have solid skeletons. The analogy is not very strong; but also, the weight assigned to it in the argument is small. *Valeat quantum valere debet.*

then, it would seem, be cartilaginous and glutinous masses; peopling the waters with minute forms: perhaps also with larger monsters; for the weight of a bulky creature, floating in the fluid, would be much more easily sustained than on solid ground. If we are resolved to have such a population, and that they shall live by food, we must suppose that the waters contain at least so much solid matter as is requisite for the sustenance of the lowest classes; for the higher classes of animals will probably find their food in consuming the lower. I do not know whether the advocates of peopled worlds will think such a population as this worth contending for: but I think the only doubt can be, between such a population, and none. If Jupiter be a mere mass of water, with perhaps a few cinders at the centre, and an envelope of clouds around it, it seems very possible that he may not be the seat of life at all. But if life be there, it does not seem in any way likely, that the living things can be anything higher in the scale of being, than such boneless, watery, pulpy creatures as I have imagined.

20. Perhaps it may occur to some one to ask, if this planet, which presents so glorious an aspect to our eyes, be thus the abode only of such imperfect and embryotic lumps of vitality as I have described; to what purpose was all that gorgeous array of satellites appended to him, which would present, to intelligent spectators on his surface, a spectacle far more splendid than any that our skies offer to us: four moons, some as great, and others hardly less, than our moon, performing their regular revolutions in the vault of heaven. To which it will suffice, at present, to reply, that the use of those moons, under such a supposition, would be precisely the same, as the use of our moon, during the myriads of years which elapsed while the earth was tenanted by corals and madrepores, shell-fish

and belemnites, the cartilaginous fishes of the Old Red Sandstone, or the Saurian monsters of the Lias; and in short, through all the countless ages which elapsed, before the last few thousand years: before man was placed upon the earth "to eye the blue vault and bless the *useful* light:' to reckon by it his months and years: to discover by means of it, the structure of the universe, and perhaps, the special care of his Creator for him alone of all his creatures. The moons of Jupiter, may in this way be of use, as our own moon is. Indeed we know that they have been turned to most important purposes, in astronomy and navigation. And knowing this, we may be content not to know how, either the satellites of Jupiter, or the satellite of the Earth, tend to the advantage of the brute inhabitants of the waters.

21. There is another point, connected with this doctrine of the watery nature of Jupiter, which I may notice, though we have little means of knowledge on the subject. Jupiter being thus covered with water, is the water ever converted into ice? The planet is more than 5 times as far from the sun as the earth is: the heat which he receives is, on that account, 25 times less than ours. The veil of clouds which covers a large part of his surface, must diminish the heat still further. What effect the absence of land produces, on the freezing of the ocean, it is not easy to say. We cannot, therefore, pronounce with any confidence whether his waters are ever frozen or not. In the next considerable planet, Mars, astronomers conceive that they do trace the effects of frost; but in Mars we have also appearances of land. In Jupiter, we are left to mere conjecture; whether continents and floating islands of ice still further chill the fluids of the slimy tribes whom we have been led to regard as the only possible inhabitants; or whether the watery globe is converted into a globe of ice;

retaining on its surface, of course, as much fluid as is requisite, under the evaporating power of the sun, to supply the currents of vapor which form the belts. In this case, perhaps, we may think it most likely that there are no inhabitants of these shallow pools in a planet of ice: at any rate, it is not worth while to provide any new speculations for such a hypothesis.

22. We may turn our consideration from Jupiter to Saturn; for in many respects the two planets are very similar. But in almost every point, which is of force against the hypothesis of inhabitants, the case is much stronger in Saturn than it is in Jupiter. Light and heat, at his distance, are only one ninetieth of those at the Earth. None but a very low degree of vitality can be sustained under such sluggish influences. The density of his mass is hardly greater than that of cork; much less than that of water: so that, it does not appear what supposition is left for us, except that a large portion of the globe, which we see as his, is vapor. That the outer part of the globe is vapor, is proved, in Saturn as in Jupiter, by the existence of several cloudy streaks or belts running round him parallel to his equator. Yet his mass, taken altogether, is considerable, on account of his great size; and gravity would be greater, at his outer surface, than it is at the earth's. For such reasons, then, as were urged in the case of Jupiter, we must either suppose that he has no inhabitants; or that they are aqueous, gelatinous creatures; too sluggish, almost to be deemed alive, floating on their ice-cold waters, shrouded forever by their humid skies.

23. Whether they have eyes or no, we cannot tell; but probably if they had, they would never see the Sun; and therefore we need not commiserate their lot in not seeing the host of Saturnian satellites; and the Ring, which to an intelli-

gent Saturnian spectator, would be so splendid a celestial object. The Ring is a glorious object for man's view, and his contemplation; and therefore is not altogether without its use. Still less need we (as some appear to do) regard as a serious misfortune to the inhabitants of certain regions of the planet, a solar eclipse of fifteen years' duration, to which they are liable by the interposition of the Ring between them and the Sun.*

24. The cases of Uranus and Neptune are similar to that of Saturn, but of course stronger, in proportion to their smaller light and heat. For Uranus, this is only 1-360th, for Neptune, as we have already said, 1-900th of the light and heat at the earth. Moreover, these two new planets agree with Jupiter and with Saturn, in being of very large size and of very small density; and also we may remark, one of them, probably both, in revolving with great rapidity, and in nearly the same period, namely, about 10 hours: at least, this has been the opinion of astronomers with regard to Uranus. The arguments against the hypothesis of these two planets being inhabited, are of course of the same kind as in the case of Jupiter and Saturn, but much increased in strength; and the supposition of the probably watery nature and low vitality of their inhabitants must be commended to the consideration of those who contend for inhabitants in those remote regions of the solar system.

25. We may now return towards the Sun, and direct our attention to the planet Mars. Here we have some approximation to the condition of the Earth, in circumstances, as in position. It is true, his light and heat, so far as distance from the Sun affects them, are less than half those at the Earth. His density appears to be nearly equal to that of the Earth, but his mass is so much smaller, that gravity at his surface is

* Herschel, 522.

only one-half of what it is here. Then, as to his physical condition, so far as we can determine it, astronomers discern in his face* the outlines of continents and seas. The ruddy color by which he is distinguished, the red and fiery aspect which he presents, arise, they think, from the color of the land, while the seas appear greenish. Clouds often seem to intercept the astronomer's view of the globe, which with its continents and oceans thus revolves under his eye; and that there is an atmosphere on which such clouds may float, appears to be further proved, by brilliant white spots at the poles of the planet, which are conjectured to be snow; for they disappear when they have been long exposed to the sun, and are greatest when just emerging from the long night of their polar winter; the snow-line then extending to about six degrees (reckoned upon the meridian of the planet) from the pole. Moreover, Mars agrees with the earth, in the period of his rotation; which is about 24 hours; and in having his axis inclined to his orbit, so as to produce a cycle of long and short days and nights, a return of summer and winter, in every revolution of the planet.

26. We have here a number of circumstances which speak far more persuasively for a similarity of condition, in this planet and the Earth, than in any of the cases previously discussed. It is true, Mars is much smaller than the earth, and has not been judged worthy of the attendance of a satellite, although further from the Sun; but still, he may have been judged worthy of inhabitants by his Creator. Perhaps we are not quite certain about the existence of an atmosphere; and without such an appendage, we can hardly accord him tenants. But if he have inhabitants, let us consider of what kind they must be conceived to be, according to any judgment which we can form. The force of his gravity is so small, that we may al-

* Herschel, 510.

low his animals to be large, without fearing that they will break down by their own weight. In a planet so dense, they may very likely have solid skeletons. The ice about his poles will cumber the seas, cold even for the want of solar heat, as it does in our arctic and antarctic oceans; and we may easily imagine that these seas are tenanted, like those, by huge creatures of the nature of whales and seals, and by other creatures which the existence of these requires and implies. Or rather, since, as we have said, we must suppose the population of other planets to be more different from our existing population, than the population of other ages of our own planet, we may suppose the population of the seas and of the land of Mars, (if there be any, and if we are not carrying it too high in the scale of vital activity,) to differ from any terrestrial animals, in something of the same way in which the great land and sea saurians, or the iguanodon and dinotherium, differed from the animals which now live on the earth.

27. That we need not discuss the question, whether there are intelligent beings living on the surface of Mars, perhaps the reader will allow, till we have some better evidence that there are living things there at all; if he calls to mind the immense proportion which, on the earth, far better fitted for the habitation of the only intelligent creature which we know or can conceive, the duration of unintelligent life has borne to that of intelligent. Here, on this Earth, a few thousand years ago, began the life of a creature who can speculate about the past and the future, the near and the absent, the Universe and its Maker, duty and immortality. This began a few thousand years ago, after ages and myriads of ages, after immense varieties of lives and generations, of corals and mollusks, saurians, iguanodons, and dinotheriums. No doubt the Creator might place an intelligent creature upon a planet, without all

this preparation, all this preliminary life. He has not chosen to do so on the earth, as we know; and that is by much the best evidence attainable by us, of what His purposes are. It is also possible that He should, on another planet, have established creatures of the nature of corals and mollusks, saurians and iguanodons, without having yet arrived at the period of intelligent creatures: especially if that other planet have longer years, a colder climate, a smaller mass, and perhaps no atmosphere. It is also possible that He should have put that smaller planet near the Earth, resembling it in some respects, as the Moon does, but without any inhabitants, as she has none; and that Mars may be such a planet. The probability against such a belief can hardly be considered as strong, if the arguments already offered be regarded as effective against the opinion of inhabitants in the other planets, and in the Moon.

28. The numerous tribe of small bodies, which revolve between Jupiter and Mars, do not admit of much of the kind of reasoning, which we have applied to the larger planets. They have, with perhaps one exception (Vesta) no disk of visible magnitude; they are mere dots, and we do not even know that their form is spherical. The near coincidence of their orbits has suggested, to astronomers, the conjecture that they have resulted from the explosion of a larger body, and from its fracture into fragments. Perhaps the general phenomena of the universe suggest rather the notion of a collapse of portions of sidereal matter, than of a sudden disruption and dispersion of any portion of it; and these small bodies may be the results of some imperfectly effected concentration of the elements of our system; which, if it had gone on more completely and regularly, might have produced another planet, like Mars or Venus. Perhaps they are only the larger masses, among a great number of smaller ones, resulting from such a process:

and it is very conceivable, that the meteoric stones which, from time to time, have fallen upon the earth's surface, are other results of the like process:—bits of planets which have failed in the making, and lost their way, till arrested by the resistance of the earth's atmosphere. A remarkable circumstance in these bodies is, that though thus coming apparently from some remote part of the system, they contain no elements but such as had already been found to exist in the mass of the earth; although some substances, as nickel and chrome, which are somewhat rare in the earth's materials, are common parts of the composition of meteoric stones. Also they are of crystalline structure, and exhibit some peculiarities in their crystallization. Such as these strange visitors are, they seem to show that the other parts of the solar system contain the same elementary substances, and are subject to the same laws of chemical synthesis and crystalline force, which obtain in the terrestrial region. The smallness of these specimens is a necessary condition of their reaching us; for if they had been more massive, they would have followed out the path of their orbits round the sun, however eccentric these might be. The great eccentricity of the smaller planets, their great deviation from the zodiacal path, which is the highway of the large planets, their great number, probably by no means yet exhausted by the discoveries of astronomers; all fall in with the supposition that there are, in the solar system, a vast multitude of such abnormal planetoidal lumps. As I have said, we do not even know that they are approximately spherical; and if they are of the nature of meteoric stones, they are mere crude and irregularly crystallized masses of metal and earth. It will therefore, probably, be deemed unnecessary to give other reasons why these planetoids are not inhabited. But if it be granted that they are not, we have here, in addition to the moon, a large array of examples, to prove how baseless is the assumption, that all the bodies of the solar system are the seats of life.

29. We have thus performed our journey from the extremest verge of the Universe, so far as we have any knowledge of it, to the orbit of our own planet; and have found, till we came into our own most immediate vicinity, strong reasons for rejecting the assumption of inhabited worlds like our own; and indeed, of the habitation of worlds in any sense. And even if Mars, in his present condition, may be some image of the Earth, in some of its remote geological periods, it is at least equally possible that he may be an image of the Earth, in the still remoter geological period before life began. Of peculiar fitnesses which make the earth suited to the sustentation of life, as we know that it is, we shall speak hereafter; and at present pass on to the other planets, Venus and Mercury. But of these, there is, in our point of view, very little to say. Venus, which, when nearest to us, fills a larger angle than any other celestial body, except the Sun and the Moon, might be expected to be the one of which we know most. Yet she is really one of the most difficult to scrutinize with our telescopes. Astronomers cannot discover in her, as in Mars, any traces of continents and seas, mountains and valleys; at least with any certainty.* Her illuminated part shines with an intense lustre which dazzles the sight;† yet she is of herself perfectly dark; and it was the discovery, that she presented the phases of the Moon, made by the telescope of Galileo, which gave the first impulse to planetary research. She is almost as large as the earth; almost as heavy. The light and heat which she re-

* According to Bessel, Schrœter *once* saw one bright point on the dark ground, near the boundary of light in Venus. This was taken as proving a mountain, estimated at 60,000 feet high. *Pop. Vorles.* p. 86.

† Herschel, 509.

10

ceives from the Sun must be about double those which come to the earth. We discern no traces of a gaseous or watery atmosphere surrounding her. Perhaps if we could see her better, we might find that she had a surface like the moon; or perhaps, in the nearer neighborhood of the sun, she may have cooled more slowly and quietly, like a glass which is annealed in the fire; and hence, may have a smooth surface, instead of the furrowed and pimpled visage which the Moon presents to us. With this ignorance of her conditions, it is hard to say what kind of animals we could place in her, if we were disposed to people her surface; except perhaps the microscopic creatures, with siliceous coverings, which, as modern explorers assert, are almost indestructible by heat. To believe that she has a surface like the earth, and tribes of animals, like terrestrial animals, and like man, is an exercise of imagination, which not only is quite gratuitous, but contrary to all the information which the telescope gives us; and with this remark, we may dismiss the hypothesis.

30. Of Mercury we know still less. He receives seven times as much light and heat as the Earth; is much smaller than the earth, but perhaps more dense; and has not, so far as we can tell, any of the conditions which make animal existence conceivable. If it is so difficult to find suitable inhabitants for Venus, the difficulty for Mercury is immensely greater.

31. So far then, we have traversed the Solar System, and have found even here, the strongest grounds that there can be no animal existence, like that which alone we can conceive as animal existence, except in the planet next beyond the earth, Mars; and there, not without great modifications. But we may make some further remarks on the condition of the several planets, with regard to what appears to us to be the necessary elements of animal life.

CHAPTER X.

THEORY OF THE SOLAR SYSTEM.

1. We have given our views respecting the various planets which constitute the Solar System;—views established, it would seem, by all that we know, of the laws of heat and moisture, density and attraction, organization and life. We have examined and reasoned upon the cases of the different planets separately. But it may serve to confirm this view, and to establish it in the reader's mind, if we give a description of the system which shall combine and connect the views which we have presented, of the constitution and peculiarities, as to physical circumstances, of each of the planets. It will help us in our speculations, if we can regard the planets not only as a collection, but as a scheme;—if we can give, not an enumeration only, but a theory. Now such a scheme, such a theory, appears to offer itself to us.

2. The planets exterior to Mars, Jupiter, and Saturn especially, as the best known of them, appear, by the best judgment which we can form, to be spheres of water, and of aqueous vapor, combined, it may be, with atmospheric air, in which their cloudy belts float over their deep oceans. Mars seems to have some portion at least of aqueous atmosphere; the earth, we know, has a considerable atmosphere of air, and

of vapor; but the Moon, so near to her mistress, has none. On Venus and Mercury, we see nothing of a gaseous or aqueous atmosphere; and they, and Mars, do not differ much in their density from the Earth. Now, does not this look as if the water and the vapor, which belong to the solar system, were driven off into the outer regions of its vast circuit; while the solid masses which are nearest to the focus of heat, are all approximately of the same nature? And if this be so, what is the peculiar physical condition which we are led to ascribe to the Earth? Plainly this: that she is situated just in that region of the system, where the existence of matter, both in a solid, a fluid, and a gaseous condition, is possible. Outside the Earth's orbit, or at least outside Mars and the small Planetoids, there is, in the planets, apparently, no solid matter; or rather, if there be, there is a vast preponderance of watery and vaporous matter. Inside the Earth's orbit, we see, in the planets, no traces of water or vapor, or gas; but solid matter, about the density of terrestrial matter. The Earth, alone, is placed at the border where the conditions of life are combined; ground to stand upon; air to breathe; water to nourish vegetables, and thus, animals; and solid matter to supply the materials for their more solid parts; and with this, a due supply of light and heat, a due energy of the force of weight. All these conditions are, in our conception, requisite for life: that all these conditions meet, elsewhere than in the neighborhood of the Earth's orbit, we see strong reasons to disbelieve. The Earth, then, it would seem, is the abode of life, not because all the globes which revolve round the Sun may be assumed to be the abodes of life; but because the Earth is fitted to be so, by a curious and complex combination of properties and relations, which do not at all apply to the others. That the Earth is inhabited, is not a reason for believing that the other Planets are so, but for believing that they are not so.

3. Can we see any physical reason, for the fact which appears to us so probable, that all the water and vapor of the system is gathered in its outward parts? It would seem that we can. Water and aqueous vapor are driven from the Sun to the outer parts of the solar system, or are allowed to be permanent there only, as they are driven off and retained at a distance by any other source of heat;—to use a homely illustration, as they are driven from wet objects placed near the kitchen-fire: as they are driven from the hot sands of Egypt into the upper air: as they are driven from the tropics to the poles. In this latter case, and generally, in all cases, in which vapor is thus driven from a hotter region, when it comes into a colder, it may again be condensed in water, and fall in rain. So the cold of the air in the temperate zone condenses the aqueous vapors which flow from the tropics; and so, we have our clouds and our showers. And as there is this rainy region, indistinctly defined, between the torrid and the frigid zones on the earth; so is there a region of clouds and rain, of air and water, much more precisely defined, in the solar system, between the central torrid zone and the external frigid zone which surrounds the Sun at a greater distance.

4. *The Earth's Orbit is the Temperate Zone of the Solar System.* In that Zone only is the play of Hot and Cold, of Moist and Dry, possible. The Torrid Zone of the Earth is not free from moisture; it has its rains, for it has its upper colder atmosphere. But how much hotter are Venus and Mercury than the Torrid Zone? There, no vapors can linger; they are expelled by the fierce solar energy; and there is no cool stratum to catch them and return them. If they were there, they must fly to the outer regions; to the cold abodes of Ju-

piter and Saturn, if on their way, the Earth did not with cold and airy finger outstretched afar, catch a few drops of their treasures, for the use of plant, and beast, and man. The solid stone only, and the metallic ore which can be fused and solidified with little loss of substance, can bear the continual force of the near solar fire, and be the material of permanent solid planets in that region. But the lava pavement of the Inner Planets bears no superstructure of life; for all life would be scorched away along with water, its first element. On the Earth first, can this superstructure be raised; and there, through we know not what graduation of forms, the waters were made to bring forth abundantly things that had life; plants, and animals nourished by plants, and conspiring with them, to feed on their respective appointed elements, in the air which surrounded them. And so, nourished by the influences of air and water, plants and animals lived and died, and were entombed in the scourings of the land, which the descending streams carried to the bottom of the waters. And then, these beds of dead generations were raised into mountain ranges; perhaps by the yet unextinguished forces of subterraneous fires. And then a new creation of plants and animals succeeded; still living under the fostering influence of the united pair, Air and Water, which never ceased to brood over the World of Life, their Nurseling; and then, perhaps, a new change of the limits of land and water, and a new creation again: till at last, Man was placed upon the Earth; with far higher powers, and far different purposes, from any of the preceding tribes of creatures: and with this, for one of his offices;—that there might be an intelligent being to learn how wonderfully the scheme of creation had been carried on, and to admire, and to worship the Creator.

5. But we have a few more remarks to make on the struc-

ture of the Solar System, in this point of view. When we say that the water and vapor of the System were driven to the outer parts, or retained there, by the central heat of the Sun, perhaps it might be supposed to be most simple and natural, that the aqueous vapor, and the water, should assume its place in a distinct circle, or rather a spherical shell, of which the Sun was the centre; thus making an elemental sphere about the centre, such as the ancients imagined in their schemes of the Universe. Nor will we venture to say that such an arrangement of elements might not be; though perhaps it might be shown that no stable equilibrium of the system would be, in this way, mechanically possible. But this at least we may say; that a rotatory motion of all the parts of the universe appears to be a universal law prevalent in it, so far as our observation can reach: and that, by such rotation of the separate masses, the whole is put in a condition which is everywhere one of stable equilibrium. It was, then, agreeable to the general scheme, that the excess of water and vapor, which must necessarily be carried away, or stored up, in the outer regions of the System, should be put into shapes in which it should have a permanent place and form. And thus, it is suitable to the general economy of creation, that this water and vapor should be packed into rotating masses, such as are Jupiter and Saturn, Uranus and Neptune. When once collected in such rotating masses, the attraction of its parts would gather it into spheroidal forms; oblate by the effect of rotation, as Jupiter, or perhaps into annular forms, like the Ring of Saturn;* for such also is a mechanically possible form of equilibrium, for a fluid mass. And these spheroids once formed, the water would form a central nucleus, over which would hang a cover of vapor,

* Other speculators also have regarded Saturn's Ring as a ring of cloud or water. See *Cosmos*, III. 527 and 553.

raised by the evaporating power of the Sun, and forming clouds, where the rarity of the upper strata of vapor allowed the cold of the external space to act; and these clouds, spun into belts by the rotation of the sphere. And thus, the vapor, which would otherwise have wandered loose about the atmosphere, was neatly wound into balls; which, again, were kept in their due place, by being made to revolve in nearly circular orbits about the Sun.

6. And thus, according to our view, water and gases, clouds and vapors, form mainly the planets in the outer part of the solar system; while masses such as result from the fusion of the most solid materials, lie nearer the sun, and are found principally within the orbit of Jupiter.* To conceive planetary systems as formed by the gradual contraction of a nebular mass, and by the solidification of some of its parts, is a favorite notion of several speculators. If we adopt this notion. we shall, I think, find additional proofs in favor of our view of the system. For, in the first place, we have the zodiacal light, a nebulous appendage to the Sun, as Herschel conceives, extending beyond the orbits of Mercury and Venus. These planets, then, have not yet fully emerged from the atmosphere in which they had their origin:—the *mother-light* and *mother-fire*, in which they began to crystallize, as crystals do in their mother-water. Though they are already opaque, they are still immersed in luminous vapor: and bearing such traces of their chaotic state being not yet ended, we need not wonder, if we find no evidence of their having inhabitants, and some evidence to the contrary. They are within a nebular region, which may

* Humboldt has already remarked (*Cosmos*, I. 95, and III. 427), that the inner planets as far as Mars, and the outer ones beginning with Jupiter, form two groups having different properties. Also Encke. (See Humboldt's Note.)

easily be conceived to be uninhabitable. And where this neb ular region, marked by the zodiacal light, terminates, the world of life begins, namely at the Earth.

7. But further, outside this region of the Earth, what dc we find in the solar system? Of solid matter, if our views are right, we find nothing but an immense number of small bodies; namely, first, Mars, who, as we have said, is only about one-eighth the earth in mass: the twenty-six small planetoids, (or whatever number may have been discovered when these pages meet the reader's eye,*) between Mars and Jupiter; the four satellites of Jupiter; the eight satellites of Saturn; the six (if that be the true number,) satellites of Uranus; and the one satellite of Neptune, already detected. It is very remarkable, that all this array of small bodies begins to be found just outside the Earth's orbit. Supposing, as we have found so much reason to suppose, that Jupiter, and the other exterior planets, are not solid bodies, but masses of water and of vapor; the existence of great solid planetary masses, such as exist in the region of the Earth's orbit, is succeeded externally by the existence of a vast number of smaller bodies. The real quantity of matter in these smaller bodies we cannot in general determine. Perhaps the largest of them, (after Mars,) may be Jupiter's third satellite; which† is reckoned, by Laplace, to have a mass less than 1-10,000th of that of Jupiter himself; and thus, since Jupiter, as we have seen, has a mass 333 times that of the Earth, the satellite would be above 1-30th of the Earth's mass.‡ That none but masses of this size, and many far below this, are found

* Printed Oct. 19, 1853.

† Herschel, 540.

‡ It is probable, from the small density of Jupiter's satellites, that they also consist in a great measure of water and vapor. Only one of them is denser than Jupiter himself.—*Cosmos.*

outside of Mars, appears to indicate, that the *planet-making* powers which were efficacious to this distance from the sun, and which produced the great globe of the Earth, were, beyond this point, feebler; so that they could only give birth to smaller masses; to planetoids, to satellites, and to meteoric stones. Perhaps we may describe this want of energy in the planet-making power, by saying, that at so great a distance from the central fire, there was not heat enough to melt together these smaller fragments into a larger globe;* or rather, when they existed in a nebular, perhaps in a gaseous state, that there was not heat enough to keep them in that state, till the attraction of the parts of all of them had drawn them into one mass, which might afterwards solidify into a single globe. The tendency of nebular matter to separate into distinct portions, which may afterwards be more and more detached from each other, so as to break the nebulous light into patches and specks, appears to be seen in the structure of the resolvable nebulæ, as we have already had occasion to notice. And according to the view we are now taking, we may conceive such patches, by further cooling and concentration, to remain luminous as comets, and perhaps shooting stars; or to become opaque as planets, planetoids, satellites, or meteoric stones. And here we may call to mind what we have already said, that the meteoric stones consist of the same elements as those of the earth, combined by the same laws; and thus appear to bring us a message from the other solid planets, that they also have the same elements and the same chemical forces as the earth has.

* It has, in our own day, even in the present year, been regarded as a great achievement of man to direct the fiery influences which he can command, so as to cast a colossal statue in a single piece, instead of casting it in several portions.

8. It has already been supposed, by many astronomers, that shooting stars, and meteoric stones, are bodies of connected nature and origin; and that they are cosmical, not terrestrial bodies;—parts of the solar system, not merely appendages to the earth. It has been conceived, that the luminous masses, which appear as shooting stars, when they are without the sphere of terrestrial influences, may, when they reach our atmosphere, collapse into such solid lumps as have from time to time fallen upon the earth's surface: many of them, with such sudden manifestations of light and heat, as implied some rapid change taking place in their chemical constitution and consistence. If shooting stars are of this nature, then, in those cases in which a great number of them appear in close succession, we have evidence that there is a region in which there is a large collection of matter of a nebulous kind, collected already into small clouds, and ready, by any additional touch of the powers that hover round the earth, to be further consolidated into planetary matter. That the earth's orbit carries her through such regions, in her annual course, we have evidence, in the curious fact, now so repeatedly observed, of showers of shooting stars, seen at particular seasons of every year; especially about the 13th of November, and the 10th of August. This phenomenon has been held, most reasonably, to imply that at those periods of the year, the earth passes through a crowd of such meteor-planets, which form a ring round the sun; and revolving round him, like the other planets, retain their place in the system from year to year.* It may be that the orbits of these meteor-planets are very elliptical. That they are to a certain extent elliptical, appears to be shown, by our falling in with them only once a year, not every half year, as we should do, if their orbit, being nearly circular,

* Herschel, 900—905.

met the earth's orbit in two opposite points. That the shooting stars, thus seen in great numbers when the earth is at certain points of her orbit, are really planetoidal bodies, appears to be further proved by this;—that they all seem to move nearly in the same direction.* They are, each of them, visible for a short time only, (indeed commonly only for a few seconds), while they are nearest the earth; much in the same way in which a comet is visible only for a small portion of its path: and this portion is described in a short time, because they move near the earth. They are so small that a little change of distance removes them beyond our vision.

9. Perhaps these revolving specks of nebulæ are the outriders of the zodiacal light; portions of it, which, being external to the permanently nebulous central mass, have broken into patches, and are seen as stars for the moment that we are near to them. And if this be true, we have to correct, in a certain way, what we have previously said of the zodiacal light;—that no one had thought of resolving it into stars: for it would thus appear, that in its outer region, it resolves itself into stars, visible, though but for a moment, to the naked eye.

10. And thus, all these phenomena concur in making it appear probable, that the Earth is placed in that region of the solar system in which the planet-forming powers are most vigorous and potent;—between the region of permanent nebulous vapor, and the region of mere shreds and specks of planetary matter, such as are the satellites and the planetoidal group. And from these views, finally it follows, that the Earth is really the largest planetary body in the Solar System. The vast globes of Jupiter and Saturn, Uranus and Neptune, which roll far above her, are still only huge masses of cloud and vapor, water and air; which, from their enormous

* Herschel, 901.

size, are ponderous enough to retain round them a body of small satellites, perhaps, in some degree at least, solid; and which have perhaps a small lump, or a few similar lumps, of planetary matter at the centre of their watery globe. The Earth is really the domestic hearth of this Solar System; adjusted between the hot and fiery haze on one side, the cold and watery vapor on the other. This region only is fit to be a domestic hearth, a seat of habitation; and in this region is placed the largest solid globe of our system; and on this globe, by a series of creative operations, entirely different from any of those which separated the solid from the vaporous, the cold from the hot, the moist from the dry, have been established, in succession, plants, and animals, and man. So that the habitation has been occupied; the domestic hearth has been surrounded by its family; the fitnesses so wonderfully combined have been employed; and the Earth alone, of all the parts of the frame which revolves round the Sun, has become a World.

11. Perhaps it may tend still further to illustrate, and to fix in the reader's mind, the view of the constitution of the solar system here given, if we remark an analogy which exists, in this respect, between the Earth in particular, and the Solar System in general. The earth, like the central parts of the system, is warmed by the sun; and hence, drives off watery vapors into the circumambient space, where they are condensed by the cold. The upper regions of the atmosphere, like the outer regions of the solar system, form the vapors thus raised into clouds, which are really only water in minute drops; while in the solar system, the cold of the outer regions, and the rotation of the masses themselves, maintain the water, and the vapor, in immense spheres. But Jupiter and Saturn may be regarded as, in many respects, immense clouds; the con-

tinuous water being collected at their centres, while the more airy and looser parts circulate above. They are the permanent receptacles of the superfluous water and air of the system. What is not wanted on the Earth, is stored up there, and hangs above us, far removed from our atmosphere; but yet, like the clouds in our atmosphere, an example, what glorious objects accumulations of vapor and water, illuminated by the rays of the sun, may become in our eyes.

12. These views are so different from those hitherto generally entertained, and considered as having a sort of religious dignity belonging to them, that we may fear, at first at least, they will appear to many, rash and fanciful, and almost, as we have said, irreverent. On the question of reverence we may hereafter say a few words; but as to the rashness of these views, we would beg the reader, calmly and dispassionately, to consider the very extraordinary number of points in the solar system, hitherto unexplained, which they account for, or, at least reduce into consistency and connection, in a manner which seems wonderful. The Theory, as we may perhaps venture to call it, brings together all these known phenomena; —the great size and small density of the exterior planets;—their belts and streaks;—Saturn's ring;—Jupiter's oblateness; —the great number of satellites of the exterior planets;—the numerous group of planetoid bodies between Jupiter and Mars;—the appearance of definite shapes of land and water on Mars;—the showers of shooting stars which appear at certain periods of the year;—the Zodiacal Light;—the appearance of Venus as different from Mars;—and finally, the material composition of meteoric stones.

13. Perhaps there are other phenomena which more readily find an explanation in this theory, than in any other: for instance, the recent discovery of a dim half-transparent ring, as

an appendage to the luminous ring of Saturn, which has hitherto alone been observed. Perhaps this is the ring of vapor which may naturally be expected to accompany the ring of water. It is the annular atmosphere of the aqueous annulus. But, the discovery of this faint ring being so new, and hitherto not fully unfolded, we shall not further press the argument, which, hereafter, perhaps, may be more confidently derived from its existence.

14. There are some other facts in the Solar System, which, we can hardly doubt, must have a bearing upon the views which we have urged; though we cannot yet undertake to explain that bearing fully. Not only do all the planetary bodies of the solar system, as well as the Sun himself, revolve upon their axes; but there is a very curious fact relative to these revolutions, which appears to point out a further connection among them. So far as has yet been ascertained, all those which we, in our theory, regard as solid bodies, Mercury, Venus, the Earth, and Mars, revolve in very nearly the same time: namely, in about twenty-four hours. All those larger masses, on the other hand, which we, in our theory, hold to be watery planets, Jupiter, Saturn, Uranus, revolve, not in a longer time, as would perhaps have been expected, from their greater size, but in a shorter time; in less than half the time; in about ten hours. The near agreement of the times of revolution in each of these two groups, is an extremely curious fact; and cannot fail to lead our thoughts to the probability of some common original cause of these motions. But no such common cause has been suggested, by any speculator on these subjects. If, in this blank, even of hypotheses, one might be admitted, as at least a mode of connecting the facts, we might say, that the compound collection of solid materials, water, and air, of which the solar system consists, and of

which our earth alone, perhaps, retains the combination, being, by whatever means, set a spinning round an axis, at the rate of one revolution in 24 hours, the solid masses which were detached from it, not being liable to much contraction, retained their rate of revolution; while the vaporous masses which were detached from the fluid and airy part, contracting much, when they came into a colder region, increased their rate of revolution on account of their contraction. That such an acceleration of the rate of revolution would be the result of contraction, is known from mechanical principles; and indeed, is evident: for the contraction of a circular ring of such matter into a narrower compass, would not diminish the linear velocity of its elements, while it would give them a smaller path to describe in their revolutions. Such an hypothesis would account, therefore, both for the nearly equal times of revolution of all the solid planets, and for the smaller period of rotation, which the larger planets show.

15. In what manner, however, portions are to be detached from such a rotating mass, so as to form solid planets on the one side, and watery planets on the other, and how these planets, so detached, are to be made to revolve round the Sun, in orbits nearly circular, we have no hypothesis ready to explain. And perhaps we may say, that no satisfactory, or even plausible, hypothesis to explain these facts, has been proposed: for the Nebular Hypothesis, the only one which is likely to be considered as worthy any notice on this subject, is too imperfectly worked out, as yet, to enable us to know, what it will or will not account for. According to that hypothesis, the nebular matter of a system, having originally a rotatory motion, gradually contracts; and separating, at various distances from the centre, forms rings; which again, breaking at some point of their circumference, are, by the mutual attraction of

their parts, gathered up into one mass; which, when cooled down, so as to be opaque, becomes a planet; still revolving round the luminous mass which remains at the centre. That such a process, if we suppose the consistency, and other properties, of the nebulous matter to be such as to render it possible, would produce planetary masses revolving round a sun in nearly circular orbits, and rotating about their own axes, seems most likely; though it does not appear that it has been very clearly shown.* But no successful attempt has been made to deduce any laws of the distances from the centre, times of rotation, or other properties of such planets; and therefore,

* Besides the curious relation of the times of rotation of the planets, just noticed, there is another curious relation, of their distanee from the Sun, which any one, wishing to frame an hypothesis on the origin of our Solar System, ought by all means to try to account for.

The distances from the Sun, of the planets, Mercury, Venus, Earth, Mars, the Planetoids, Jupiter, Saturn, Uranus, are nearly as the numbers,

4, 7, 10, 16, 28, 52, 100, 196:

now the excesses of each of these numbers above the first are,

3, 3, 6, 12, 24, 48, 96:

a series in which each term (after the first,) is double of the preceding one. Hence, the distances of the planets conform to a series following this law, (*Bode's law,* as it is termed.) And though the law is by no means exact, yet it was so far considered a probable expression of a general fact, that the deviation from this law, in the interval between Mars and Jupiter, was the principal cause which led first to the suspicion of a planet interposed in the seemingly vacant space; and thus led to the discovery of the planetoids, which really occupy that region. It is true, that the law is found not to hold, in the case of the newly-discovered planet Neptune; for his distance from the Sun, which according to this law, should be 388, is really only 300, 30 times the Earth's distance, instead of 39 times. Still, Bode's law has a comprehensive approximate reality in the Solar System, sufficient to make it a strong recommendation of any hypothesis of the origin of the system, that it shall account for this law. This, howhowever, the nebular hypothesis does not.

we cannot say that the nebular hypothesis is yet in any degree confirmed.

16. The Theory which we have ventured to propose, of the Solar System, agrees with the Nebular Hypothesis, so far as that hypothesis goes; if we suppose that there is, at the centre of the exterior planets, Jupiter, Saturn, Uranus, and Neptune, a solid nucleus, probably small, of the same nature as the other planets. Such an addition to our theory is, perhaps, on all accounts, probable: for that circumstance would seem to determine, to particular points, the accumulation of water and vapors, to which we hold that those planets owe the greater part of their bulk. Those planets then, Jupiter, Saturn, and the others, are really small solid planets, with enormous oceans and atmospheres. The Nebular Hypothesis, in that case, is that part of our Hypothesis, which relates to the condensation of luminous nebular matter; while *we* consider, further, the causes which, scorching the inner planets, and driving the vapors to the outer orbs, would make the region of the earth the only habitable part of the system.

17. The belief that other planets, as well as our own, are the seats of habitation of living things, has been entertained, in general, not in consequence of physical reasons, but in spite of physical reasons; and because there were conceived to be other reasons, of another kind, theological or philosophical, for such a belief. It was held that Venus, or that Saturn, was inhabited, not because any one could devise, with any degree of probability, any organized structure which would be suitable to animal existence on the surfaces of those planets; but because it was conceived that the greatness or goodness of the Creator, or His wisdom, or some other of His attributes, would be manifestly imperfect, if these planets were not tenanted by living creatures. The evidences of design, of

which we can trace so many, and such striking examples, in our own sphere, the sphere of life, must, it was assumed, exist, in the like form, in every other part of the universe. The disposition to regard the Universe in this point of view, is very general; the disinclination to accept any change in our belief which seems, for a time, to interfere with this view, is very strong; and the attempt to establish the necessity of new views discrepant from these has, in many eyes, an appearance as if it were unfriendly to the best established doctrines of Natural Theology. All these apprehensions will, we trust, be shown, in the sequel, to be utterly unfounded: and in order that any such repugnance to the doctrines here urged, may not linger in the reader's mind, we shall next proceed to contemplate the phenomena of the universe in their bearing upon such speculations.

CHAPTER XI.

THE ARGUMENT FROM DESIGN.

1. THERE is no more worthy or suitable employment of the human mind, than to trace the evidences of Design and Purpose in the Creator, which are visible in many parts of the Creation. The conviction thus obtained, that man was formed by the wisdom, and is governed by the providence, of an intelligent and benevolent Being, is the basis of Natural Religion, and thus, of all Religion. We trust that some new lights will be thrown upon the traces of Design which the Universe offers, even in the work now before the reader; and as our views, regarding the plan of such Design, are different, in some respects, and especially as relates to the Planets and Stars, from those which have of late been generally entertained, it will be proper to make some general remarks, mainly tending to show, that the argument remains undisturbed, though the physical theory is changed.

2. It cannot surprise any one who has attended to the history of science, to find that the views, even of the most philosophical minds, with regard to the plan of the universe, alter, as man advances from falsehood to truth: or rather, from very imperfect truth to truth less imperfect. But yet such a one will not be disposed to look, with any other feeling than pro-

found respect, upon the reasonings by which the wisest men of former times ascended from their erroneous views of nature to the truth of Natural Religion. It cannot seem strange to us that man at any point, and perhaps at every point, of his intellectual progress, should have an imperfect insight into the plan of the Universe; but, in the most imperfect condition of such knowledge, he has light enough from it, to see vestiges of the Wisdom and Benevolence of the Creating Deity; and at the highest point of his scientific progress, he can probably discover little more, by the light which physical science supplies. We can hardly hope, therefore, that any new truths with regard to the material universe, which may now be attainable, will add very much to the evidence of creative design; but we may be confident, also, that they will not, when rightly understood, shake or weaken such evidence. It has indeed happened, in the history of mankind, that new views of the constitution of the universe, brought to the light by scientific researches, and established beyond doubt, in the conviction of impartial persons, have disturbed the thoughts of religious men; because they did not fall in with the view then entertained, of the mode in which God effects his purpose in the universe. But in these cases, it soon came to be seen, after a season of controversy, reproach, and alarm, that the old argument for design was capable of being translated into the language of the new theory, with no loss of force; and the minds of men were gradually tranquillized and pacified. It may be hoped that the world is now so much wiser than it was two or three centuries ago, that if any modification of the current arguments for the Divine Attributes, drawn from the aspect of the universe, become necessary, in consequence of the rectification of received errors, it will take place without producing pain, fear, or anger. To promote this purpose, we proceed to make a few remarks.

3. The proof of Design, as shown in the works of Creation, is seen most clearly, not in mere physical arrangement, but in the structure of organized things;—in the constitution of plants and animals. In those parts of nature, the evidences of intelligent purpose, of wise adaptation, of skilful selection of means to ends, of provident contrivance, are, in many instances, of the most striking kind. Such, for example, are the structure of the human eye, so curiously adapted for its office of seeing; the muscles, cords, and pullies by which the limbs of animals are moved, exceeding far the mechanical ingenuity shown in human inventions; the provisions which exist, before the birth of offspring, for its sustenance and well-being when it shall have been born;—these are lucid and convincing proofs of an intelligent Creator, to which no ordinary mind can refuse its conviction. Nor is the evidence, which we here recognize, deprived of its force, when we see that many parts of the structure of animals, though adapted for particular purposes, are yet framed as a portion of a system which does not seem, in its general form, to have any bearing on such purposes.* The beautiful contrivances which exist in the skeleton of man, and the contrivances, possessing the same kind of beauty, in the skeleton of a sparrow, do not appear to any reasonable person less beautiful, because the skeleton of a man, and of a sparrow, have an agreement, bone for bone, for which we see no reason, and which appears to us to answer no purpose. The way in which the human hand and arm are made capable of their in-

* The greatest anatomists, and especially Mr. Owen, have recently expressed their conviction, that researches on the structure of animals must be guided by the principle of *unity of composition* as well as the principle of *final causes*. See Owen *On the Nature of Limbs.*

finite variety of use, by the play of the radius and ulna, the bones of the wrist and the fingers, is not the less admirable, because we can trace the representatives and rudiments of each of these bones, in cases where they answer no such ends;—in the foreleg of the pig, the ox, the horse, or the seal. The provision for feeding the young creature, which is made, with such bounteous liberality, and such opportune punctuality, by the breasts of the mother, has not any doubt thrown upon its reality, by the teats of male animals and the paps of man, which answer no such purpose. That in these cases there is manifested a wider plan, which does not show any reference to the needs of particular cases; as well as peculiar contrivances for the particular cases, does not disturb our impression of design in each case. Why should so large a portion of the animal kingdom, intended, as it seems, for such different fields of life and modes of living;—beasts, birds, fishes;—still have a skeleton of the same plan, and even of the same parts, bone for bone; though many of the parts, in special cases, appear to be altogether useless (namely, the vertebrate plan)? We cannot tell. Our naturalists and comparative anatomists, it would seem, cannot point out any definite end, which is answered by making so many classes of animals on this one vertebrate plan. And since they cannot do this, and since we cannot tell why animals are so made, we must be content to say that we do not know; and therefore, to leave this feature in the structure of animals out of our argument for design. Hence we do not say that the making of beasts, birds, and fishes, on the same vertebrate plan, proves design in the Creator, in any way in which we can understand design. That plan is not of itself a proof of design; it is something in addition to the proofs of design; a general law of the animal creation, established, it may be, for some other reason. But this common plan being given, we can discern and admire, in every kind of animal, the manner in which the common plan is adapted to the particular purpose which the animal's kind of life involves.* The general law is not all; there is also, in every instance, a special care for the species. The general law may seem, in many cases, to remove further from us the proof of providential care; by showing that the elements of the benevolent contrivance are not provided in the cases alone where they are needed, but in others also. But yet this seeming, this obscuration of the evidence of design, by interposing the form of general law, cannot last long. If the general law supplies the elements, still a special adaptation is needed to make the elements answer such a purpose; and what is this adaptation, but design? The radius and ulna, the carpal and metacarpal bones, are all in the general type of the vertebrate skeleton. But does this fact make it the less wonderful, that man's arm and hand and fingers should be constructed so that he can make and use the spade, the plow, the loom, the pen, the pencil, the chisel, the lute, the telescope, the microscope, and all other instruments? Is it not, rather, very wonderful that the bones which are to be found rudimentally, in the leg-bone of a horse, or the hoof of an ox, should be capable of such a curious and fertile development and modification? And is not such development and modification a work, and a proof, of design and intention in the Creator? And so in other cases. The teats of male animals, the nipples of man, may arise from this, that the general plan of the animal frame includes paps, as portions of it; and that the frame is so far moulded in the embryo, before the sex of the offspring is determined. Be it so. Yet still this provision of paps in the animal form in gen-

* This has been termed by physiologists *The Law of the Development from the General to the Special.*

eral, has reference to offspring; and the development of that part of the frame, when the sex is determined, is evidence of design, as clear as it is possible to conceive in the works of nature. The general law is moulded to the special purpose, at the proper stage; and this play of general laws, and special contrivances, into each other's provinces, though it may make the phenomena a little more complex, and modify our notion as to the mode of the Creator's working, will not, in philosophical minds, disturb the conviction that there is design in the special adaptations: besides which, some other feature of the operation of the Creative Mind may be suggested by the prevalence of general laws in the Creation.

4. There is, however, one caution suggested by this view. Since, besides, and mixed with the examples of Design which the creation offers, there are also results of General Laws, in which we cannot trace the purpose and object of the law; we may fall into error, if we fasten upon something which is a result of such mere general laws, and imagine that we can discern its object and purpose. Thus, for instance, we might possibly persuade ourselves that we had discovered the use and purpose of the teats of male animals; or of the trace of separation into parts which the leg-bone of a horse offers; or of the false toes of a pig: all which are, as we have seen, the rudiments of a plan more general than is developed in the particular case. And if, when we had made such a fancied discovery, it were found that the uses and purposes which we had imagined to belong to these parts or features, were not really served by them; at first, perhaps, we might be somewhat disturbed, as having lost one of the evidences of the design of the Creator, all which are precious to a reverent mind. But it is not likely that any disturbance of a reverent mind on such grounds as this, would continue long, or go far. We

should soon come to recollect, how light and precarious, perhaps how arbitrary and ill-supported by our real knowledge, were the grounds on which we had assigned such uses to such parts. We should turn back from them to the more solid and certain evidences, not shaken, nor likely to be shaken, by any change in prevalent zoological or anatomical doctrines, which those who love to contemplate such subjects habitually dwell upon; and, holding ourselves ready to entertain any speculations by which the bearing of those general Laws upon Natural Religion could be shown, in such a way as to convince our reason, we should rest in the confident and tranquil persuasion that no success or failure in such speculations could vitally affect our belief in a wise and benevolent Deity:—that though additional illustrations of his attributes might be interesting and welcome, no change of our scientific point of view could make his being or action doubtful.

5. This is, it would seem, the manner in which a reasonable and reverent man would regard the proof of a Supreme Creator and Governor, which is derived from Design, as seen in the organic creation; and the mode in which such proof would be affected by changes in the knowledge which we may acquire of the general laws by which the organic creation is constituted and governed. And hence, if it should be found to be established by the researches of the most comprehensive and exact philosophy, that there are, in any province of the universe, resemblances, gradations, general laws, indications of the mode in which one form approaches to another, and seems to pass into and generate another, which tend to obliterate distinctions which at first appeared broad and conspicuous; still the argument, from the design which appears in the parts of which we most clearly see the purpose, would not lose its force. If, for instance, it should be made apparent, by geo-

logical investigations of the extinct fossil creation, that the animal forms which have inhabited the earth, have gradually approached to that type in which the human form is included, passing from the rudest and most imperfect animal organizations, mollusks, or even organic monads, to vertebrate animals, to warm-blooded animals, to monkeys, and to men; still, the evidences of design in the anatomy of man are not less striking than they were, when no such gradation was thought of. And what is more to the purpose of our argument, the evidences of the peculiar nature and destination of man, as shown in other characters than his anatomy,—his moral and intellectual nature, his history and capacities,—stand where they stood before; nor is the vast chasm which separates man, as a being with such characters as these latter, from all other animals, at all filled up or bridged over.

6. The evidence of design in the inorganic world,—in the relation of earth, air, water, heat and light,—is, to most persons, less striking and impressive, than it is in the organic creation. But even among these mere physical elements of the world, when we consider them with reference to living things, we find many arrangements which, on a reflective view, excite our admiration, by the beneficial effect, and seemingly beneficent purpose. Our condition is furnished with the solid earth, on which we stand, and in which we find the materials of man's handiworks; stone and metal, clay and sand;—with the atmosphere which we breathe, and which is the vehicle of oral intercourse between man and man;—with revolutions of the sun, by which are brought round the successions of day and night, through all their varying lengths, and of summer and winter;—with the clouds above us, which pour upon the earth their fertilizing showers. All this furniture of the earth, so marvellously adapting it for the abode of living creatures,

and especially of man, may well be regarded as a collection of provisions for his benefit:—as *intended* to do him the good, which they do. Nor would this impression be removed, or even weakened, if we were to discover that some of these arrangements, instead of being produced by a machinery confined to that single purpose, were only partial results of a more general plan. For instance; we learn that the varying lengths of days and nights through the year, and the varying declination of the sun, are produced, not, as was at first supposed, by the sun moving round the earth, in a complex diurnal and annual path, but by the earth revolving in an annual orbit round the sun; while at the same time she has a diurnal rotation about her own axis, which axis, by the laws of mechanics, remains always parallel to itself. When we learn that this is so, we see that the effect is produced by a mechanical arrangement far more simple than any which the imagination of man had devised; but in this case, the effect is plainly rather an increased admiration at the simplicity of the mechanism, than a wavering belief in the reality of the purpose. In like manner when, instead of supposing water to exist in a continuous reservoir in a firmament above the earth, and to fall in the earlier and in the latter rain, by some special agency for that purpose; men learnt to see that the water in the upper regions of the air must exist in clouds and in vapors only, and must fall in showers by the condensing influence of cold currents of air; they needed not to cease to admire the kindness of the Creator, in providing the rain to water the earth, and the wind to dry it; although the mechanism by which the effect was produced was of a larger kind than they had before imagined. And even if this mechanism extend through the solar system: if the arrangement by which the Earth's atmosphere is the special region in which there are winds hot and cold, clouds compact or dissolving,—be an arrangement which extends its influence to other planets, as well as to ours;—if this mixed atmosphere be placed, not only at the meeting point of clear aqueous vapor above, and warmer airs below, but also at the meeting point of a hot central region surrounding the Sun, and a cold exterior zone in which water and vapor can exist in immense collected masses, such as are Jupiter and Saturn;—still it would not appear, to a reasonable view, that this larger expansion of the machinery by which the effect is produced, makes the machinery less remarkable; or can at all tend to diminish the belief that it was *intended* to produce the effect which it does produce. Hot and cold, moist and dry, are constantly mixed together for the support of vegetable and animal life; and not the less so, if we believe that, though elements of this kind pervade the whole solar system, it is only at the Earth that they are combined so as to foster and nourish living things.

7. But it will perhaps be said, that to suppose the whole Solar System to be a machine merely operating for the benefit of the Earth and its population, is to give to the Earth and its population an importance in the scheme of creation which is quite extravagant and improbable:—it is to make the greater orbs, Jupiter and Saturn, minister to the less; instead of having their own purpose, and their own population, which their size naturally leads us to expect. To this we reply, that, in the first place, we have shown good reason for believing that the Earth is really the largest dense solid globe which exists in the solar system, and that the size of Jupiter and Saturn arises from their being composed mainly of water and vapor. And with regard to the difficulty of the greater ministering to the less;—if by *greater*, mere size and extent be understood, it appears to be the universal law of creation, that the greater, in

that sense, *should* minister to the less, when the less includes living things. Even if the planets be all inhabited, the sun, which is greater far than all of them together, ministers light and heat to all of them. Even on this supposition, the vast spaces by which the planets are separated have no use, that we can discern, except to place them at suitable distances from the sun. Even on this supposition, their solid globes within, their atmospheres without are all merely subservient to the benefit of a thin and scattered population on the surface. The space occupied by men and animals on the earth's surface, even taking into account the highest buildings and the deepest seas, is only a few hundreds, or a thousand feet. The benefit of this minute shell, interrupted in many places for vast distances, everywhere loosely and sparsely filled, is ministered to by the solidity and attraction of a mass below it 20 millions of feet deep; by the influence of an atmosphere above it 200 thousand feet high at least, and it may be, much more. And this being so, if we increase the depth of the centre 20 thousand times; if we carry the extreme verge of air and vapor to thirty times the radius of the earth's orbit from us, how does the construction of the machine become more improbable, or the disproportion of its size to its purpose more incongruous? Is mere size,—extent of brute matter or blank space,—so majestic a thing? Is not infinite space large enough to admit of machines of any size without grudging? But if we thus move the centre of the Earth's peopled surface 20 thousand times further off, we reach the Sun. If we carry the limit of air and vapor to the distance of 30 times the radius of the Earth's orbit we arrive at Neptune. Are these new numbers monstrous, while the old ones were accepted without scruple? Is number such an alarming feature in the description of the Universe? Does not the description of every part and every aspect of it, present us with numbers so large, that wonder and repugnance, on that ground are long ago exhausted? Surely this is so: and if the evidence really tend to prove to us that all the solar system ministers to the earth's population; the mere size of the system, compared with the space occupied by the population, will not long standin the way of the reception of such a doctrine.

8. But the objection will perhaps be urged in another form. It will be said that the other Planets have so many points of resemblance with the Earth, that we must suppose their nature and purpose the same. They, like the Earth, revolve in circles round the sun, rotate on their own axes, have, several of them, satellites, are opaque bodies, deriving light and probably heat from the sun. To an external spectator of the Solar System, they would not be distinguishable from the Earth. Such a spectator would never be tempted to guess that the Earth alone, of all these, neither the greatest nor the least, neither the one with the most satellites, nor the fewest, neither the innermost nor the outermost of the planets, is the only one inhabited; or at any rate the only one inhabited by an intelligent population. And to this we reply; that the largest of the other planets, if we judge rightly, are *not* like the Earth in one most essential respect, their density; and none of them, in having a surface consisting of land and water; except perhaps Mars: that if the supposed external spectator could see that this was so, he might see that the earth was different from the rest; and he might be able to see the vaporous nature of the outer planets, so that he would no more think of peopling them, than we do, of peopling the grand Alpine ridges and vallies which we see in the clouds of a summer-sky.

9. But even if the supposed spectator attended only to the obvious and superficial resemblances between one of the planets and another, he might still, if he were acquainted with the

general economy of the Universe, have great hesitation in inferring that, if one of them were inhabited, the others also must be inhabited. For, as we have said, in the plan of creation, we have a profusion of examples, where similar visible structures do not answer a similar purpose; where, so far as we can see, the structure answers no purpose in many cases; but exists, as we may say, for the sake of similarity: the similarity being a general Law, the result, it would seem, of a creative energy, which is wider in its operation than the particular purpose. Such examples are, as we have said, the finger-bones which are packed into the hoofs of a horse, or the paps and nipples of a male animal. Now the spectator, recollecting such cases might say: I know that the earth is inhabited; no doubt Mars and Jupiter are a good deal like the Earth; but are they inhabited? They look like the terrestrial breast of Nature: but are they really nursing breasts? Do they, like that, give food to living offspring? Or are they mere images of such breasts? male teats, dry of all nutritive power? sports, or rather overworks of nature; marks of a wider law than the needs of Mother Earth require? many sketches of a design, of which only one was to be executed? many specimens of the preparatory process of making a Planet, of which only one was to be carried out into the making of a World? Such questions might naturally occur to a person acquainted with the course of creation in general; even before he remarked the features which tend to show that Jupiter and Saturn, that Venus and Mercury, have not been developed into peopled worlds, like our Earth.

10. Perhaps it may be said, that to hold this, is to make Nature work in vain; to waste her powers; to suppose her to produce the frame work, and not to build; to make the skeleton, and not to clothe it with living flesh; to delude us with

appearances of analogy and promises of fertility, which are fallacious. What can we reply to this?

11. We reply, that to work in vain, in the sense of producing means of life which are not used, embryos which are never vivified, germs which are not developed; is so far from being contrary to the usual proceedings of nature, that it is an operation which is constantly going on, in every part of nature. Of the vegetable seeds which are produced, what an infinitely small proportion ever grow into plants! Of animal ova, how exceedingly few become animals, in proportion to those that do not; and that are wasted, if this be waste! It is an old calculation, which used to be repeated as a wonderful thing, that a single female fish contains in its body 200 millions of ova, and thus, might, of itself alone, replenish the seas, if all these were fostered into life. But in truth, this, though it may excite wonder, cannot excite wonder as anything uncommon. It is only one example of what occurs everywhere. Every tree, every plant, produces innumerable flowers, the flowers innumerable seeds, which drop to the earth, or are carried abroad by the winds, and perish, without having their powers unfolded. When we see a field of thistles shed its downy seeds upon the wind, so that they roll away like a cloud, what a vast host of possible thistles are there! Yet very probably none of them become actual thistles. Few are able to take hold of the ground at all; and those that do, die for lack of congenial nutriment, or are crushed by external causes before they are grown. The like is the case with every tribe of plants.* The

* Every reader of physiological works knows how easy it would be to multiply examples of this kind to any extent. Thus it is held by physiologists, that the sporules of fungi are universally diffused through the atmosphere, ready to vegetate whenever an opportunity presents itself: and that a single individual produces not less than ten millions of germs. It is held also that innumerable seeds of plants

like with every tribe of animals. The possible fertility of some kinds of insects is as portentous as anything of this kind can be. If allowed to proceed unchecked, if the possible life were not perpetually extinguished, the multiplying energies perpetually frustrated, they would gain dominion over the largest animals, and occupy the earth. And the same is the case, in different degrees, in the larger animals. The female is stocked with innumerable ovules, capable of becoming living things: of which incomparably the greatest number end as they began, mere ovules;—marks of mere possibility, of vitality frustrated. The universe is so full of such rudiments of things, that they far outnumber the things which outgrow their rudiments. The marks of possibility are much more numerous than the tale of actuality. The vitality which is frustrated is far more copious than the vitality which is consummated. So far, then, as this analogy goes, if the earth alone, of all the planetary harvest, has been a fertile seed of creation;—if the terrestrial embryo have alone been evolved into life, while all the other masses have remained barren and dead:—we have, in this, nothing which we need regard as an unprecedented waste, an improbable prodigality, an unusual failure in the operations of nature: but on the contrary, such a single case of success among many of failure, is exactly the order of nature in the production of life. It is quite agreeable to analogy, that the Solar System, of which the *flowers* are not many, should have borne but one *fertile* flower. One in eight, or in twice eight, reared into such wondrous fertility as belongs to the Earth, is an abundant produce, compared with the result in the most fertile provinces of Nature. And even if any number

still capable of vegetation, lie in strata far below the earth's surface, finding the occasion to vegetate only by the rarest and most exceptional occurrences.—Carpenter, *Manual of Physiology.* 1851, Art. 44.

of the Fixed Stars were also found to be barren flowers of the sky; objects, however beautiful, yet not sources of life or development, we need not think the powers of creation wasted or frustrated, thrown away or perverted. One such fertile result as the Earth, with all its hosts of plants and animals, and especially with Man, an intelligent being, to stand at the head of those hosts, is a worthy and sufficient produce, so far as we can judge of the Creator's ways by analogy, of all the Universal Scheme.

12. But when we follow this analogy, so far as to speak of the mere material mass of a planet as an *embryo world*;—a barren flower;—a seed which has never been developed into a plant;—we are in danger of allowing the analogy to mislead us. For a planet, as to its brute mass, has really nothing in common with a seed or an embryo. It has no organization, or tendency to organization; no principle of life, however obscure. So far as we can judge, no progress of time, or operation of mere natural influence, would clothe a brute mass with vegetables, or stock it with animals. No species of living thing would have its place upon the surface, by the mere order of unintelligent nature. So much is this so, according to all that our best knowledge teaches, that those geologists who must most have desired, for the sake of giving completeness and consistency to their systems, to make the production of vegetable and animal species from brute matter, a part of the order of nature, (inasmuch as they have explained everything else by the order of nature,) have not ventured to do so. They allow, generally at least, each separate species to require a special act of creative power, to bring it into being. They make the peopling of the earth, with its successive races of inhabitants, a series of events altogether different from the operation of physical laws in the sustentation of existing species.

The creation of life is, they allow, something out of the range of the ordinary laws of nature. And therefore, when we speak of uninhabited planets, as cases in which vital tendencies have been defeated; in which their apparent destiny, as worlds of life, has been frustrated; we really do injustice to our argument. The planets had no vital tendencies: they could have had such given, only by an additional act, or a series of additional acts, of Creative power. As mere inert globes, they had no settled destiny to be seats of life: they could have such a destiny, only by the appointment of Him who creates living things, and puts them in the places which he chooses for them. If, when a planetary mass had come into being, (in virtue of the same general physical law, suppose, which produced the earth,) the Creator placed a host of living things upon the earth, and none upon the other planet; there was still no violation of analogy, no seeming change of purpose, no unfinished plan. In the solar system, we can see what seem to be good reasons why he did this; but if we could not see such reasons, still we should be yet further from being able to see reasons why he necessarily must place inhabitants upon the other planet.

13. It is sometimes said, that it is agreeable to the goodness of God, that all parts of the creation should swarm with life; that life is enjoyment; and that the benevolence of the Supreme Being is shown in the diffusion of such enjoyment into every quarter of the universe. To leave a planet without inhabitants, would, it is thought, be to throw away an opportunity of producing happiness. Now we shall not here dwell upon the consideration, that the enjoyment thus spoken of, is, in a great degree, the enjoyment which the mere life of the lower tribes of animals implies;—the enjoyment of madrepores and oysters, cuttle-fish and sharks, tortoises and serpents; but we reply more broadly, that it is not the rule followed by the

Creator, to fill all places with living things. To say nothing of the vast intervals between planet and planet, which, it is presumed, no one supposes to be occupied by living things; how large a portion of the surface of the earth is uninhabited, or inhabited only in the scantiest manner. Vast desert tracts exist in Africa and in Asia, where the barren sand nourishes neither animal nor vegetable life. The highest regions of mountain-ranges, clothed with perpetual snow, and with far-reaching sheets of glacier ice, are untenanted, except by the chamois at their outskirts. There are many uninhabited islands; and were formerly many more. The ocean, covering nearly three-fourths of the globe, is no seat of habitation for land animals or for man; and though it has a large population of the fishy tribes, is probably peopled in smaller numbers than if it were land, as well as by inferior orders. We see, in the Earth then, which is the only seat of life of which we really know anything, nothing to support the belief that every field in the material universe is tenanted by living inhabitants.

14. That vegetables and animals, being once placed upon the earth, have multiplied or are multiplying, so as to occupy every part of the land and water which is suited for their habitation, we can see much reason to believe. Philosophical natural-historians have been generally led to the conviction that each species has had an original centre of dispersion, where it was first native, and that from this centre it has been diffused in all directions, as far as the circumstances of climate and soil were favorable to its production. But we can see also much reason to believe that this general diffusion of vegetable and animal life from centres, is a part of the order of nature which may often be made to give way to other and higher purposes;—to the diffusion, over the whole surface of the earth, of a race of intelligent, moral agents. This process may often interfere

with the general law of diffusion: as for instance, when man exterminates noxious animals. And whatever may be the laws which tend to replenish the earth, on which such centres of the diffusion of life exist for animals and plants; according to all analogy, these laws can have no force on any other planet, till such origins and centres of life are established on their surfaces. And even if any of the species which have ever tenanted the earth were so established on any other planet, we have the strongest reason to believe that they could not survive to a second generation.

15. Perhaps it may be said that we unjustifiably limit the power and skill of the Supreme Creator, if we deny that he could frame creatures fitted to live on any of the other planets, as well as in the Earth:—that the wonderful variety, and unexpected resource, of the ways in which animals are adapted for all kinds of climates, habitations, and conditions, upon the earth, may give us confidence that, under conditions still more extended, in habitations still further removed, in climates going beyond the terrestrial extremes, still the same wisdom and skill may well be supposed to have devised possible modes of animal life.

16. To this we reply, that we are so far from saying that the Creator could not place inhabitants in the other planets, that we have attempted to show what kind of inhabitants would be most likely to be placed there, by considering the way in which animals are accommodated to special conditions in their habitation. In judging of such modes of accommodating animals to an abode on other planets, as well as the earth, we have reasoned from what we know, of the mode in which animals are accommodated to their different habitations on the earth. We believe this to be the only safe and philosophical way of treating the question. If we are to reason

at all about the possibility of animal life, we must suppose that heat and light, gravity and buoyancy, materials and affinities, air and moisture, produce the same effect, require the same adaptations, in Jupiter or in Venus, as they do on the Earth. If we do not suppose this, we run into the error which so long prevented many from accepting the Newtonian system:—the error of thinking that matter in the heavens is governed by quite different laws from matter on the earth. We must adopt that belief, if we hold that animals may live under relations of heat and moisture, materials and affinities, in Jupiter or Venus, under which they could not live on our planet. And that belief, as we have said, appears to us contrary to all the teaching which the history of science offers us.

17. And not only is it contrary to the teaching of the history of science, to suppose the laws, which connect elemental and organic nature, to be different in the other planets from what they are on ours; but moreover the supposition would not at all answer the purpose, of making it probable that the planets are inhabited. For if we begin to imagine new and unknown laws of nature for those abodes, what is there to limit or determine our assumptions in any degree? What extravagant mixtures of the attributes and properties of mind and matter may we not then accept as probable truths? We know how difficult the poets have found it to describe, with any degree of consistency, the actions and events of a world of angels, or of evil spirits, souls or shades, embodied in forms so as to admit of description, and yet not subject to the laws of human bodies. Virgil, Tasso, Milton, Klopstock, and many others, have struggled with this difficulty:—no one of them, it will be probably agreed, with any great success; at least, regarding his representation as a hypothesis of a possible form of life, different from all the forms which we know.

Yet if we are to reject the laws which govern the known forms of life, in order that we may be able to maintain the possibility of some unknown form in a different planet, we must accept some of these hypotheses, or find a better. We must suppose that weight and cohesion, wounds and mutilations, wings and plumage, would have, either the effect which the poets represent them as having, or some different effect: and in either case it will be impossible to give any sufficient reason why we should confine the population to the surface of a planet. If gravity have not, upon any set of beings, the effect which it has upon us, such beings may live upon the surface of Saturn, though it be mere vapor: but then, on that supposition, they may equally well live in the vast space between Saturn and Jupiter, without needing any planet for their mansion. If we are ready to suppose that there are, in the solar system, conscious beings, not subject to the ordinary laws of life, we may go on to imagine creatures constituted of vaporous elements, floating in the fiery haze of a nebula, or close to the body of a sun; and cloudy forms which soar as vapors in the region of vapor. But such imaginations, besides being rather fitted for the employment of poets than of philosophers, will not, as we have said, find a population for the planets; since such forms may just as easily be conceived swimming round the sun in empty space, or darting from star to star, as confining themselves to the neighborhood of any of the solid globes which revolve about the central sun.

18. We should not, then add anything to the probability of inhabitants on the other planets of our system, even if we were arbitrarily to assume unlimited changes in the laws of nature, when we pass from our region to theirs. But probably, all readers will be of opinion that such assumptions are contrary to the whole scheme and spirit of such speculations

as we are here presuming:—that if we speculate on such subjects at all, it must be done by supposing that the same laws of nature operate in the same manner, in planetary, as in terrestrial spaces;—and that as we suppose, and prove, gravity and attraction, inertia and momentum, to follow the same rules, and produce the same effects, on brute matter there, which they do here; so, both these forces, and others, as light and heat, moisture and air, if, in the planets, they go beyond the extremes which limit them here, yet must imply, in any organized beings which exist in the planets, changes, though greater in amount, of the same kind as those which occur in approaching the terrestrial extremes of those elementary agents. And what kind of a population that would lead us to suppose in Jupiter or Saturn, Mars or Venus, the reader has already seen our attempt to determine; and may thence judge whether, when we go so far beyond the terrestrial extremes of heat and cold, light and dimness, vapor and water, air and airlessness, any population at all is probable.

19. Perhaps some persons, even if they cannot resist the force of these reasons, may still yield to them with regret; and may feel as if, having hitherto believed that the planets were inhabited, and having now to give up that belief, their view of the solar system, as one of the provinces of God's creation, were made narrower and poorer than it was before. And this feeling may be still further increased, if they are led to believe also that many of the fixed stars are not the centres of inhabited systems; or that very few, or none are. It may seem to them, as if, by such a change of belief, the field of God's greatness, benevolence, and government, were narrowed and impoverished, to an extent painful and shocking;—as if, instead of being the Maker and Governor of innumerable worlds, of the most varied constitution, we were called upon to

regard him as merely the Master of the single world in which we live:—as if, instead of being the object of reverence and adoration to the intelligent population of these thousand spheres, he was recognized and worshipped on one only, and on that, how scantily and imperfectly!

20. It is not to be denied that there may be such a regret and disturbance naturally felt, at having to give up our belief that the planets and the stars probably contain servants and worshippers of God. It must always be a matter of pain and trouble, to be urged with tenderness, and to be performed in time, to untwine our reverential religious sentiments from erroneous views of the constitution of the universe with which they have been involved. But the change once made, it is found that religion is uninjured, and reverence undiminished. And therefore we trust that the reader will receive with candor and patience the argument which we have to offer with reference to this view, or rather, this sentiment.

21. We remark, in the first place, that however repugnant it may be to us to believe a state of any part of the universe in which there are not creatures who can know, obey and worship God; we are compelled, by geological evidence, to admit that such a state of things has existed upon the earth, during a far longer period than the whole duration of man's race. If we suppose that the human race, if not by their actual knowledge, obedience, and worship of God, yet at least by their faculties for knowing, obeying, and worshipping, are a sufficient reason why there should be such a province in God's empire; still in fact, this race has existed only for a few thousand years, out of the, perhaps, millions of years of the earth's existence; and during all the previous period, the earth, if tenanted, was tenanted by brute creatures, fishes and lizards, beasts and birds, of which none had any faculty, intellectual,

moral, or religious. By the same analogy, therefore, on which we have already insisted, we may argue that there is reason to believe, that if other planets, and other stars, are the seats of habitation, it is rather of such habitation as has prevailed upon the earth during the millions, than during the six thousand years; and that if we have, in consequence of physical reasons, to give up the belief of a population in the other planets, or in the stars; we are giving up, not anything with which we might dwell with religious pleasure—hosts of fellow-servants and fellow-worshippers of the Divine Author of all:—but the mere brute tribes, of the land and of the water, things that creep and crawl, prowl and spring;—none that can lift its visage to the sky, with a feeling that it is looking for its Maker and Master. There have not existed upon the Earth, during the immense ages of its præhuman existence, beings who could recognize and think of the Creator of the world: and if astronomy introduces us, as geology has done, to a new order of material structures, thus barren of an intelligent and religious population, we must learn to accept the prospect, in the one case, as in the other. Nor need we fear that on a further contemplation of the universe, we shall find every part of it ministering, though perhaps not in the way our first thoughts had guessed, to sentiments of reverence and adoration towards the Maker of the universe.

22. The truth is, as the slightest recollection of the course of opinion about the stars may satisfy us, that men have had repeatedly to give up the notions which they had adopted, of the manner in which the material heavens, the stars and the skies, are to minister to man's feeling of reverence for the Creator. It was long ago said, that the heavens declare the glory of God, and the firmament showeth his handiwork: that day and night, sun and moon, clouds and stars, unite in impressing upon us this sentiment. And this language still

finds a sympathetic echo, in the breasts of all religious persons. Nor will it ever cease to do so, however our opinions of the structure and nature of the heavenly bodies may alter. When the new aspects of things become familiar, they will show us the handiwork of God, and declare his glory, as plainly as the old ones. But in the progress of opinions, man has often had to resign what seemed to him, at the time, visions so beautiful, sublime, and glorious, that they could not be dismissed without regret. The Universal Lord was at one time conceived as directing the motions of all the spheres by means of Ruling Angels, appointed to preside over each. The prevalence of proportion and number, in the dimensions of these spheres, was assumed to point to the existence of harmonious sounds, accompanying their movements, though unheard by man; as proportion and number had been found to be the accompaniments and conditions of harmony upon earth. The time came, when these opinions were no longer consistent with man's knowledge of the heavenly motions, and of the wide-spreading causes by which they are produced. Then "Ruling Angels from their spheres were hurled," as a matter of belief; though still the poets loved to refer to imagery in which so many lofty and reverent thoughts had so long been clothed. The aspect of the stars was most naturally turned to a lesson of cheerful and thoughtful piety, by the adoption of such a view of their nature and office; and thus, the midnight contemplator of an Italian sky teaches his companion concerning the starry host;

Sit, Jessica; look how the floor of heav'n
Is thick inlaid with patterns of bright gold.
There's not the meanest orb, which thou behold'st,
But in his motion like an angel sings,
Still quiring to the young-eyed cherubims;
Such harmony is in immortal souls.

Meaning, apparently, the harmony between the immortal spirits that govern each star, and the cherubims that sing before the throne of God. But however beautiful and sublime may be this representation, the philosopher has had to abandon it in its literal sense. He may have adopted, instead, the opinion that each of the stars is the seat, or the centre of a group of seats, of choirs of worshippers; but this again, is still to suppose the nature of those orbs to be entirely different from that of this earth; though in many respects, we know that they are governed by the same laws. And if he will be content to know no more than he has the means of knowing, or even to know only according to his best means of knowing, he must be prepared, if the force of proof so requires, to give up this belief also; at least for the present.

23. Indeed, those who have not been content with this, and have sought to combine with the visible splendor of the skies, some scheme, founded upon astronomical views, which shall people them with intelligent beings and worshippers, have drawn upon their fancy quite as much as Lorenzo in his lesson to Jessica; or rather, they have done what he and those from whom his love was derived, had done before. They have taken the truths which astronomers have discovered and taught, and made the objects and regions so revealed, the scenes and occasions of such sentiments of piety as they themselves have, or feel that they ought to have. Even in Shakspeare, the stars are already *orbs*, each orb has his *motion*, and in his motion produces the music of the spheres. More recent preachers, following sounder views of the nature of these orbs and motions, have been equally poetical when they come to their religious reflection. When the poet of the *Night Thoughts* says,

"Each of these stars is a religious house;
I saw their altars smoke, their incense rise,
And heard hosannas ring through every sphere."

he is no less imaginative than the poet of that *Midsummer Night's Dream*, which we have in the *Merchant of Venice*. And we are compelled, by all the evidence which we can discern, to say the same of the preacher who speaks, from the pulpit, of these orbs of worlds, and tells us of the stars which "give animation to other systems*;" when he says† "worlds roll in these distant regions; and these worlds must be the centres of life and intelligence;" when he speaks of the earth‡ as "the humblest of the provinces of God's empire." But then we must recollect that these thoughts still prove the religious nature of man; they show how he is impelled to endeavor to elevate his mind to God by every part of the universe; and it is not too much to say, that through the faculties of man, thus regarding the starry heavens, every star does really testify to the greatness of God, and minister to His worship.

24. We may trust that this mere material magnificence does not require inhabitants, to make it lift man's heart towards the Universal Creator, and to make him accept it as a sublime evidence of His greatness. The grandest objects in nature are blank and void of life;—the mountain-peaks that stand, ridge beyond ridge, serene in the region of perpetual snow;—the summer-clouds, images of such mountain tracts, even upon a grander scale, and tinted with more gorgeous colors;—the thunder-cloud with its dazzling bolt;—the stormy ocean with its mountainous waves;—the Aurora Borealis, with its mysterious pillars of fire;—all these are sublime; all these elevate the soul, and make it acknowledge a mighty Worker in the elements, in spite of any teaching of a material philosophy. And if we have to regard the planets as merely parts of the same great spectacle of nature, we shall not the less regard them with an admiration which ministers to pious awe. Even merely as

* Chalmers, p. 35. † Ibid. p. 21. ‡ Ibid. p. 119.

a spectacle, Saturn made visible in his real shape, only by a vast exertion of human skill, yet shining like a star, in form so curiously complex, symmetrical and seemingly artificial, will never cease to be an object of the ardent and contemplative gaze of all who catch a sight of him. And however much the philosopher may teach that he is merely a mass of water and vapor, ice and snow, he must be far more interesting to the eye than the Alps, or the clouds that crown them, or the ocean with its icebergs; where the same elements occur in forms comparatively shapeless and lawless, irregular and chaotic.

25. But perhaps there is in the minds of many persons, a sentiment connected with this regular and symmetrical form of the heavenly bodies; that being thus beautifully formed and finished they must have been the objects of especial care to the Creator. These regular globes, these nearly circular orbits, these families of satellites, they too so regular in their movements; this ring of Saturn; all the adjustments by which the planetary motions are secured from going wrong, as the profoundest researches into the mechanics of the universe show; —all these things seem to indicate a peculiar attention bestowed by the Maker on each part of the machine. So much of law and order, of symmetry and beauty in every part, implies, it may be thought, that every part has been framed with a view to some use;—that its symmetry and its beauty are the marks of some noble purpose.

26. To reply to this argument, so far as it is requisite for us to do so, we must recur to what we have already said; that though we see in many parts of the universe, inorganic as well as organic, marks which we cannot mistake, of design and purpose; yet that this design and purpose are often effected by laws which are of a much wider sweep than the design, so far as we can trace its bearing. These laws, besides answering the

purpose, produce many other effects, in which we can see no purpose. We have now to observe further that these laws, thus ranging widely through the universe, and working everywhere, as if the Creator delighted in the generality of the law, independently of its special application, do often produce innumerable results of beauty and symmetry, as if the Creator delighted in beauty and symmetry, independently of the purpose answered.

27. Thus, to exemplify this reflection : the powers of aggregation and cohesion, which hold together the parts of solid bodies, as metals and stones, salts and ice,—which solidify matter, in short,—we can easily see, to be necessary, in order to the formation and preservation of solid terrestrial bodies. They are requisite, in order that man may have the firm earth to stand upon, and firm materials to use. But let us observe, what a wonderful and beautiful variety of phenomena grows out of this law, with no apparent bearing upon that which seems to us its main purpose. The power of aggregation of solid bodies is, in fact, the force of crystallization. It binds together the particles of bodies by molecular forces, which not only hold the particles together, but are exerted in special directions, which form triangles, squares, hexagons, and the like. And hence we have all the variety of crystalline forms which sparkle in gems, ores, earths, pyrites, blendes ; and which, when examined by the crystallographers, are found to be an inexhaustible field of the play of symmetrical complexity. The diamond, the emerald, the topaz, have got each its peculiar kind of symmetry. Gold and other metals have, for the basis of their forms, the cube, but run from this into a vastly greater variety of regular solids than ever geometer dreamt of. Some single species of minerals, as calc-spar, present hundreds of forms, all rigorously regular, and have been alone the subject

of volumes. Ice crystalizes by the same laws as other solid bodies; and our Arctic voyagers have sometimes relieved the weariness of their sojourn in those regions, by collecting some of the innumerable forms, resembling an endless collection of hexagonal flowers, sporting into different shapes, which are assumed by flakes of snow*. In these and many other ways, the power of crystallization produces an inexhaustible supply of examples of symmetrical beauty. And what are we to conceive to be the object and purpose of this? As we have said, that part of the purpose which is intelligible to us is, that we have here a force holding together the particles of bodies, so as to make them solid. But all these pretty shapes add nothing to this intelligible use. Why then are they there? They are there, it would seem, for their own sake;—because they are pretty;—symmetry and beauty are there on their own account; or because they are universal adjuncts of the general laws by which the creator works. Or rather we may say, combining different branches of our knowledge, that crystallization is the mark and accompaniment of chemical composition: and that as chemical composition takes place according to definite numbers, so crystaline aggregation takes place according to definite forms. The symmetrical relations of space in crystals correspond to the simple relations of number in synthesis; and thus, because there is rule, there is regularity, and regularity assumes the form of beauty.

28. This, which thus shows itself throughout the mineral kingdom, or, speaking more widely and truly, throughout the whole range of chemical composition, is still more manifest in the vegetable domain. All the vast array of flowers, so infi-

* Dr. Scoresby, in his *Account of the Artic Regions* (1820) Vol. II. has given figures of 96 such forms, selected for their eminent regularity from many more.

nitely various, and so beautiful in their variety, are the results of a few general laws; and show, in the degree of their symmetry, the alternate operation of one law and another. The rose, the lily, the cowslip, the violet, differ in something of the same way, in which the crystalline forms of the several gems differ. Their parts are arranged in fives or in threes, in pentagons or in hexagons, and in these regular forms, one part or another is expanded or contracted, rendered conspicuous by color or by shape, so as to produce all the multiplicity of beauty which the florist admires. Or rather, in the eye of the philosophical botanist, the whole of the structure of plants, with all their array of stems and leaves, blossoms and fruits, is but the manifestation of one Law; and all these members of the vegetable form, are, in their natures, the same, developed more or less in this way or in that. The daisy consists of a close cluster of flowers of which each has, in its form, the rudiments of the valerian. The peablossom is a rose, with some of its petals expanded into butterfly-like wings. Even without changing the species, this general law leads to endless changes. The garden-rose is the common hedge-rose with innumerable filaments changed into glowing petals. By the addition of whorl to whorl, of vegetable coronet over coronet, green and colored, broad and narrow, filmy and rigid, every plant is generated, and the glory of the field and of the garden, of the jungle and of the forest, is brought forth in all its magnificence. Here, then, we have an immeasurable wealth of beauty and regularity, brought to view by the operation of a single law. And to what use? What purpose do these beauties answer? What is the object for which the lilies of the field are clothed so gaily and gorgeously? Some plants, indeed, are subservient to the use of animals and of man: but how small is the number in which we can trace this, as an intelligent purpose of their existence! And does it not, in fact, better express the impression which the survey of this province of nature suggests to us, to say, that they grow because the Creator willed that they should grow? Their vegetable life was an object of His care and contrivance, as well as animal and human life. And they are beautiful, also because He willed that they should be so:—because He delights in producing beauty;—and, as we have further tried to make it appear, because He acts by general law, and law produces beauty. Is not such a tendency here apparent, as a part of the general scheme of Creation?

29. We have already attempted to show, that in the structure of animals, especially that large class best known to us, vertebrate animals, there is also a general plan which, so far as we can see, goes beyond the circuit of the special adaptation of each animal to its mode of living: and is a rule of creative action, in addition to the rule that the parts shall be subservient to an intelligible purpose of animal life. We have noticed several phenomena in the animal kingdon, where parts and features appear, rudimentary and inert, discharging no office in their economy, and speaking to us, not of purpose, but of law:—consistent with an end which is visible, but seemingly the results of a rule whose end is in itself.

30. And do we not, in innumerable cases, see beauties of color and form, texture and lustre, which suggests to us irresistibly the belief that beauty and regular form are rules of the Creative agency, even when they seem to us, looking at the creation for uses only, idle and wanton expenditure of beauty and regularity. To what purpose are the host of splendid circles which decorate the tail of the peacock, more beautiful, each of them, than Saturn with his rings? To what purpose the exquisite textures of microscopic objects, more curiously

regular than anything which the telescope discloses? To what purpose the gorgeous colors of tropical birds and insects, that live and die where human eye never approaches to admire them? To what purpose the thousands of species of butterflies with the gay and varied embroidery of their microscopic plumage, of which one in millions, if seen at all, only draws the admiration of the wandering schoolboy? To what purpose the delicate and brilliant markings of shells, which live, generation after generation, in the sunless and sightless depths of the ocean? Do not all these examples, to which we might add countless others, (for the world, so far as human eye has scanned it, is full of them,) prove that beauty and regularity are universal features of the work of Creation, in all its parts, small and great: and that we judge in a way contrary to a vast range of analogy, which runs through the whole of the Universe, when we infer that, because the objects which are presented to our contemplation are beautiful in aspect and regular in form, they must, in each case, be means for some special end, of those which we commonly fix upon, as the main ends of the Creation, the support and advantage of animals or of man?

31. If this be so, then the beautiful and regular objects which the telescope reveals to us; Jupiter and his Moons, Saturn and his Rings, the most regular of the Double Stars, Clusters and Nebulæ; cannot reasonably be inferred, because they are beautiful and regular, to be also fields of life, or scenes of thought. They may be, as to the poet's eye they often appear, the gems of the robe of Night, the flowers of the celestial fields. Like gems and like flowers, they are beautiful and regular, because they are brought into being by vast and general laws. These laws, although, in the mind of the Creator, they have their sufficient reason, as far as they extend, may

have, in no other region than that which we inhabit, the reason which we seek to discover everywhere, the sustentation of a life like ours. That we should connect with the existence of such laws, the existence of Mind like our own mind, is most natural; and, as we might easily show, is justifiable, reasonable, even necessary. But that we should suppose the result of such laws are so connected with Mind, that wherever the laws gather matter into globes, and whirl it round the central body, *there* is also a local seat of minds like ours; is an assumption altogether unwarranted; and is, without strong evidence, of which we have as yet no particle, quite visionary.

32. But finally, it may be said that by this our view of the universe, we diminish the greatness of the work of creation, and the majesty of the Creator. Such a view appears to represent the other planets as mere fragments, which have flown off in the fabrication of this our earth, and of the mechanism by which it answers its purpose. Instead of a vast array of completed worlds, we have one world, surrounded by abortive worlds and inert masses. Instead of perfection everywhere, we have imperfection everywhere, except at one spot; if even there the workmanship be perfect.

33. To this, the reply is contained in what we have already said: but we may add, that it cannot be wise or right, to prop up our notions of God's greatness, by physical doctrines which will not bear discussion. God's greatness has no need of man's inventions for its support. The very conviction that the Creation must be such as to confirm our belief in the greatness of God, shows that such a belief is more deeply seated than any special views of the structure of the universe, and will triumphantly survive the removal of error in such views. We may add, that till within a few thousand years, this earth, compared with what it now is, having upon it no intelligent beings,

might be regarded as an abortive world; that all the parts of the solar system which we can best scrutinize, the moon, and meteoric stones, are inert masses; and further, that there is everywhere the perfection which results from the operation of law, and that *that* seems to be the perfection with which the Creator is contented.

34. And perhaps, when the view of the universe which we here present has become familiar, we may be led to think that the aspect which it gives to the mode of working of the Creator, is sufficiently grand and majestic. Instead of manufacturing a multitude of worlds on patterns more or less similar, He has been employed in one great work, which we cannot call imperfect, since it includes and suggests all that we can conceive of perfection. It may be that all the other bodies, which we can discover in the universe, show the greatness of this work, and are rolled into forms of symmetry and order, into masses of light and splendor, by the vast whirl which the original creative energy imparted to the luminous element. The planets and the stars are the lumps which have flown from the potter's wheel of the Great Worker;—the shred-coils which, in the working, sprang from His mighty lathe:—the sparks which darted from His awful anvil when the solar system lay incandescent thereon;—the curls of vapor which rose from the great cauldron of creation when its elements were separated. If even these superfluous portions of the material are marked with universal traces of regularity and order, this shows that universal rules are his implements, and that Order is the first and universal Law of the heavenly work.

35. And, that we may see the full dignity of this work, we must always recollect that Man is a part of it, and the crowning part. The workmanship which is employed on mere matter is, after all, of small account, in the eyes of intellectual

and moral creatures, when compared with the creation and government of intellectual and moral creatures. The majesty of God does not reside in planets and stars, in orbs and systems; which are, after all, only stone and vapor, materials and means. If, as we believe, God has not only made the material world, but has made and governs man, we need not regret to have to depress any portion of the material world below the place which we had previously assigned to it; for, when all is done, the material world *must* be put in an inferior place, compared with the world of mind. If there be a World of Mind, *that*, according to all that we can conceive, must have been better worth creating, must be more worthy to exist, as an object of care in the eyes of the Creator, than thousands and millions of stars and planets, even if they were occupied by a myriad times as many species of brute animals as have lived upon the earth since its vivification. In saying this, we are only echoing the common voice of mankind, uttered, as so often it is, by the tongues of poets. One such speaks thus of stellar systems:

> Behold this midnight splendor, worlds on worlds;
> Ten thousand add and twice ten thousand more,
> Then weigh the whole: one soul outweighs them all,
> And calls the seeming vast magnificence
> Of unintelligent creation, poor.

And as this is true of intelligence, with the suggestion which that faculty so naturally offers, of the inextinguishable nature of mind, so is it true of the moral nature of man. No accumulation of material grandeur, even if it fill the universe, has any dignity in our eyes, compared with moral grandeur: as poetry has also expressed:

> Look then abroad through nature, to the range
> Of planets, suns, and adamantine spheres,

> Wheeling unshaken through the void immense,
> And speak, O man! Can this capacious scene
> With half that kindling majesty exalt
> Thy strong conception, as when Brutus rose
> Refulgent from the stroke of Cæsar's fate
> Amid the band of patriots; and his arm
> Aloft extending, like eternal Jove
> When guilt calls down the thunder, call'd aloud
> On Tully's name, and shook his crimson steel,
> And bade the Father of his Country, Hail!
> For lo! the tyrant prostrate in the dust,
> And Rome again is free.

This action being taken, as it is here meant to be conceived, for one of the highest examples of moral greatness. And however we may judge of this action, we must allow that the characters which are implied in this praise of it,—the loftiest kinds of moral excellence,—are more suitable to the highest idea of the object and purpose of a Deity creating worlds, than would be any mere material structure of planets and suns, whether kept in their places by adamantine spheres, wheeling unshaken through the void immense, or themselves wheeling unshaken by the power of a universal law. The thoughts of Rights and Obligations, Duty and Virtue, of Law and Liberty, of Country and Constitution, of the Glory of our Ancestors, the Elevation of our Fellow-Citizens, the Freedom and Happiness and Dignity of Posterity,—are thoughts which belong to a world, a race, a body of beings, of which any one individual, with the capacities which such thoughts imply, is more worthy of account, than millions of millions of mollusks and belemnites, lizards and fishes, sloths and pachyderms, diffused through myriads of worlds.

36. We might illustrate this argument further, by taking actions of the moral character of which there will be less doubt. If we look at the great acts which render Greece

illustrious and interesting in our eyes,—such as the death of Socrates, for instance, the triumph of a reverence for Law and a love of country;—can we think it any real diminution of the glory of the universe, if we are reduced to the necessity of rejecting the belief in a multitude of worlds, which though, it may be, peopled with lower animals, contain none endowed with any higher principle than hunger and thirst?

37. That the human race possesses a worth in the eyes of Reason beyond that which any material structure, or any brute population can possess, might be maintained on still higher and stronger grounds; namely, on religious grounds: but we do not intend here to dwell on that part of the subject. If man be, not merely (and he alone of all animals) capable of Virtue and Duty, of Universal Love and Self-Devotion, but be also immortal; if his being be of infinite duration, his soul created never to die; then, indeed, we may well say that one soul outweighs the whole unintelligent creation. And if the Earth have been the scene of an action of Love and Self-Devotion for the incalculable benefit of the whole human race, in comparison with which the death of Socrates fades into a mere act of cheerful resignation to the common lot of humanity; and if this action, and its consequences to the whole race of man, in his temporal and eternal destiny, and in his history on earth before and after it, were the main object for which man was created, the cardinal point round which the capacities and the fortunes of the race were to turn; then indeed we see that the Earth has a pre-eminence in the scheme of creation, which may well reconcile us to regard all the material splendour which surrounds it, all the array of mere visible luminaries and masses which accompany it, as no unfitting appendages to such a drama. The elevation of millions of intellectual, moral, religious, spiritual creatures, to a destiny

so prepared, consummated, and developed, is no unworthy occupation of all the capacities of space, time, and matter. And, so far as any one has yet shown, to regard this great scheme as other than the central point of the divine plan; to consider it as one part among other parts, similar, co-ordinate, or superior; involves those who so speculate, in difficulties, even with regard to the plan itself, which they strive in vain to reconcile; while the assumption of the subjects of such a plan, in other regions of the universe, is at variance with all which we, looking at the analogies of space and time, of earth and stars, of life in brutes and in man, have found reason to deem in any degree probable.

38. And thus that conjecture of the Plurality of Worlds, to which a wide and careful examination of the physical constitution of the Universe supplied no confirmation, derives also little support from a contemplation of the Design which the Creator may be supposed to have had in the work of the Creation; when such Design is regarded in a comprehensive manner, and in all its bearings. Such a survey seems to speak rather in favor of the Unity of the World, than of a Plurality of Worlds. A further consideration of the intellectual, moral, and religious nature of man may still further illustrate this view; and with that object, we shall make a few additional remarks.

CHAPTER XII.

THE UNITY OF THE WORLD.

1. The two doctrines which we have here to weigh against each other are the Plurality of Worlds, and the Unity of the World. In so saying, we include in our present view, a necessary part of the conception of a *World*, a collection of intelligent creatures: for even if the suppositions to which we have been led, respecting the kind of unintelligent living things which may inhabit other parts of the Universe, be conceived to be probable; such a belief will have little interest for most persons, compared with the belief of other worlds, where reside intelligence, perception of truth, recognition of moral Law, and reverence for a Divine Creator and Governor. In looking outwards at the Universe, there are certain aspects which suggest to man, at first sight, a conjecture that there may be other bodies like the Earth, tenanted by other creatures like man. This conjecture, however, receives no confirmation from a closer inquiry, with increased means of observation. Let us now look inwards, at the constitution of man; and consider some characters of his nature, which seem to remove or lessen the difficulties which we may at first feel, in regarding the Earth as, in a unique and special manner, the field of God's Providence and Government.

2. In the first place, the Earth, as the abode of man, the in-

tellectual creature, contains a being, whose mind is, in some measure, of the same nature as the Divine Mind of the Creator. The Laws which man discovers in the Creation must be Laws known to God. The truths,—for instance the truths of geometry,—which man sees to be true, God also must see to be true. That there were, from the beginning, in the Creative Mind, Creative Thoughts, is a doctrine involved in every intelligent view of Creation.

3. This doctrine was presented by the ancients in various forms; and the most recent scientific discoveries have supplied new illustrations of it. The mode in which Plato expressed the doctrine which we are here urging was, that there were in the Divine Mind, before or during the work of creation, certain archetypal Ideas, certain exemplars or patterns of the world and its parts, according to which the work was performed: so that these Ideas or Exemplars existed in the objects around us being in so many cases discernible by man, and being the proper objects of human reason. If a mere metaphysician were to attempt to revive this mode of expressing the doctrine, probably his speculations would be disregarded, or treated as a pedantic resuscitation of obsolete Platonic dreams. But the adoption of such language must needs be received in a very different manner, when it proceeds from a great discoverer in the field of natural knowledge: when it is, as it were, forced upon *him*, as the obvious and appropriate expression of the result of the most profound and comprehensive researches into the frame of the whole animal creation. The recent works of Mr. Owen, and especially one work, *On the Nature of Limbs*, are full of the most energetic and striking passages, inculcating the doctrine which we have been endeavoring to maintain. We may take the liberty of enriching our pages with one passage bearing upon the present part of the subject.

"If the world were made by any antecedent Mind or Understanding, that is by a Deity, then there must needs be an Idea and Exemplar of the whole world before it was made, and consequently actual knowledge, both in the order of Time and Nature, before Things. But conceiving of knowledge as it was got by their own finite minds, and ignorant of any evidence of an ideal Archetype for the world or any part of it, they [the Democritic Philosophers who denied a Divine Creative Mind] affirmed that there was none, and concluded that there could be no knowledge or mind before the world was, as its cause." Plato's assertion of Archetypal Ideas was a protest against this doctrine, but was rather a guess, suggested by the nature of mathematical demonstration, than a doctrine derived from a contemplation of the external world.

"Now however," Mr. Owen continues, "the recognition of an ideal exemplar for the vertebrated animals proves that the knowledge of such a being as Man must have existed before Man appeared. For the Divine Mind which planned the Archetypal also foreknew all its modifications. The Archetypal Idea was manifested in the flesh under divers modifications upon this planet, long prior to the existence of those animal species which actually exemplify it. To what natural or secondary causes the orderly succession and progression of such organic phenomena may have been committed, we are as yet ignorant. But if without derogation to the Divine Power, we may conceive such ministers and personify them by the term *Nature*, we learn from the past history of our globe that she has advanced with slow and stately steps, guided by the archetypal light amidst the wreck of worlds, from the first embodiment of the vertebrate idea, under its old ichthyic vestment, until it became arrayed in the glorious garb of the human form."

4. Law implies a Lawgiver, even when we do not see the object of the Law; even as Design implies a Designer, when we do not see the object of the Design. The Laws of Nature are the indications of the operation of the Divine Mind; and are revealed to us, as such, by the operations of our minds, by which we come to discover them. They are the utterances of the Creator, delivered in language which we can understand; and being thus Language, they are the utterances of an Intelligent Spirit.

5. It may seem to some persons too bold a view, to identify, so far as we thus do, certain truths as seen by man, and as seen by God:*—to make the Divine Mind thus cognizant of the truths of geometry, for instance. If any one has such a scruple, we may remark that truth, when of so luminous and stable a kind as are the truths of geometry, must be alike *Truth* for all minds, even for the highest. The mode of arriving at the knowledge of such truths, may be very different, even for different human minds;—deduction for some;—intuition for others. But the intuitive apprehension of necessary truth is an act so purely intellectual, that even in the Supreme Intellect, we may suppose that it has its place. Can we conceive otherwise, than that God does contemplate the universe as existing in space, since it really does so;—and subject to the relations of space, since these are as real as space itself? We are well aware that the Supreme Being must contemplate the world under many other aspects than this;—even man does so. But that does not prevent the truths, which belong to the aspect of the world, contemplated as existing in space, from being truths, regarded as such, even by the Divine Mind.

* Among the most recent expositors of this doctrine we may place M. Henri Martin, whose *Philosophie Spiritualiste de la Nature* is full of striking views of the universe in its relation to God. (Paris. 1849.)

6. If these reflections are well founded, as we trust they will, on consideration, be seen to be, we may adopt many of the expressions by which philosophers heretofore have attempted to convey similar views; for in fact, this view, in its general bearing at least, is by no means new. The Mind of Man is a partaker of the thoughts of the Divine Mind. The Intellect of Man is a spark of the Light by which the world was created. The Ideas according to which man builds up his knowledge, are emanations of the archetypal Ideas according to which the work of creation was planned and executed. These, and many the like expressions, have been often used; and we now see, we may trust, that there is a great philosophical truth, which they all tend to convey; and this truth shows at the same time, how man may have some knowledge respecting the Laws of Nature, and how this knowledge may, in some cases, seem to be a knowledge of necessary relations, as in the case of space.*

* Most readers who have given any attention to speculations of this kind, will recollect Newton's remarkable expressions concerning the Deity: "Æternus est et infinitus, omnipotens et omnisciens; id est, durat ab æterno in æternum, et adest ab infinito in infinitum . . . Non est æternitas et infinitas, sed æternus et infinitus; non est duratio et spatium, sed durat et adest. Durat semper et adest ubique, et existendo semper et ubique durationem et spatium constituit."

To say that God by existing always and everywhere *constitutes duration and space*, appears to be a form of expression better avoided. Besides that it approaches too near to the opinion, which the writer rejects, that He *is* duration and space, it assumes a knowledge of the nature of the Divine existence, beyond our means of knowing, and therefore rashly. It appears to be safer, and more in conformity with what we really know, to say, not that the existence of God constitutes time and space; but that God has constituted *man*, so that *he* can apprehend the works of creation, only as existing in time and space. That God has constituted time and space as conditions of man's knowledge of the creation, is certain: that God has constituted time and space as results of his own existence in any other way, *we* cannot know.

7. Now, the views to which we have been led, bear very strongly upon that argument. For if man, when he attains to a knowledge of such laws, is really admitted, in some degree, to the view with which the Creator himself beholds his creation;—if we can gather, from the conditions of such knowledge, that his intellect partakes of the Nature of the Supreme Intellect;—if his Mind, in its clearest and largest contemplations, harmonizes with the Divine Mind;—we have, in this, a reason which may well seem to us very powerful, why, even if the Earth alone be the habitation of intelligent beings, still, the great work of Creation is not wasted. If God have placed upon the earth a creature who can so far sympathize with Him, if we may venture upon the expression;—who can raise his intellect into some accordance with the Creative Intellect; and that, not once only, nor by few steps, but through an indefinite gradation of discoveries, more and more comprehensive, more and more profound; each, an advance, however slight, towards a Divine Insight;—then, so far as intellect alone (and we are here speaking of intellect alone) can make Man a worthy object of all the vast magnificence of Creative Power, we can hardly shrink from believing that he is so.

8. We may remark further, that this view of God, as the Author of the Laws of the Universe, leads to a view of all the phenomena and objects of the world, as the work of God; not a work made, and laid out of hand, but a field of his present activity and energy. And such a view cannot fail to give an aspect of dignity to all that is great in creation, and of beauty to all that is symmetrical, which otherwise they could not have. Accordingly, it is by calling to their thoughts the presence of God as suggested by scenes of grandeur or splendor, that poets often reach the sympathies of their readers. And this dignity and sublimity appear especially to belong to the larger

objects, which are destitute of conscious life; as the mountain, the glacier, the pine-forest, the ocean; since in these, we are, as it were, alone with God, and the only present witnesses of His mysterious working.

9. Now if this reflection be true, the vast bodies which hang in the sky, at such immense distances from us, and roll on their courses, and spin round their axles with such exceeding rapidity; Jupiter and his array of Moons, Saturn with his still larger host of Satellites, and with his wonderful Ring, and the other large and distant Planets, will lose nothing of their majesty, in our eyes, by being uninhabited; any more than the summer-clouds, which perhaps are formed of the same materials, lose their dignity from the same cause;—any more than our Moon, one of the tribe of satellites, loses her soft and tender beauty, when we have ascertained that she is more barren of inhabitants than the top of Mount Blanc. However destitute the planets and moons and rings may be of inhabitants, they are at least vast scenes of God's presence, and of the activity with which he carries into effect, everywhere, the laws of nature. The light which comes to us from them is transmitted according to laws which He has established, by an energy which He maintains. The remotest planet is not devoid of life, for God lives there. At each stage which we make, from planet to planet, from star to star, into the regions of infinity, we may say, with the patriarch, "Surely God is here, and I knew it not." And when those who question the habitability of the remote planets and stars are reproached as presenting a view of the universe, which takes something from the magnificence hitherto ascribed to it, as the scene of God's glory, shown in the things which He has created; they may reply, that they do not at all disturb that glory of the creation which arises from its being, not only the product, but the constant field of God's

activity and thought, wisdom and power; and they may perhaps ask, in return, whether the dignity of the Moon would be greatly augmented if her surface were ascertained to be abundantly peopled with lizards; or whether Mount Blanc would be more sublime, if millions of frogs were known to live in the crevasses of its glaciers.

10. Again: the Earth is a scene of Moral Trial. Man is subject to a Moral Law; and this Moral Law is a Law of which God is the Legislator. It is a law which man has the power of discovering, by the use of the faculties which God has given him. By considering the nature and consequences of actions, man is able to discern, in a great measure, what is right and what is wrong;—what he ought and what he ought not to do;—what his duty and virtue, what his crime and vice. Man has a Law on such subjects, written on his heart, as the Apostle Paul says. He has a conscience which accuses or excuses him; and thus, recognizes his acts as worthy of condemnation or approval. And thus, man is, and knows himself to be, the subject of Divine Law, commanding and prohibiting; and is here, in a state of probation, as to how far he will obey or disobey this Law. He has impulses, springs of action, which urge him to the violation of this Law. Appetite, Desire, Anger, Lust, Greediness, Envy, Malice, impel him to courses which are vicious. But these impulses he is capable of resisting and controlling;—of avoiding the vices and practising the opposite virtues;—and of rising from one stage of Virtue to another, by a gradual and successive purification and elevation of the desires, affections and habits, in a degree, so far as we know, without limit.

11. Now in considering the bearing of this view upon our original subject, we have, in the first place, to make this remark: that the existence of a body of creatures, capable of

such a Law, of such a Trial, and of such an Elevation as this, is, according to all that we can conceive, an object infinitely more worthy of the exertion of the Divine Power and Wisdom, in the Creation of the universe, than any number of planets occupied by creatures having no such lot, no such law, no such capacities, and no such responsibilities. However imperfectly the moral law be obeyed; however ill the greater part of mankind may respond to the appointment which places them here in a state of moral probation; however few those may be who use the capacities and means of their moral purification and elevation;—still, that there is such a plan in the creation, and that any respond to its appointments,—is really a view of the Universe which we can conceive to be suitable to the nature of God, because we can approve of it, in virtue of the moral nature which He has given us. One school of moral discipline, one theatre of moral action, one arena of moral contests for the highest prizes, is a sufficient centre for innumerable hosts of stars and planets, globes of fire and earth, water and air, whether or not tenanted by corals and madrepores, fishes and creeping things. So great and majestic are those names of *Right* and *Good*, *Duty* and *Virtue*, that all mere material or animal existence is worthless in the comparison.

12. But further: let us consider what is this moral progress of which we have spoken;—this purification and elevation of man's inner being. Man's intellectual progress, his advance in the knowledge of the general laws of the Universe, we found reason to believe that we were not describing unfitly, when we spoke of it as bringing us nearer to God;—as making our thoughts, in some degree, resemble His thoughts;—as enabling us to see things as He sees them. And on that account, we held that the placing man, with his intellectual powers, in a condition in which he was impelled, and enabled, to seek such

knowledge, was of itself a great thing, and tended much to give to the Creation a worthy end. Now the moral elevation of man's being is the elevation of his sentiments and affections towards a standard or idea, which God, by his Law, has indicated as that point towards which man ought to tend. We do not ascribe *Virtue* to God, adapting to Him our notions taken from man's attributes, as we do when we ascribe Knowledge to God: for Virtue implies the control and direction of human springs of action;—implies human efforts and human habits. But we ascribe to God infinite Goodness, Justice, and Truth, as well as infinite Wisdom and Power; and Goodness, Justice, Truth, form elements of the character at which man also is, by the Moral Law, directed to aim. So far, therefore, man's moral progress is a progress towards a likeness with God; and such a progress, even more than a progress towards an intellectual likeness with God, may be conceived as making the soul of man fit to endure forever with God; and therefore, as making this earth a prefatory stage of human souls, to fit them for eternity;—a nursery of plants which are to be fully unfolded in a celestial garden.

13. And to this, we must add that, on other accounts also, as well as on account of the capacity of the human soul for moral and intellectual progress, thoughtful men have always been disposed, on grounds supplied by the light of nature, to believe in the existence of human souls after this present earthly life is past. Such a belief has been cherished in all ages and nations, as the mode in which we naturally conceive that which is apparently imperfect and deficient in the moral government of the world, to be completed and perfected. And if this mortal life be thus really only the commencement of an infinite Divine Plan, beginning upon earth and destined to endure for endless ages after our earthly life; we need no array

of other worlds in the universe to give sufficient dignity and majesty to the scheme of the Creation.

14. We may make another remark which may have an important bearing upon our estimate of the value of the moral scheme of the world which occupies the earth. If, by any act of the Divine Government, the number of those men should be much increased, who raise themselves towards the moral standard which God has appointed, and thus, towards a likeness to God, and a prospect of a future eternal union with him;—such an act of Divine Government would do far more towards making the Universe a scene in which God's goodness and greatness were largely displayed, than could be done by any amount of peopling of planets with creatures who were incapable of moral agency; or with creatures whose capacity for the development of their moral faculties was small, and would continue to be smali till such an act of Divine Government were performed. The Interposition of God, in the history of man, to remedy man's feebleness in moral and spiritual tasks, and to enable those who profit by the Interposition, to ascend towards a union with God, is an event entirely out of the range of those natural courses of events which belong to our subject; and to such an Interposition, therefore, we must refer with great reserve; using great caution that we do not mix up speculations and conjectures of our own, with what has been revealed to man concerning such an Interposition. But this, it would seem, we may say:—that such a Divine Interposition for the moral and spiritual elevation of the human race, and for the encouragement and aid of those who seek the purification and elevation of their nature, and an eternal union with God, is far more suitable to the Idea of a God of Infinite Goodness, Purity, and Greatness, than any supposed multiplication of a population, (on our planet or

on any other,) not provided with such means of moral and spiritual progress.

15. And if we were, instead of such a supposition, to imagine to ourselves, in other regions of the Universe, a moral population purified and elevated without the aid or need of any such Divine Interposition; the supposed possibility of such a moral race would make the sin and misery, which deform and sadden the aspect of our earth, appear more dark and dismal still. We should therefore, it would seem, find no theological congruity, and no religious consolation, in the assumption of a Plurality of Worlds of Moral Beings: while, to place the seats of such worlds in the Stars and the Planets, would be, as we have already shown, a step discountenanced by physical reasons; and discountenanced the more, the more the light of science is thrown upon it.

16. Perhaps it may be said, that all which we have urged to show that other animals, in comparison with man, are less worthy objects of creative design, may be used as an argument to prove that other planets are tenanted by men, or by moral and intellectual creatures like man; since, if the creation of *one* world of such creatures exalts so highly our views of the dignity and importance of the plan of creation, the belief in *many* such worlds must elevate still more our sentiments of admiration and reverence of the greatness and goodness of the Creator; and must be a belief, on that account, to be accepted and cherished by pious minds.

17. To this we reply, that we cannot think ourselves authorized to assert cosmological doctrines, selected arbitrarily by ourselves, on the ground of their exalting our sentiments of admiration and reverence for the Deity, *when the weight of all the evidence which we can obtain respecting the constitution of the universe is against them.* It appears to us, that to dis-

cern one great scheme of moral and religious government, which is the spiritual centre of the universe, may well suffice for the religious sentiments of men in the present age; as in former ages such a view of creation was sufficient to overwhelm men with feelings of awe, and gratitude, and love; and to make them confess, in the most emphatic language, that all such feelings were an inadequate response to the view of the scheme of Providence which was revealed to them. The thousands of millions of inhabitants of the Earth to whom the effects of the Divine Plan extend, will not seem, to the greater part of religious persons, to need the addition of more, to fill our minds with sufficiently vast and affecting contemplations, so far as we are capable of pursuing such contemplations. The possible extension of God's spiritual kingdom upon the earth will probably appear to them a far more interesting field of devout meditation, than the possible addition to it of the inhabitants of distant stars, connected in some inscrutable manner with the Divine Plan.

18. To justify our saying that the weight of the evidence is against such cosmological doctrines, we must recall to the reader's recollection the whole course of the argument which we have been pursuing.

It is a possible conjecture, at first, that there may be other Worlds, having, as this has, their moral and intellectual attributes, and their relations to the Creator. It is also a possible conjecture, that this World, having such attributes, and such relations, may, on that account, be necessarily unique and incapable of repetition, peculiar, and spiritually central. These two opposite possibilities may be placed, at first, front to front, as balancing each other. We must then weigh such evidence and such analogies as we can find on the one side or on the other. We see much in the intellectual and moral nature of man, and in his history, to confirm the opinion that the human race is thus unique, peculiar and central. In the views which Religion presents, we find much more, tending the same way, and involving the opposite supposition in great difficulties. We find, in our knowledge of what we ourselves are, reasons to believe that if there be, in any other planet, intellectual and moral beings, they must not only be *like* men, but must *be* men, in all the attributes which we can conceive as belonging to such beings. And yet to suppose other groups of the human species, in other parts of the universe, must be allowed to be a very bold hypothesis, to be justified only by some positive evidence in its favor. When from these views, drawn from the attributes and relations of man, we turn to the evidence drawn from physical conditions, we find very strong reason to believe that, so far as the Solar System is concerned, the Earth *is*, with regard to the conditions of life, in a peculiar and central position; so that the conditions of any life approaching at all to human life, exist on the Earth alone. As to other systems which may circle other suns, the possibility of their being inhabited by men, remains, as at first, a mere conjecture, without any trace of confirmatory evidence. It was suggested at first by the supposed analogy of other stars to our sun; but this analogy has not been verified in any instance; and has been, we conceive, shown in many cases, to vanish altogether. And that there may be such a plan of creation,—one in which the moral and intelligent race of man is the climax and central point to which innumerable races of mere unintelligent species tend,—we have the most striking evidence, in the history of our own earth, as disclosed by geology. We are left, therefore, with nothing to cling to, on one side, but the bare possibility that some of the stars are the centres of systems like the Solar System;—an opinion founded upon the single fact, shown to be highly ambiguous, of those stars being self-luminous; and to this possibility, we oppose all the considerations, flowing from moral, historical, and religious views, which represent the human race as unique and peculiar. The force of these considerations will, of course, be different in different minds, according to the importance which each person attaches to such moral, historical, and religious views; but whatever the weight of them may be deemed, it is to be recollected that we have on the other side a bare possibility, a mere conjecture; which, though suggested at first by astronomical discoveries, all more recent astronomical researches have failed to confirm in the smallest degree. In this state of our knowledge, and with such grounds of belief, to dwell upon the Plurality of Worlds of intellectual and moral creatures, as a highly probable doctrine, must, we think, be held to be eminently rash and unphilosophical.

19. On such a subject, where the evidences are so imperfect, and our power of estimating analogies so small, far be it from us to speak positively and dogmatically. And if any one holds the opinion, on whatever evidence, that there are other spheres of the Divine Government than this earth,—other regions in which God has subjects and servants,—other beings who do his will, and who, it may be, are connected with the moral and religious interests of man;—we do not breathe a syllable against such a belief; but, on the contrary, regard it with a ready and respectful sympathy. It is a belief which finds an echo in pious and reverent hearts;* and it is, of itself,

* "For doubt not that in other worlds above
There must be other offices of love,
That other tasks and ministries there are,
Since it is promised that His servants, there,
Shall serve Him still."—TRENCH.

an evidence of that religious and spiritual character in man, which is one of the points of our argument. But the discussion of such a belief does not belong to the present occasion, any further than to observe, that it would be very rash and unadvised,—a proceeding unwarranted, we think, by Religion, and certainly at variance with all that Science teaches,—to place those other, extra-human spheres of Divine Government, in the Planets and in the Stars. With regard to the planets and the stars, if we reason at all, we must reason on physical grounds; we must suppose, as to a great extent we can prove. that the laws and properties of terrestrial matter and motion apply to them also. On such grounds, it is as improbable that visitants from Jupiter or from Sirius can come to the Earth, as that men can pass to those stars: as unlikely that inhabitants of those stars know and take an interest in human affairs, as that we can learn what they are doing. A belief in the Divine Government of other races of spiritual creatures besides the human race, and in Divine Ministrations committed to such beings, cannot be connected with our physical and astronomical views of the nature of the stars and the planets, without making a mixture altogether incongruous and incoherent; a mixture of what is material and what is spiritual, adverse alike to sound religion and to sound philosophy.

20. Perhaps again, it may be said, that in speaking of the shortness of the time during which man has occupied the earth, in comparison with the previous ages of irrational life, and of blank matter, we are taking man at his present period of existence on the earth:—that we do not know that the race may not be destined to continue upon the earth for as many ages as preceded the creation of man. And to this we reply, that in reasoning, as we must do, at the present period, we can only proceed upon that which has happened up to the present period.

If we do not know how long man will continue to inhabit the earth, we cannot reason as if we did know that he will inhabit it longer than any other species has done. We may not dwell upon a mere possibility, which, it is assumed, may at some indefinitely future period, alter the aspect of the facts now before us. For it would be as easy to assume possibilities which may come hereafter to alter the aspect of the facts, in favor of the one side, as of the other.* What the future destinies of our race, and of the earth, may be, is a subject which is, for us, shrouded in deep darkness. It would be very rash to assume that they will be such as to alter the impression derived from what we now know, and to alter it in a certain preconceived manner. But yet it is natural to form conjectures on this subject; and perhaps we may be allowed to consider for a moment what kind of conjectures the existing stage of our knowledge suggests, when we allow ourselves the license of conjecturing. The next Chapter contains some remarks bearing upon such conjectures.

* For instance, we may assume that in two or three hundred years, by the improvement of telescopes, or by other means, it may be ascertained that the other planets of the Solar System are not inhabited, and that the other Stars are not the centres of regular systems.

CHAPTER XIII.

THE FUTURE.

1. We proceed then to a few reflections to which we cannot but feel ourselves invited by the views which we have already presented in these pages. What will be the future history of the human race, and what the future destination of each individual, most persons will, and most wisely, judge on far other grounds than the analogies which physical science can supply. Analogies derived from such a quarter can throw little light on those grave and lofty questions. Yet perhaps a few thoughts on this subject, even if they serve only to show how little the light thus attainable really is, may not be an unfit conclusion to what has been said; and the more so, if these analogies of science, so far as they have any specific tendency, tend to confirm some of the convictions, with regard to those weighty and solemn points,—the destiny of Man, and of Mankind,—which we derive from other and higher sources of knowledge.

2. Man is capable of looking back upon the past history of himself, his Race, the Earth, and the Universe. So far as he has the means of doing so, and so far as his reflective powers are unfolded, he cannot refrain from such a retrospect. As we have seen, man has occupied his thoughts with such contemplations, and has been led to convictions thereupon, of the most

remarkable and striking kind. Man is also capable of looking forwards to the future probable or possible history of himself, his race, the earth, and the universe. He is irresistibly tempted to do this, and to endeavor to shape his conjectures on the Future, by what he knows of the Past. He attempts to discern what future change and progress may be imagined or expected, by the analogy of past change and progress, which have been ascertained. Such analogies may be necessarily very vague and loose; but they are the peculiar ground of speculation, with which we have here to deal. Perhaps man cannot discover with certainty any fixed and permanent laws which have regulated those past changes which have modified the surface and population of the earth; still less, any laws which have produced a visible progression in the constitution of the rest of the universe. He cannot, therefore, avail himself of any close analogies, to help him to conjecture the future course of events, on the earth or in the universe; still less can he apply any known laws, which may enable him to predict the future configurations of the elements of the world; as he can predict the future configurations of the planets for indefinite periods. He can foresee the astronomical revolutions of the heavens, so long as the known laws subsist. He cannot foresee the future geological revolutions of the earth, even if they are to be produced by the same causes which have produced the past revolutions, of which he has learnt the series and order. Still less can he foresee the future revolutions which may take place in the condition of man, of society, of philosophy, of religion; still less, again, the course which the Divine Government of the world will take, or the state of things to which, even as now conducted, it will lead.

3. All these subjects are covered with a veil of mystery, which science and philosophy can do little in raising. Yet these

are subjects to which the mind turns, with a far more eager curiosity, than that which it feels with regard to mere geological or astronomical revolutions. Man is naturally, and reasonably, the greatest object of interest to man. What shall happen to the human race, after thousands of years, is a far dearer concern to him, than what shall happen to Jupiter or Sirius; and even, than what shall happen to the continents and oceans of the globe on which he lives, except so far as the changes of his domicile affect himself. If our knowledge of the earth and of the heavens, of animals and of man, of the past condition and present laws of the world, is quite barren of all suggestion of what may or may not hereafter be the lot of man, such knowledge will lose the charm which would have made it most precious and attractive in the eyes of mankind in general. And if, on such subjects, any conjectures, however dubious,—any analogies, however loose,—can be collected from what we know, they will probably be received as acceptable, in spite of their insecurity; and will be deemed a fit offering from the scientific faculty, to those hopes and expectations,—to that curiosity and desire of all knowledge,—which gladly receive their nutriment and gratification from every province of man's being.

4. Now if we ask, what is likely to be the future condition of the population of the earth as compared with the present; we are naturally led to recollect, what has been the past condition of that population as compared with the present. And here, our thoughts are at once struck by that great fact, to which we have so often referred; which we conceive to be established by irrefragable geological evidence, and of which the importance cannot be overrated:—namely, the fact that the existence of man upon the earth has been for only a few thousand years:—that for thousands, and myriads, and it may be

for millions of years, previous to that period, the earth was tenanted, entirely and solely, by brute creatures, destitute of reason, incapable of progress, and guided merely by animal instincts, in the preservation and continuation of their races. After this period of mere brute existence, in innumerable forms, had endured for a vast series of cycles, there appeared upon the earth a creature, even in his organization, superior far to all; but still more superior, in his possession of peculiar endowments;—reason, language, the power of indefinite progress, and of raising his thoughts towards his Creator and Governor: in short, to use terms already employed, an intellectual, moral, religious, and spiritual creature. After the ages of intellectual darkness, there took place this creation of intellectual light. After the long-continued play of mere appetite and sensual life, there came the operation of thought, reflection, invention, art, science, moral sentiments, religious belief and hope; and thus, life and being, in a far higher sense than had ever existed, even in the hightest degree, in the long ages of the earth's previous existence.

5. Now, this great and capital fact cannot fail to excite in us many reflections, which, however vaguely and dimly, carry us to the prospect of the future. The present being *so* related to the past, how may we suppose that the future will be related to the present?

In the first place, *this* is a natural reflection. The terrestrial world having made this advance from brute to human life, can we think it at all likely, that the present condition of the earth's inhabitants is a final condition? Has the vast step from animal to human life, exhausted the progressive powers of nature? or to speak more reverently and justly, has it completed the progressive plan of the Creator? After the great revolution by which man became what he is, can and will nothing be done, to bring into being something better than now is; however that future creature may be related to man? We leave out of consideration any supposed progression, which may have taken place in the animal creation previous to man's existence; any progression by which the animal organization was made to approximate, gradually or by sudden steps, to the human organization; partly, because such successive approximation is questioned by some geologists; and is, at any rate, obscure and perplexed: but much more, because it is not really to our purpose. Similarity of organization is not the point in question. The endowments and capacities of man, by which he is Man, are the great distinction, which places all other animals at an immeasurable distance below him. The closest approximation of form or organs, does nothing to obliterate this distinction. It does not bring the monkey nearer to man, that his tongue has the same muscular apparatus as man's, so long as he cannot talk; and so long as he has not the thought and idea which language implies, and which are unfolded indefinitely in the use of language. The step, then, by which the earth became a *human* habitation, was an immeasurable advance on all that existed before; and therefore there is a question which we are, it seems, irresistibly prompted to ask, Is this the last such step? Is there nothing beyond it? Man is the head of creation, in his present condition; but is that condition the final result and ultimate goal of the progress of creation in the plan of the Creator? As there was found and produced something so far beyond animals, as man is, may there not also, in some course of the revolutions of the world, be produced something far beyond what man is? The question is put, as implying a difficulty in believing that it should be so; and this difficulty must be very generally felt. Considering how vast the resources of the Creative Power have been shown to be, it is difficult to suppose they are exhausted. Considering how great things have been done, in the progress of the work of creation, we naturally think that even greater things than these, still remain to be done.

6. But then, on the other hand, there is an immense difficulty in supposing, even in imagining, any further change, at all commensurate in kind and degree, with the step which carried the world from a mere brute population, to a human population. In a proportion in which the two first terms are *brute* and *man*, what can be the third term? In the progress from mere Instinct to Reason, we have a progress from blindness to sight; and what can we do more than see? When pure Intellect is evolved in man, he approaches to the nature of the Supreme Mind: how can a creature rise higher? When mere impulse, appetite, and passion are placed under the control and direction of duty and virtue, man is put under Divine Government: what greater lot can any created being have?

7. And the difficulty of conceiving any ulterior step at all analogous to the last and most wonderful of the revolutions which have taken place in the condition of the earth's inhabitants, will be found to grow upon us, as it is more closely examined. For it may truly be said, the change which occurred when man was placed on the earth, was not one which could have been imagined and constructed beforehand, by a speculator merely looking at the endowments and capacities of the creatures which were previously living. Even in the way of organization, could any intelligent spectator, contemplating anything which then existed in the animal world, have guessed the wonderful new and powerful purposes to which it was to be made subservient in man? Could such a spectator, from seeing the *rudiments of a Hand*, in the horse or the cow, or even from seeing the hand of a quadrumanous animal, have conjectured, that

the Hand was, in man, to be made an instrument by which infinite numbers of new instruments were to be constructed, subduing the elements to man's uses, giving him a command over nature which might seem supernatural, taming or conquering all other animals, enabling him to scrutinize the farthest regions of the universe, and the subtlest combinations of material things?

8. Or again; could such a spectator, by dissecting the tongues of animals, have divined that the Tongue, in man, was to be the means of communicating the finest movements of thought and feeling; of giving one man, weak and feeble, an unbounded ascendency over robust and angry multitudes; and, assisted by the (writing) hand, of influencing the intimate thoughts, laws, and habits of the most remote posterity?

9. And again, could such a spectator, seeing animals entirely occupied by their appetites and desires, and the objects subservient to their individual gratification, have ever dreamt that there should appear on earth a creature who should desire to know, and should know, the distances and motions of the stars, future as well as present; the causes of their motions, the history of the earth, and his own history; and even should know truths by which all possible objects and events not only are, but must be regulated?

10. And yet again, could such a spectator, seeing that animals obeyed their appetites with no restraint but external fear, and knew of no difference of good and bad except the sensual difference, ever have imagined that there should be a creature acknowledging a difference of right and wrong, as a distinction supreme over what was good or bad to the sense; and a rule of duty which might forbid and prevent gratification by an internal prohibition?

11. And finally, could such a spectator, seeing nothing but

animals with all their faculties thus entirely immersed in the elements of their bodily being, have supposed that a creature should come, who should raise his thoughts to his Creator, acknowledge Him as his Master and Governor, look to His Judgment, and aspire to live eternally in His presence?

12. If it would have been impossible for a spectator of the præhuman creation, however intelligent, imaginative, bold and inventive, to have conjectured beforehand the endowments of such a creature as Man, taking only those which we have thus indicated; it may well be thought, that if there is to be a creature which is to succeed man, as man has succeeded the animals, it must be equally impossible for us to conjecture beforehand, what kind of creature *that* must be, and what will be *his* endowments and privileges.

13. Thus a spectator who should thus have studied the præhuman creation, and who should have had nothing else to help him in his conjectures and conceptions, (of course, by the supposition of a præhuman period, not any knowledge of the operation of intelligence, though a most active intelligence would be necessary for such speculations,) would not have been able to divine the future appearance of a creature, so excellent as Man; or to guess at his endowments and privileges, or his relation to the previous animal creation; and just as little able may we be, even if there is to exist at some time, a creature more excellent and glorious than man, to divine what kind of creature he will be, and how related to man. And here, therefore, it would perhaps be best, that we should quit the subject; and not offer conjectures which we thus acknowledge to have no value. Perhaps, however, the few brief remarks which we have still to make, put forwards, as they are, merely as suggestions to be weighed by others, can

not reasonably give offence, or trouble even the most reverent thinker.

14. To suppose a higher development of endowments which already exist in man, is a natural mode of rising to the imagination of a being nobler than man is; but we shall find that such hypotheses do not lead us to any satisfactory result. Looking at the first of those features of the superiority of man over brutes, which we have just pointed out, the Human Hand, we can imagine this superiority carried further. Indeed, in the course of human progress, and especially in recent times, and in our own country, man employs instead of, or in addition to the hand, innumerable instruments to make nature serve his needs and do his will. He works by Tools and Machinery, derivative hands, which increase a hundredfold the power of the natural hand. Shall we try to ascend to a New Period, to imagine a New Creature, by supposing this power increased hundreds and thousands of times more, so that nature should obey man, and minister to his needs, in an incomparably greater degree than she now does? We may imagine this carried so far, that all need for manual labor shall be superseded; and thus, abundant time shall be left to the creature thus gifted, for developing the intellectual and moral powers which must be the higher part of its nature. But still, that higher nature of the creature itself, and not its command over external material nature, must be the quarter in which we are to find anything which shall elevate the creature above man, as man is elevated above brutes.

15. Or, looking at the second of the features of human superiority, shall we suppose that the means of Communication of their thoughts to each other, which exist for the human race, are to be immensely increased, and that this is to be the leading feature of a New Period? Already, in addition to

the use of the tongue, other means of communication have vastly multiplied man's original means of carrying on the intercourse of thought:—writing, employed in epistles, books, newspapers; roads, horses and posting establishments; ships; railways; and, as the last and most notable step, made in our time, electric telegraphs, extending across continents and even oceans. We can imagine this facility and activity of communication, in which man so immeasurably exceeds all animals, still further increased, and more widely extended. But yet so long as what is thus communicated is nothing greater or better than what is now communicated among men;—such news, such thoughts, such questions and answers, as now dart along our roads;—we could hardly think that the creature, whatever wonderful means of intercourse with its fellow-creatures it might possess, was elevated above man, so as to be of a higher nature than man is.

16. Thus, such improved endowments as we have now spoken of, increased power over materials, and increased means of motion and communication, arising from improved mechanism, do little, and we may say, nothing, to satisfy our idea of a more excellent condition than that of man. For such extensions of man's present powers are consistent with the absence of all intellectual and moral improvement. Men might be able to dart from place to place, and even from planet to planet, and from star to star, on wings, such as we ascribe to angels in our imagination: they might be able to make the elements obey them at a beck; and yet they might not be better, nor even wiser, than they are. It is not found generally, that the improvement of machinery, and of means of locomotion, among men, produces an improvement in morality, nor even an improvement in intelligence, except as to particular points. We must therefore look somewhat further,

in order to find possible characters, which may enable us to imagine a creature more excellent than man.

17. Among the distinctions which elevate man above brutes, there is one which we have not mentioned, but which is really one of the most eminent. We mean, his faculty and habit of forming himself into Societies, united by laws and language for some common object, the furtherance of which requires such union. The most general and primary kind of such societies, is that Civil Society which is bound together by Law and Government, and which secures to men the Rights of property, person, family, external peace, and the like. That this kind of society may be conceived, as taking a more excellent character than it now possesses, we can easily see: for not only does it often very imperfectly attain its direct object, the preservation of Rights, but it becomes the means and source of wrong. Not only does it often fail to secure peace with strangers, but it acts as if its main object were to enable men to make wars with strangers. If we were to conceive a Universal and Perpetual Peace to be established among the nations of the earth; (for instance by some general agreement for that purpose;) and if we were to suppose, further, that those nations should employ all their powers and means in fully unfolding the intellectual and moral capacities of their members, by early education, constant teaching, and ready help in all ways; we might then, perhaps, look forwards to a state of the earth in which it should be inhabited, not indeed by a being exalted above Man, but by Man exalted above himself as he now is.

18. That by such combinations of communities of men, even with their present powers, results may be obtained, which at present appear impossible, or inconceivable, we may find good reason to believe; looking at what has already been

done, or planned as attainable by such means, in the promotion of knowledge, and the extension of man's intellectual empire. The greatest discovery ever made, the discovery, by Newton, of the laws which regulate the motions of the cosmical system, has been carried to its present state of completeness, only by the united efforts of all the most intellectual nations upon earth; in addition to vast labors of individuals, and of smaller societies, voluntarily associated for the purpose. Astronomical observatories have been established in every land; scientific voyages, and expeditions for the purpose of observation, wherever they could throw light upon the theory, have been sent forth; costly instruments have been constructed, achievements of discovery have been rewarded; and all nations have shown a ready sympathy with every attempt to forward this part of knowledge. Yet the largest and wisest plans for the extension of human knowledge in other provinces of science by the like means, have remained hitherto almost entirely unexecuted, and have been treated as mere dreams. The exhortations of Francis Bacon to men, to seek, by such means, an elevation of their intellectual condition, have been assented to in words; but his plans of a methodical and organized combination of society for this purpose, it has never been even attempted to realize. If the nations of the earth were to employ, for the promotion of human knowledge, a small fraction only of the means, the wealth, the ingenuity, the energy, the combination, which they have employed in every age, for the destruction of human life and of human means of enjoyment; we might soon find that what we hitherto knew, is little compared with what man has the power of knowing.

19. But there is another kind of Society, or another object of Society among men, which in a still more important manner

aims at the elevation of their nature. Man sympathizes with man, not only in his intellectual aspirations, but in his moral sentiments, in his religious beliefs and hopes, in his efforts after spiritual life. Society, even Civil Society, has generally recognized this sympathy, in a greater or less degree; and has included Morality and Religion, among the objects which it endeavored to uphold and promote. But any one who has any deep and comprehensive perception of man's capacities and aspirations, on such subjects, must feel that what has commonly, or indeed ever, been done by nations for such a purpose, has been far below that which the full development of man's moral, religious, and spiritual nature requires. Can we not conceive a Society among men, which should have for its purpose, to promote this development, far more than any human society has yet done?—a Body selected from all nations, or rather, including all nations, the purpose of which should be to bind men together by a universal feeling of kindness and mutual regard, to associate them in the acknowledgment of a common Divine Lawgiver, Governor, and Father;—to unite them in their efforts to divest themselves of the evil of their human nature, and to bring themselves nearer and nearer to a conformity with the Divine Idea; and finally, a Society which should unite them in the hope of such a union with God that the parts of their nature which seem to claim immortality, the Mind, the Soul, and the Spirit, should endure forever in a state of happiness arising from their exalted and perfected condition? And if we can suppose such a Society, fully established and fully operative, would not this be a condition, as far elevated above the ordinary earthly condition of man, as that of man is elevated above the beasts that perish?

20. Yet one more question; though we hesitate to mix such

suggestions from analogy, with trains of thought and belief, which have their proper nutriment from other quarters. We know, even from the evidence of natural science, that God *has* interposed in the history of this Earth, in order to place Man upon it. In that case, there was a clear, and, in the strongest sense of the term, a *supernatural interposition* of the Divine Creative Power. God interposed to place upon the earth, Man, the social and rational being. God thus directly instituted Human Society; gave man his privileges and his prospects in such society; placed him far above the previously existing creation; and endowed him with the means of an elevation of nature entirely unlike anything which had previously appeared. Would it then be a violation of analogy, if God were to interpose again, to institute a Divine Society, such as we have attempted to describe; to give to its members their privileges; to assure to them their prospects; to supply to them his aid in pursuing the objects of such a union with each other; and thus, to draw them, as they aspire to be drawn, to a spiritual union with Him?

It would seem that those who believe, as the records of the earth's history seem to show, that the establishment of Man, and of Human Society, or of the germ of human society, upon the earth, was an interposition of Creative Power beyond the ordinary course of nature; may also readily believe that another supernatural Interposition of Divine Power might take place, in order to plant upon the earth the Germ of a more Divine Society; and to introduce a period in which the earth should be tenanted by a more excellent creature than at present.

21. But though we may thus prepare ourselves to assent to the possibility, or even probability, of such a Divine Interposition, exercised for the purpose of establishing upon earth a

Divine Society: it would be a rash and unauthorized step,—especially taking into account the vast differences between material and spiritual things,—to assume that such an Interposition would have any resemblance to the commencement of a New Period in the earth's history, analogous to the Periods by which that history has already been marked. What the manner and the operation of such a Divine Interposition would be, Philosophy would attempt in vain to conjecture. It is conceivable that such an event should produce its effect, not at once, by a general and simultaneous change in the aspect of terrestrial things, but gradually, by an almost imperceptible progression. It is possible also that there may be such an Interposition, which is only one step in the Divine Plan;—a preparation for some other subsequent Interposition, by which the change in the Earth's inhabitants is to be consummated. Or it is possible that such a Divine Interposition in the history of man, as we have hinted at, may be a preparation, not for a new form of terrestrial life, but for a new form of human life;—not for a new peopling of the Earth, but for a new existence of Man. These possibilities are so vague and doubtful, so far as any scientific analogies lead, that it would be most unwise to attempt to claim for them any value, as points in which Science supplies support to Religion. Those persons who most deely feel the value of religion, and are most strongly convinced of its truths, will be the most willing to declare, that religious belief is, and ought to be, independent of any such support, and must be, and may be, firmly established on its own proper basis.

22. We find no encouragement, then, for any attempt to obtain, from Science, by the light of the analogy of the past, any definite view of a future condition of the Creation. And that this is so, we cannot, for reasons which have been given,

feel any surprise. Yet the reasonings which we have, in various parts of this Essay, pursued, will not have been without profit, even in their influence upon our religious thoughts, if they have left upon our minds these convictions :—That if the analogy of science proves anything, it proves that the Creator of man can make a Creator as far superior to Man, as Man, when most intellectual, moral, religious, and spiritual, is superior to the brutes :—and again, That Man's Intellect is of a divine, and therefore of an immortal nature. Those persons who can, on any basis of belief, combine these two convictions, so as to feel that they have a personal interest in both of them; —those who have such grounds as Religion, happily appealed to, can furnish, for hoping that their imperishable element may, hereafter, be clothed with a new and more glorious apparel by the hand of its Almighty Maker;—may be well content to acknowledge that Science and Philosophy could not give them this combined conviction, in any manner in which it could minister that consolation, and that trust in the Divine Power and Goodness, which human nature, in its present condition, requires.

THE END.

IMPORTANT

LITERARY AND SCIENTIFIC WORKS

PUBLISHED BY

GOULD AND LINCOLN,

59 WASHINGTON STREET, BOSTON,

ANNUAL OF SCIENTIFIC DISCOVERY; or, Year Book of Facts in Science and Art, exhibiting the most important Discoveries and Improvements in Mechanics, Useful Arts, Natural Philosophy, Chemistry, Astronomy, Meteorology, Zoölogy, Botany, Mineralogy, Geology, Geography, Antiquities, etc.; together with a list of recent Scientific Publications, a classified list of Patents, Obituaries of eminent Scientific Men, an Index of important Papers in Scientific Journals, Reports, &c. Edited by DAVID A. WELLS, A. M. 12mo, cloth, 1,25.

This work, commenced in the year 1850, and issued on the first of March annually, contains all important facts discovered or announced during the year. Each volume is distinct in itself, and contains *entirely new matter*, with a fine portrait of some distinguished scientific man. As it is not intended exclusively for scientific men, but to meet the wants of the general reader, it has been the aim of the editor that the articles should be brief, and intelligible to all. The editor has received the approbation, counsel, and personal contributions of the prominent scientific men throughout the country.

THE FOOTPRINTS OF THE CREATOR; or, The Asterolepis of Stromness. With numerous Illustrations. By HUGH MILLER, author of "The Old Red Sandstone," &c. From the third London Edition. With a Memoir of the Author, by LOUIS AGASSIZ. 12mo, cloth, 1,00.

Dr. BUCKLAND, at a meeting of the British Association, said he had never been so much astonished in his life, by the powers of any man, as he had been by the geological descriptions of Mr. Miller. That wonderful man described these objects with a facility which made him ashamed of the comparative meagreness and poverty of his own descriptions in the "Bridgewater Treatise," which had cost him hours and days of labor. *He would give his left hand to possess such powers of description as this man:* and if it pleased Providence to spare his useful life, he, if any one, would certainly render science attractive and popular, and do equal service to theology and geology.

Mr. Miller's style is remarkably pleasing; his mode of popularizing geological knowledge unsurpassed, perhaps unequalled; and the deep reverence for divine revelation pervading all adds interest and value to the volume. — *N. Y. Com. Advertiser.*

The publishers have again covered themselves with honor, by giving to the American public, with the author's permission, an elegant reprint of a foreign work of science. We earnestly bespeak for this work a wide and free circulation among all who love science much and religion more. — *Puritan Recorder.*

THE OLD RED SANDSTONE; or, New Walks in an Old Field. By HUGH MILLER. Illustrated with Plates and Geological Sections. 12mo, cloth, 1,00.

Mr. Miller's exceedingly interesting book on this formation is just the sort of work to render any subject popular. It is written in a remarkably pleasing style, and contains a wonderful amount of information. — *Westminster Review.*

It is, withal, one of the most beautiful specimens of English composition to be found, conveying information on a most difficult and profound science, in a style at once novel, pleasing, and elegant. It contains the results of twenty years' close observation and experiment, resulting in an accumulation of facts which not only dissipate some dark and knotty old theories with regard to ancient formations, but establish the great truths of geology in more perfect and harmonious consistency with the great truths of revelation. — *Albany Spectator.*

GUYOT'S WORKS.

THE EARTH AND MAN: Lectures on COMPARATIVE PHYSICAL GEOGRAPHY, in its relation to the History of Mankind. By Prof. ARNOLD GUYOT. Translated from the French, by Prof. C. C. FELTON, with numerous Illustrations. Eighth thousand. 12mo, cloth, 1,25.

From Prof. Louis Agassiz, of Harvard University.

It will not only render the study of Geography more attractive, but actually show it in its true light, namely, as the science of the relations which exist between nature and man throughout history; of the contrasts observed between the different parts of the globe; of the laws of horizontal and vertical forms of the dry land, in its contact with the sea; of climate, &c. It would be highly serviceable, it seems to me, for the benefit of schools and teachers, that you should induce Mr. Guyot to write a series of graduated text books of geography, from the first elements up to a scientific treatise. It would give new life to these studies in this country, and be the best preparation for sound statistical investigations.

From George S. Hillard, Esq., of Boston.

Professor Guyot's Lectures are marked by learning, ability, and taste. His bold and comprehensive generalizations rest upon a careful foundation of facts. The essential value of his statements is enhanced by his luminous arrangement, and by a vein of philosophical reflection which gives life and dignity to dry details. To teachers of youth it will be especially important. They may learn from it how to make Geography, which I recall as the least interesting of studies, one of the most attractive; and I earnestly commend it to their careful consideration.

Those who have been accustomed to regard Geography as a merely descriptive branch of learning, drier than the remainder biscuit after a voyage, will be delighted to find this hitherto unattractive pursuit converted into a science, the principles of which are definite and the results conclusive.—*North American Review.*

The grand idea of the work is happily expressed by the author, where he calls it the *geographical march of history.* Faith, science, learning, poetry, taste, in a word, genius, have liberally contributed to the production of the work under review. Sometimes we feel as if we were studying a treatise on the exact sciences; at others, it strikes the ear like an epic poem. Now it reads like history, and now it sounds like prophecy. It will find readers in whatever language it may be published.—*Christian Examiner.*

The work is one of high merit, exhibiting a wide range of knowledge, great research, and a philosophical spirit of investigation. Its perusal will well repay the most learned in such subjects, and give new views to all of man's relation to the globe he inhabits.—*Silliman's Journal.*

COMPARATIVE PHYSICAL AND HISTORICAL GEOGRAPHY; or, the Study of the Earth and its Inhabitants. A series of graduated courses for the use of Schools. By ARNOLD GUYOT, author of "Earth and Man," etc.

The series hereby announced will consist of three courses, adapted to the capacity of three different ages and periods of study. The first is intended for primary schools and for children of from seven to ten years. The second is adapted for higher schools, and for young persons of from ten to fifteen years. The third is to be used as a scientific manual in Academies and Colleges.

Each course will be divided into two parts, one on purely Physical Geography, the other for Ethnography, Statistics, Political and Historical Geography. Each part will be illustrated by a colored Physical and Political Atlas, prepared expressly for this purpose, delineating, with the greatest care, the configuration of the surface, and the other physical phenomena alluded to in the corresponding work, the distribution of the races of men, and the political divisions into states, &c., &c.

The two parts of the first or preparatory course are now in a forward state of preparation, and will be issued at an early day.

GUYOT'S MURAL MAPS; a Series of elegant Colored Maps, projected on a large scale, for the Recitation Room, consisting of a Map of the World, North and South America, Europe, Asia, Africa, &c., exhibiting the Physical Phenomena of the Globe, etc. By Prof. ARNOLD GUYOT. Price, mounted, 10,00 each.

MAP OF THE WORLD,—Now ready.
MAP OF NORTH AMERICA,—Now ready.
MAP OF SOUTH AMERICA,—Nearly ready.
MAP OF GEOGRAPHICAL ELEMENTS,—Now ready.

☞ *Other Maps of the Series are in preparation.*

C

VALUABLE SCIENTIFIC WORKS.

A TREATISE ON THE COMPARATIVE ANATOMY OF THE Animal Kingdom. By Profs. C. TH. VON SIEBOLD and H. STANNIUS. Translated from the German, with Notes, Additions, &c., By WALDO J. BURNETT, M. D., Boston. Two volumes, octavo, cloth.

This is unquestionably the best and most complete work of its class yet published; and its appearance in an English dress, with the corrections, improvements, additions, etc., of the American Editor, will no doubt be welcomed by the men of science in this country and in Europe, from whence orders for supplies of the work have been received.

THE POETRY OF SCIENCE; or, the Physical Phenomena of Nature. By ROBERT HUNT, Author of "Panthea," "Researches of Light," &c. 12mo, cloth, 1,25.

We are heartily glad to see this interesting work republished in America. It is a book that *is* a book.—*Scientific American.*

It is one of the most readable, interesting, and instructive works of the kind that we have ever seen.—*Phil. Christian Observer.*

THE NATURAL HISTORY OF THE SPECIES: its Typical Forms and Primeval Distribution. By CHARLES HAMILTON SMITH. With an Introduction, containing an Abstract of the Views of Blumenbach, Prichard, Bachman, Agassiz, and other writers of repute. By SAMUEL KNEELAND, JR., M. D. With elegant Illustrations. 12mo, cloth, 1,25.

The history of the species is thoroughly considered by Colonel Smith, with regard to its origin, typical forms, distribution, filiations, &c. The marks of practical good sense, careful observation, and deep research are displayed in every page. An introductory essay of some seventy or eighty pages forms a valuable addition to the work. It comprises an abstract of the opinions advocated by the most eminent writers on the subject. The statements are made with strict impartiality, and, without a comment, left to the judgment of the reader.—*Sartain's Magazine.*

This work exhibits great research, as well as an evident taste and talent, on the part of the author, for the study of the history of man, upon zoological principles. It is a book of learning, and full of interest, and may be regarded as among the comparatively few real contributions to science, that serve to redeem, in some measure, the mass of useless stuff under which the press groans.—*Chris. Witness.*

This book is characterized by more curious and interesting research than any one that has recently come under our examination.—*Albany Journal and Register.*

It contains a learned and thorough treatment of an important subject, always interesting, and of late attracting more than usual attention.—*Ch. Register.*

The volume before us is one of the best of the publishers' series of publications, replete with rare and valuable information, presented in a style at once clear and entertaining, illustrated in the most copious manner with plates of all the various forms of the human race, tracing with the most minute precision analogies and resemblances, and hence origin. The more it is read, the more widely opens this field of research before the mind, again and again to be returned to, with fresh zest and satisfaction. It is the result of the researches, collections, and labors of a long and valuable lifetime, presented in the most popular form imaginable.—*Albany Spectator.*

LAKE SUPERIOR: its Physical Character, Vegetation, and Animals, compared with those of other and similar regions. By L. AGASSIZ, and Contributions from other eminent Scientific Gentlemen. With a Narrative of the Expedition, and Illustrations. By J. E. CABOT. One volume, octavo, elegantly illustrated. Cloth, 3,50.

The illustrations, seventeen in number, are in the finest style of the art, by Sonrel; embracing lake and landscape scenery, fishes, and other objects of natural history, with an outline map of Lake Superior.

This work is one of the most valuable scientific works that has appeared in this country. Embodying the researches of our best scientific men relating to a hitherto comparatively unknown region, it will be found to contain a great amount of scientific information.

B

www.ingramcontent.com/pod-product-compliance
Lightning Source LLC
LaVergne TN
LVHW020236110826
845151LV00003B/939

* 9 7 8 1 4 2 5 5 3 1 1 1 9 *